The Muslim Community of India-Pakistan Subcontinent

The Muslim Community of India-Pakistan Subcontinent

Brig. V. K.Negi .AVSM (Retd.)

NEHA PUBLISHERS & DISTRIBUTORS
DELHI

Publisher
NEHA PUBLISHERS & DISTRIBUTORS
4832/24,Prahlad Lane,S-207 Ansari
Road, Daryaganj, Delhi-110002
Ph.: 43570976, 23278261
Email: nehapubdistributors@gmail.com

Edition: 2015

ISBN: 978-93-80318-73-8

Laser Typesetting
JEE-VEE Graphics, Delhi

Price: 1195/-

Printed
Vikas Computers, Delhi

Preface

The first great expansion of Islam into India came during the Umayyad Dynasty of caliphs, who were based in Damascus. In 711, the Umayyads appointed a young 17 year old man from Ta'if to extend Umayyad control into Sindh: Muhammad bin Qasim. Sindh is the land around the Indus River in the Northwestern part of the subcontinent, in present-day Pakistan.

Muslim conquests on the Indian subcontinent mainly took place from the 12th to the 16th centuries, though earlier Muslim conquests made limited inroads into modern Afghanistan and Pakistan as early as the time of the Rajput kingdoms in the 8th century. With the establishment of the Delhi Sultanate, Islam spread across large parts of the subcontinent. In 1204, Bakhtiar Khilji led the Muslim conquest of Bengal, marking the eastern-most expansion of Islam at the time.

Muhammad bin Qasim led his army of 6,000 soldiers to the far eastern reaches of Persia, Makran. He encountered little resistance as he made his way into India. When he reached the city of Nerun, on the banks of the Indus River, he was welcomed into the city by the Buddhist monks that controlled it. Most cities along the Indus thus voluntarily came under Muslim control, with no fighting. In some cases, oppressed Buddhist minorities reached out to the Muslim armies for protection against Hindu governors.

This book contains the fundamental and basic information of the subject and useful for teachers, students and researchers.

—*Editor*

Contents

1

Muslim Conquests on the Indian Subcontinent

Muslim conquests on the Indian subcontinent mainly took place from the 12th to the 16th centuries, though earlier Muslim conquests made limited inroads into modern Afghanistan and Pakistan as early as the time of the Rajput kingdoms in the 8th century. With the establishment of the Delhi Sultanate, Islam spread across large parts of the subcontinent. In 1204, Bakhtiar Khilji led the Muslim conquest of Bengal, marking the eastern-most expansion of Islam at the time.

Prior to the rise of the Maratha Empire which was followed by the conquest of India by the British East India Company, the MuslimMoghul Empire was able to annex or subjugate most of India's Hindu kings. However, it was never able to conquer the Hindu kingdoms in upper reaches of the Himalayas such as the regions of today's Himachal Pradesh, Uttarakhand, Sikkim, Nepal andBhutan and the extreme south of India such as Travancore.

BACKGROUND

Like other societies in history, South Asia has been attacked by nomadic tribes throughout its long history. In evaluating the impact of Islam on the sub-continent, one must also note that the northwestern sub-continent was a frequent target of tribes from Central Asia who arrived from the North West. With the fall of the Sassanids and the arrival of theCaliphate's domination of the region these tribes began to contest with the new power and were subsequently integrated into it giving rise to Muslim dynasties of Central Asian heritage, generally Turkic - Persians. In that sense, the Muslim invasions of the 10th century onwards were not dissimilar to those of the earlier invasions in the History of Central Asia during the 1st through to the 6th century.

What does however, make the Muslim invasions different is that unlike the preceding invaders who assimilated into the prevalent social system, the Muslim conquerors retained their Islamic identity and created new legal and administrative systems that challenged and usually superseded the existing systems of social conduct and ethics.

They also introduced new cultural mores that in some ways were very different from the existing cultural codes. While this was often a source of friction and conflict, it should also be noted that there were also Muslim rulers, notably Akbar, who in much of their secular practice absorbed or accommodated local traditions.

The first incursion by the new Muslim successor states of the Arab World occurred around 664 CE during the Umayyad Caliphate, led by Al Muhallab ibn Abi Suffrah towardsMultan in Southern Punjab, in modern day Pakistan.

Muhallab's expeditions were not aimed at conquest, though they penetrated only as far as the capital of the Maili, he returned with wealth and prisoners of war. This was an Arab incursion and part of the early Umayyad push onwards from the Islamic conquest of Persia into Central Asia, and within the limits of the eastern borders of previous Persian empires. The last Arab push in the region would be towards the end of Umayyad reign under Muhammad bin Qasim, after whom the Arabs would be defeated by the south Indian Emperor Vikramaditya II of the Chalukya dynasty and the Rajputs like Nagabhata of the Pratihara Dynasty at theBattle of Rajasthan in 738, and Muslim incursions would only be resumed under later Turkic and Central Asian mongol dynasties with more local capitals, who supplanted the Caliphate and expanded their domains both northwards and eastwards.

It took several centuries for Islam to spread across India and how it did so is a topic of intense debate.

Conversion Theories

Considerable controversy exists both in scholarly and public opinion as to how conversion to Islam came about in Indian subcontinent, typically represented by the following schools of thought:

1. That Muslims sought conversion through *jihad* or violence
2. That the bulk of Muslims are descendants of migrants from the Iranians or Arabs.
3. Conversion was a result of the actions of Sufi saints and involved a genuine change of heart.
4. Conversion came from Buddhists and the masses of conversions of lower castes as they were the vulnerable and enticed by uniformity under Islam. (See Indian caste structures.
5. Conversion was a combination, initially by violence, threat or other pressure against the person followed by a genuine change of heart.
6. As a socio-cultural process of diffusion and integration over an extended period of time into the sphere of the dominant Muslim civilization and global polity at large.
7. That conversions occurred for relief from the jizya, the tax only imposed on non-Muslims.
8. That conversions occurred for non-religious reasons of pragmatism and patronage such as social mobility among the Muslim ruling elite

An estimate of the number of people killed remains unknown. Based on the Muslim chronicles and demographic calculations, an estimate was done by K.S. Lal in his book *Growth of Muslim Population in Medieval India,* who claimed that between 1000 CE and 1500 CE, the population of Hindus decreased by 80 million. Although this estimate was disputedby Simon Digby in (School of Oriental and African Studies), Digby suggested that estimate lacks accurate data in pre-census times. In particular the records kept by al-Utbi, Mahmud al-Ghazni's secretary, in the Tarikh-i-Yamini document several episodes of bloody military campaigns. Hindus who converted to Islam however were not completely immune to persecution due to the caste system among Muslims in India established by Ziauddin al-Barani in the *Fatawa-i Jahandari,* where they were regarded as an "Ajlaf" caste and subjected to discrimination by the "Ashraf" castes.

Critics of the "religion of the sword theory" point to the presence of the strong Muslim communities found in Southern India, modern day Bangladesh, Sri Lanka, western Burma,Indonesia and the Philippines coupled with the distinctive lack of equivalent Muslim communities around the heartland of historical Muslim empires in South Asia as refutation to the "conversion by the sword theory". The legacy of Muslim conquest of South Asia is a hotly debated issue even today. Not all Muslim invaders were simply raiders. Later rulers fought on to win kingdoms and stayed to create new ruling dynasties. The practices of these new rulers and their subsequent heirs (some of whom were borne of Hindu wives of Muslim rulers) varied considerably. While some were uniformly hated, others developed a popular following. According to the memoirs of Ibn Battuta who traveled throughDelhi in the 14th century, one of the previous sultans had been especially brutal and was deeply hated by Delhi's population. His memoirs also indicate that Muslims from the Arab world, Persia and Turkey were often favored with important posts at the royal courts suggesting that locals may have played a somewhat subordinate role in the Delhi administration. The term "Turk" was commonly used to refer to their higher social status. However S.A.A. Rizvi points to Muhammad bin Tughlaq as not only encouraging locals but promoting artisan groups such as cooks, barbers and gardeners to high administrative posts. In his reign, it is likely that conversions to Islam took place as a means of seeking greater social mobility and improved social standing.

IMPACT OF ISLAM AND MUSLIMS IN INDIA

Expansion of Trade

Islam's impact was the most notable in the expansion of trade. The first contact of Muslims with India was the Arab attack on a nest of pirates near modern-day Mumbai to safeguard their trade in the Arabian Sea. Around the same time many Arabs settled at Indian ports, giving rise to small Muslm communities. The growth of these communities was not only due to conversion but also the fact that many Hindu kings of south India (such as those from Cholas) hired Muslims as mercenaries.

A significant aspect of the Muslim period in world history was the emergence of Islamic Sharia courts capable of imposing a common commercial and legal system that extended from Morocco in the West to Mongolia in the North East and Indonesia in the South East. While southern India was already in trade with Arabs/ Muslims, northern India found new opportunities. As the Hindu and Buddhist kingdoms of Asia were subjugated by Islam, and as Islam spread through Africa – it became a highly centralising force that facilitated in the creation of a common legal system that allowed letters of credit issued in say Egypt or Tunisia to be honoured in India or Indonesia (The Sharia has laws on the transaction of business with both Muslims and non-Muslims). In order to cement their rule, Muslim rulers initially promoted a system in which there was a revolving door between the clergy, the administrative nobility and the mercantile classes. The travels of explorer Muhammad Ibn-Abdullah Ibn-Batuta were eased because of this system. He served as an Imam in Delhi, as a judicial official in the Maldives, and as an envoy and trader in the Malabar. There was never a contradiction in any of his positions because each of these roles complemented the other. Islam created a compact under which political power, law and religion became fused in a manner so as to safeguard the interests of the mercantile class. This led world trade to expand to the maximum extent possible in the medieval world. Sher Shah Suri took initiatives in improvement of trade by abolishing all taxes which hindered progress of free trade. He built large networks of roads and constructed Grand Trunk Road (1540–1544), which connects Chittagong to Kabul. Parts of it are still in use today. The geographic regions add to the diversity of languages and politics.

Cultural Influence

The divide and rule policies, two-nation theory, and subsequent partition of India in the wake of Independence from the British Empire has polarised the sub-continental psyche, making objective assessment hard in comparison to the other settled agricultural societies of India from the North West. Muslim rule differed from these others in the level of assimilation and syncretism that occurred. They retained their identity and introduced legal and administrative systems that superseded existing systems of social conduct and ethics. While this was a source of friction it resulted in a unique experience the legacy of which is a Muslim community strongly Islamic in character while at the same time distinctive and unique among its peers.

The impact of Islam on Indian culture has been inestimable. It permanently influenced the development of all areas of human endeavour – language, dress, cuisine, all the art forms, architecture and urban design, and social customs and values. Conversely, the languages of the Muslim invaders were modified by contact with local languages, to Urdu, which uses the Arabic script. This language was also known as Hindustani, an umbrella term used for the vernacular terminology of Hindi as well as Urdu, both major languages in South Asia today derived primarily from Sanskrit grammatical structures and vocabulary.

Muslim rule saw a greater urbanisation of India and the rise of many cities and their urban cultures. The biggest impact was upon trade resulting from a common commercial and legal system extending from Morocco to Indonesia. This change of emphasis on mercantilism and trade from the more strongly centralised governance systems further clashed with the agricultural based traditional economy and also provided fuel for social and political tensions.

A related development to the shifting economic conditions was the establishment of Karkhanas, or small factories and the import and dissemination of technology through India and the rest of the world. The use of ceramic tiles was adopted from architectural traditions of Iraq, Iran, and Central Asia. Rajasthan's blue pottery was a local variation of imported Chinese pottery. There is also the example of Sultan Abidin (1420–70) sending Kashmiri artisans to Samarqand to learn book-binding and paper making. Khurja and Siwan became renowned for pottery, Moradabad for brass ware, Mirzapur for carpets, Firozabad for glass wares, Farrukhabad for printing, Sahranpur and Nagina for wood-carving, Bidar and Lucknow for bidriware, Srinagar for papier-mache, Benaras for jewellery and textiles, and so on. On the flip-side encouraging such growth also resulted in higher taxes on the peasantry.

Numerous Indian scientific and mathematical advances and the Hindu numerals were spread to the rest of the world and much of the scholarly work and advances in the sciences of the age under Muslim nations across the globe were imported by the liberal patronage of Arts and Sciences by the rulers. The languages brought by Islam were modified by contact with local languages leading to the creation of several new languages, such as Urdu, which uses the modified Arabic script, but with more Persian words. The influences of these languages exist in several dialects in India today.

Islamic and Mughal architecture and art is widely noticeable in India, examples being the Taj Mahal and Jama Masjid. At the same time, muslim rulers destroyed most of the ancient Indian architectural marvels and converted them into Islamic structures, most notably at Varanasi, Mathura, Ayodhya and the Kutub Complex in New Delhi.

HISTORY OF THE SUB-CONTINENT MUSLIMS

Muslims in India have been an exceptionally fortunate minority throughout for most of their history. For large phases in the last thousand years, most of the subcontinent was ruled by a variety of Muslim nobility, enabling the community to exist with a sense of security that is extremely rare for minorities. In fact, the word 'minority' itself is a comparatively modern term. For Muslims never saw themselves as a 'minority' under, say, the Mughal empire, just as the Christians never felt oppressed or discriminated under British or Portuguese rule.

During the Muslim rule belonging to Islam was a great cementing force, and, whatever the color of the skin, all Muslim nobles tried to feel as one, as belonging to the ruling elite, as searching for exotic roots. It was aristocratic on the part of the orthodox Muslim to feel that he was in India, *but not of it*. He dare not strike his roots deep into the native soil. He must import traditions, language and culture. His civil and criminal law must be *derived* from the writings of jurists and the decisions of judges in Baghdad and Cairo. The Muslim in India was an intellectual exotic; he considered it *infra dig* to adapt himself to his environment. This concept of importing everything from outside created a perception among the elite that there is nothing worthwhile from India. Similar feeling was created that everything good in modern India is due to the influence of the outside.

Right through the Muslim rule, low origin foreigners used to come as individuals and in groups to seek employment in India. Writing about the foreign element in the Mughal nobility in seventeenth century Bernier says "the Omarahs mostly consist of adventurers from different nations who entice one another to the court; and are generally persons of low descent, some having been originally slaves, and the majority being destitute of education. The Mogul raises them to dignities, or degrades them to obscurity; according to his own pleasure and caprice." W.H. Moreland, nevertheless, does not consider all foreign immigrants as of low descent. He says that in Mughal India "there were huge prizes to be won... and one need not wonder that the service should have attracted to the court the ablest and most enterprising men from a large portion of Western Asia." High and low, foreign and Indian, the Muslim nobles after all belonged to one and the same cadre, and they tried to come closer together. On the one hand, foreign Muslims used to become locals after the lapse of a few generations. Bernier writes "the children of the third and fourth generation (of Uzbegs, Persians, Arabs and Turks)... are held in much less respect than the new corners." On the other hand, the low-born Indian Muslim became elitist with rise in economic status.

In order to provide suitable legitimacy to their claims of social superiority, medieval Indian ashraf scholars wrote numerous texts that sought to interpret the Quran to suit their purposes, thus effectively denying the Qumran's message of radical social equality. Pre-Islamic Persian notions of the divine right of kings and the nobility, as opposed to the actual practice of the Prophet and the early Muslim community, seem to have exercised a powerful influence on these writers. A classical, oft-quoted example in this regard is provided by the Fatawa-i -Jahandari, written by the fourteenth century Turkish scholar, Ziauddin

Barani, a leading courtier of Muhammad bin Tughlaq, Sultan of Delhi. This text is the only known surviving Indo-Persian treatise exclusively devoted to political theory from the period of the Delhi Sultanate. The Fatawa-i Jahandari shows Barani as a fervent champion of ashraf supremacy and as vehemently opposed to the ajlaf. In appealing to the Sultan to protect the ashraf and keep the ajlaf firmly under their control and submission he repeatedly refers to the Quran, from which he seeks to derive legitimacy from his arguments. His is not a rigorous scholarly approach to the Quran, nevertheless, for he conveniently misinterprets it to support the hegemonic claims of the ashraf, completely ignoring the Qumran's insistence on social equality. In the process, he develops a doctrine and social vision for the ideal Muslim ruler, which, in their implications for what Barani calls the 'low-born', are hardly different in their severity than the classical Hindu law of caste as contained in the Manusmriti, the Brahminical law code.

Historically the majority of Muslims, originally low-caste Hindus, affected a superiority complex, particularly in Northern India. They feared being falling down into the vast assimilative sea of Hindudom surrounding them wherein they will be at the bottom of social heap. May be they would be punished for former uppishness and for real or imagined wrongs. That explained their demonstrative adherence to Islam, which is what distinguished them from Hindus. Their religious exhibitionism and a superiority complex led to emphases on differences with Hindus and regarding themselves as rulers' kith and kin deserving privileges and safeguards — the leitmotif of pre-independence Indian Muslim politics.

It is said that saint-worship among Muslims is a practice unique to India. *Dargahs* of Sufis, real or figurative, are found all over the country and Muslims flock to them in large numbers. It is a legacy of medieval times. One reason for this can be that most Indian Muslims are converted Hindus, who, when their places of worship were converted into (*khanqahs* and later) *dargahs*, did not give up visiting them. For instance, at the most holy *dargah* of Sheikh Muinuddin Chishti, the Sandal Khana mosque is believed to have been built on the site of a Dev temple. The other is that stories of miracles of saints give a hope and a chance to people to obtain fulfillment of their desires. Hence besides Muslims, a few Hindus also resort to such shrines.

After the fall of Moghul rule there was uneasiness among the Indian Muslims regarding their status and their position under the infidels. The Europeans were expanding trade and taking political control of the country. They considered that they are not a minority in the periphery of the Islamic region like heartland of Ottoman Empire but at the core culture of the civilized world and felt vulnerable.

Had they lost touch with their roots? The Sufi thinker Shah Valli-Ullah (1703-62) believed that the answer lay in Sirhindi's position, and his views would continue to influence the Muslims of India well into the twentieth century. Ahmad Sirhindi (d. 1625): Sufi reformer who opposed the pluralism of the Moghul emperor Akbar influenced WaliUllah.

Shah expressed the new embattled vision, and as Muslims felt their power slipping away in other parts of the world and experienced similar fears about the survival of Islam, other philosophers and reformers would reach similar conclusions. First Muslims must unite, bury their sectarian differences with one another and present a united front against their enemies.

The Shariah must be adapted to meet the special conditions of the subcontinent, and become a means of resisting Hinduisation. It was essential for Muslims to retain the upper hand militarily and politically.

So concerned was he, that Shah WaliUllah even supported the disastrous Afghan attempt to revive Muslim power. A defensive strain had entered Muslim thinking, and this would continue to characterize Islamic piety in the modern world.

The Pakistani perception of their history and Muslim rule has a different angle.

During the course of the conversation with JN Dixit the ambassador to Pakistan , Gohar Khan FM proceeded to give a holistic analysis of the sub continental history.

- Partition of India was inevitable as the minimal solution to the Hindu-Muslim relations.
- Muslims had ruled India for nearly a thousand years and that they could not stay in unified India as a minority.
- Partition not only geographically conformed to the religious affiliations of Muslims and Hindus, but it affirmed the basic difference in the nature of the Hindu, Muslim populations.
- Muslims are religiously committed, war like and aggressive and not given to softness and compromises
- Hindus were exactly opposite submissive, maneuvering and clever.
- Even the flora and fauna had a linkage with Partition. While East and West Pakistan had tigers, wild boars, leopards, bulls etc. India had bison, nilgai, gazelle and deer most of which are vegetarian and natural prey to the former.
- The momin (Muslim faithful) had profound capacity to struggle
- If he lost his life, he became a shaheed and if he won he became a gazi.

EARLY MUSLIM COMMUNITIES

Several reasons existed for the desire of the rising Islamic Empire to gain a foothold in Makran and Sindh; ranging from the participation of armies from Sindh fighting alongside the Persians in battles such as Nehawand, Salasal, Qadisia and Makran, pirate raids on Arab shipping to the granting of refuge to rebel chiefs.

The Punjab and Sindh region had also been historically under considerable flux as Central Asian Kingdoms, the Persian Empire, Buddhist Kingdoms and Rajput Kingdoms vied for control prior to the arrival of the Muslim influence. Afghan warlord Mahmud Ghazni made numerous incursions into Gujarat in order to effectively loot and destroy the Somnath Temple, using the acquired wealth to fund his famous military campaigns in Northern India and Central Asia.

Islam in India existed in communities along the Arab coastal trade routes in Sindh, Bengal, Gujarat, Kerala, and Ceylon as soon as the religion originated and had early gained widespread acceptance in the Arabian Peninsula, being brought over by merchants, sufis and missionaries, who often times settled down and intermarried with the local women, adopting local customs.

Arab Invasion of Sindh

In 711, the Umayyad Caliph in Damascus sent two failed expeditions to Balochistan (an arid region on the Iranian Plateau in Southwest Asia, presently split between Iran,Afghanistan, and Pakistan) and Sindh.

According to Muslim historical accounts such as the Chach Nama, the nature of the expeditions was punitive, and in response to raids carried out by pirates on Arab shipping, operating around Debal. The allegation was made that the King of Sindh, Raja Dahir. The third expedition was led by a 20-year-old arabian chieftain named Muhammad bin Qasim. The expedition went as far North as Multan, then called the "City of Gold," that contained the extremely large Hindu temple of Sun god.

Bin Qasim invaded the sub-continent at the orders of Al-Hajjaj bin Yousef, the governor of Iraq. Qasim's armies defeated Raja Dahir at what is now Hyderabad in Sindh in 712. He then proceeded to subdue the lands from Karachi to Multan with an initial force of only six thousand arabian tribesmen; thereby establishing the dominion of the Umayyad Caliphate from Lisbon in Portugal to the Indus Valley. Qasim's stay was brief as he was soon recalled to Iraq, and the Caliphates rule in South Asia shrank to Sindh and Southern Punjab in the form of Arab states, the principal of whom were Al Mansura and Multan.

Battle of Rajasthan

The Battle of Rajasthan is a battle (or series of battles) where the Hindu alliance of Vikramaditya II of the Chalukya dynasty,

Gurjara-Pratiharas and Rajputs defeated the Arabinvaders in 738 CE and removed the Arabs from the area east of the Indus River. The final battle took place somewhere on the borders of modern Sindh-Rajasthan. Following their defeat the remnants of the Arab army fled to the other bank of the River Indus. The Muslim conquest of Persia by Arab forces in a short space of time contrasts sharply to the defeat of the Arab armies by the Hindus.

Communities in the North-West

Subsequent to Qasim's recall the Caliphates control in Sindh was extremely weak under governors who only nominally acknowledged Arab control and shared power with coexisting local Hindu, Jain and Buddhist rulers. Ismaili missionaries found a receptive audience among both the Sunni and non-Muslim populations here. In 985, a group aroundMultan declared themselves an independent Ismaili Fatimid State.

Coastal trade and the presence of a colony in Sindh permitted significant cultural exchange and the introduction of Muslim teachers into the subcontinent. Considerable conversions took place, especially amongst the Buddhist majority. Multan became a center of the Ismaili sect of Islam, which still has many adherents in Sindh today. This region under generous patronage of the arts provided a conduit for Arab scholars to absorb and expand on Indian sciences and pass them onwards to the West.

North of Multan, non-Muslim groups remained numerous. From this period, the conquered area was divided into two parts: the Northern region comprising the Punjab remained under the control of Hindu Rajas, while the Southern coastal areas comprising Balochistan, Sindh, and Multan came under Muslim control.

LATER MUSLIM INVASIONS

Ghaznavid Period

Under Sabuktigin, Ghazni found itself in conflict with the Shahi Raja Jayapala. When Sabuktigin died and his son Mahmud ascended the throne in 998, Ghazni was engaged in the North with the Qarakhanids when the Shahi Raja renewed hostilities.

In the early 11th century, Mahmud of Ghazni launched seventeen expeditions into South Asia. In 1001, Sultan Mahmud of Ghazni defeated Raja Jayapala of the Hindu Shahi Dynasty of Gandhara (in modern Afghanistan), the Battle of Peshawar and marched further into Peshawar (in modern Pakistan) and, in 1005, made it the center for his forces.

The Ghaznavid conquests were initially directed against the Ismaili Fatimids of Multan, who were engaged in an on-going struggle with theAbbasid Caliphate in conjunction with their compatriots of the Fatimid Caliphate in North Africa and the Middle East; Mahmud apparently hoped to curry the favor of the Abbasids in this fashion. However, once this aim was accomplished, he moved onto the richness of the loot of wealthy temples and monasteries. By 1027, Mahmud had captured parts of North India and obtained formal recognition of Ghazni's sovereignty from the Abbassid Caliph, al-Qadir Billah.

Ghaznavid rule in Northwestern India (modern Afghanistan and Pakistan) lasted over 175 years, from 1010 to 1187. It was during this period that Lahore assumed considerable importance apart from being the second capital, and later the only capital, of the Ghaznavid Empire.

At the end of his reign, Mahmud's empire extended from Kurdistan in the west to Samarkand in the Northeast, and from the Caspian Sea to the Punjab. Although his raids carried his forces across Northern and Western India, only Punjab came under his permanent rule; Kashmir, the Doab, Rajasthan, and Gujarat remained under the control of the local Indian dynasties.

In 1030, Mahmud fell gravely ill and died at age 59. He had been a gifted military commander.

As with the invaders of three centuries ago, Mahmud's armies looted temples in Varanasi, Mathura, Ujjain, Maheshwar, Jwalamukhi, Somnath and Dwarka.

Mu'izz al-Din

Mu'izz al-Din better known as Shahâb-ud-Din Muhammad Ghori was a Afghan conqueror from the region of Ghor in

Afghanistan. Before 1160, the Ghaznavid Empire covered an area running from central Afghanistan east to the Punjab, with capitals at Ghazni on the banks of Ghazni river in present-day Afghanistan, and at Lahore in present-day Pakistan. In 1160, the Ghorids conquered Ghazni from the Ghaznavids, and in 1173 Muhammad Bin Sâm was made governor of Ghazni. He raided eastwards into the remaining Ghaznavid territory, and invaded Gujarat in the 1180s but was defeated by the Indian queen Naikidevi of Gujarat. In 1186 and 1187 he conquered Lahore in alliance with a local Hindu ruler, ending the Ghaznavid empire and bringing the last of Ghaznavid territory under his control, and seemed to be the first Muslim ruler seriously interested in expanding his domain in the sub-continent, and like his predecessor Mahmud initially started off against the Ismaili kingdom of Multan that had regained independence during the Nizariconflicts, and then onto booty and power.

In 1191, he invaded the territory of Prithviraj III of Ajmer, who ruled much of present-day Rajasthan and Punjab, but was defeated at Tarain by Govindraj of Delhi, Prithviraj's vassal. The following year, Mu'izz al-Din assembled 120,000 horsemen and once again invaded India. Mu'izz al-Din's army met Prithviraj's army again at Tarain, and this time Mu'izz al-Din won; Govindraj was slain, Prithviraj captured and Mu'izz al-Din advanced onto Delhi. Within a year, Mu'izz al-Din controlled Northern Rajasthan and Northern Ganges-Yamuna Doab. After these victories in India, and Mu'izz al-Din's establishment of a capital in Delhi, Multan was also incorporated into his empire. Mu'izz al-Din then returned east to Ghazni to deal with the threat on his eastern frontiers from the Turks and Mongols, whiles his armies continued to advance through Northern India, raiding as far east as Bengal.

Mu'izz al-Din returned to Lahore after 1200. In 1206, Mu'izz al-Din had to travel to Lahore to crush a revolt. On his way back to Ghazni, his caravan rested at Damik near Sohawa(which is near the city of Jhelum in the Punjab province of modern-day Pakistan). He was assassinated on 15 March 1206, while offering his evening prayers. The identity of Ghori's assassins is disputed, with some claiming that he was assassinated by local Hindu Gakhars and others claiming he was assassinated by Hindu Khokhars, both being different tribes.

The Khokhars were killed in large numbers, and the province was pacified. After settling the affairs in the Punjab. Mu'izz al-Din marched back to Ghazni. While camping at Dhamayak in 1206 AD in the Jehlum district, the sultan was murdered by the Khokhars

Hasan Nizami and Ferishta record the killing of Mu'izz al-Din at the hands of the Gakhars. However, Ferishta may have confused the Ghakars with the Khokhars. Other historians have also blamed Shahabuddin Ghori's assassination *to a band of Hindu Khokhars.*

All the historians before the time of Ferishta agree that the Khokhars, not the Gakhars killed Mu'izz al-Din.

Some also claim that Mu'izz al-Din was assassinated by the Hashshashin, a radical Ismaili Muslim sect.

According to his wishes, Mu'izz al-Din was buried where he fell, in Damik. Upon his death his most capable general, Qutb-ud-din Aybak, took control of Mu'izz al-Din's Indian conquests and declared himself the first Sultan of Delhi.

The Delhi Sultanate

Muhammad's successors established the first dynasty of the Delhi Sultanate, while the Mamluk Dynasty in 1211 (however, the Delhi Sultanate is traditionally held to have been founded in 1206) seized the reins of the empire. *Mamluk* means "slave" and referred to the Turkic slave soldiers who became rulers. The territory under control of the Muslim rulers in Delhi expanded rapidly. By mid-century, Bengal and much of central India was under the Delhi Sultanate. Several Turko-Afghan dynasties ruled from Delhi: the Mamluk (1206–1290), the Khalji (1290–1320), the Tughlaq (1320–1414), the Sayyid (1414–51), and the Lodhi (1451–1526). Muslim Kings extended their domains into Southern India, Kingdom of Vijayanagar resisted until falling to the Deccan Sultanate in 1565. Certain kingdoms remained independent of Delhi such as the larger kingdoms ofPunjab, Rajasthan, parts of the Deccan, Gujarat, Malwa (central India), and Bengal, nevertheless all of the area in present-day Pakistan came under the rule of Delhi.

The Sultans of Delhi enjoyed cordial, if superficial, relations with Muslim rulers in the Near East but owed them no allegiance. They based their laws on the *Quran* and the *sharia* and permitted non-Muslim subjects to practice their religion only if they paid the *jizya* (poll tax). They ruled from urban centres, while military camps and trading posts provided the nuclei for towns that sprang up in the countryside.

Perhaps the most significant contribution of the Sultanate was its temporary success in insulating the subcontinent from the potential devastation of the Mongol invasion from Central Asia in the 13th century, which nonetheless led to the capture of Afghanistan and western Pakistan by the Mongols (see the Ilkhanate Dynasty). The Sultanate ushered in a period of Indian cultural renaissance, The resulting "Indo-Muslim" fusion left lasting monuments in architecture, music, literature, and religion. In addition it is surmised that the language of Urdu (literally meaning "horde" or "camp" in various Turkic dialects) was born during the Delhi Sultanate period as a result of the mingling of Sanskritic Hindi and the Persian, Turkish, Arabic favoured by the Muslim invaders of India .

The Sultanate suffered significantly from the sacking of Delhi in 1398 by Timur, but revived briefly under the Lodi Dynasty, the final dynasty of the Sultanate before it was conquered by Zahiruddin Babur in 1526, who subsequently founded the Mughal Dynasty that ruled from the 16th to the 18th centuries.

Timur

Tîmûr bin Taraghay Barlas, known in the West as Tamerlane or "Timur the lame", was a 14th-century warlord of Turco-Mongol descent, conqueror of much of western and central Asia, and founder of the Timurid Empire and Timurid dynasty (1370–1405) in Central Asia, which survived until 1857 as the Mughal dynasty of India.

Informed about civil war in South Asia, Timur began a trek starting in 1398 to invade the reigning Sultan Nasir-u Din Mehmud of the Tughlaq Dynasty in the north Indian city ofDelhi. His campaign was politically pretexted that the Muslim Delhi Sultanate was too tolerant toward its Hindu subjects, but that could not mask the real reason being to amass the wealth of the Delhi Sultanate.

Timur crossed the Indus River at Attock (now Pakistan) on 24 September. The capture of towns and villages was often followed by the looting, massacre of their inhabitants and raping of their women, as well as pillaging to support his massive army. Timur wrote many times in his memoirs of his specific disdain for the 'idolatrous' Hindus

Timur's invasion did not go unopposed and he did meet some resistance during his march to Delhi, most notably with the Sarv Khap coalition in northern India, and the Governorof Meerut. Although impressed and momentarily stalled by the valour of Ilyaas Awan, Timur was able to continue his relentless approach to Delhi, arriving in 1398 to combat the armies of Sultan Mehmud, already weakened by an internal battle for ascension within the royal family.

The Sultan's army was easily defeated on 17 December 1398. Timur entered Delhi and the city was sacked, destroyed, and left in ruins. Before the battle for Delhi, Timur executed more than 100,000 Hindu captives.

Timur himself recorded the invasions in his memoirs, collectively known as *Tuzk-i-Timuri*. Timur's purported autobiography, the *Tuzk-e-Taimuri* ("Memoirs of Temur") is a later fabrication, although most of the historical facts are accurate.

As per Malfuzat-i-Timuri, Timur targeted Hindus. In his own words, "Excepting the quarter of the saiyids, the 'ulama and the other Musalmans [sic], the whole city was sacked". In his descriptions of the Loni massacre he wrote, "..Next day I gave orders that the Musalman prisoners should be separated and saved."

During the ransacking of Delhi, almost all inhabitants not killed were captured and enslaved.

Timur's memoirs on his invasion of India describe in detail the massacre of Hindus, looting plundering and raping of their women and children, their forced conversions to Islam and the plunder of the wealth of Hindustan (Greater India). It gives details of how villages, towns and entire cities were rid of their Hindu male population through systematic mass slaughters and genocide and their women and children forcefully converted en masse to Islam from Hinduism.

Timur left Delhi in approximately January 1399. In April he had returned to his own capital beyond the Oxus (Amu Darya). Immense quantities of spoils were taken from India. According to Ruy Gonzáles de Clavijo, 90 captured elephants were employed merely to carry precious stones looted from his conquest, so as to to erect a mosque at Samarkand — what historians today believe is the enormous Bibi-Khanym Mosque. Ironically, the mosque was constructed too quickly and suffered greatly from disrepair within a few decades of its construction.

THE MUGHAL EMPIRE

India in the 16th century presented a fragmented picture of rulers, both Muslim and Hindu, who lacked concern for their subjects and failed to create a common body of laws or institutions. } Outside developments also played a role in shaping events. The circumnavigation of Africa by the Portuguese explorer Vasco da Gama in 1498 allowed Europeans to challenge Muslim control of the trading routes between Europe and Asia. In Central Asia and Afghanistan, shifts in power pushed Babur of Ferghana (in present-day Uzbekistan) southward, first to Kabul and then to India. The dynasty he founded endured for more than three centuries.

Babur

Claiming descent from both Genghis Khan and Timur, Babur combined strength and courage with a love of beauty, and military ability with cultivation. He concentrated on gaining control of Northwestern India, doing so in 1526 by defeating the last Lodhi Sultan at the First battle of Panipat, a town north of Delhi. Babur then turned to the tasks of persuading his Central Asian followers to stay on in India and of overcoming other contenders for power, mainly the Rajputs and the Afghans. He succeeded in both tasks but died shortly thereafter in 1530. The Mughal Empire was one of the largest centralised states in premodern history and was the precursor to the British Indian Empire.

Babur was followed by his great-grandson, Shah Jahan (r. 1628–58), builder of the Taj Mahal and other magnificent buildings. Two other towering figures of the Mughal era were Akbar (r. 1556–1605) and Aurangzeb (r. 1658–1707). Both rulers expanded the empire greatly and were able administrators. However, Akbar was known for his religious tolerance and administrative genius while Aurangzeb was a pious Muslim and fierce advocate of more orthodox Islam.

Aurangzeb

While some rulers were zealous in their spread of Islam, others were relatively liberal. Moghul emperor Akbar was relatively liberal and established a new religion, Din E Elahi, which included beliefs from different religions. He abolished the jizya for some time. In contrast, his great-grandson Aurangazeb was a more zealous and ruthless ruler .

In the century-and-a-half that followed the death of Aurangzeb, effective Muslim control weakened. Succession to imperial and even provincial power, which had often become hereditary, was subject to intrigue and force. The mansabdari system gave way to thezamindari system, in which high-ranking officials took on the appearance of hereditary landed aristocracy with powers of collecting rents. As Delhi's control waned, other contenders for power emerged and clashed, thus preparing the way for the eventual British takeover.

Durrani Empire

The decay of the Mughal power saw a series of invasions by the Persian adventurer, Nadir Shah, but no occupation per se. Following his death, his Royal Guardsman Ahmed Shah Abdali – aPashtun – embarked on an invasion of conquest. In the short space of just over a quarter of a century, he forged one of the largest Muslim empires of the 18th century. The high point of his conquests was his victory over the powerful Marathas in the third Battle of Panipat 1761. In South Asia his empire stretched from the Indus at Attock all the way to the outskirts of Delhi. Uninterested in long term of conquest or in replacing the Mughal Empire, he became increasingly pre occupied with revolts in Persia and by the Sikhs. His empire started to unravel not long after his death.

DECLINE OF MUSLIM RULE IN INDIAN SUBCONTINENT

Maratha Empire(1674-1818) ruled large parts of India following the decline of the Mughals. The long and futile war bankrupted one of the most powerful empires in the world. Mountstart Elphinstone termed this a demoralizing period for the Mussalmans as many of them lost the will to fight against the Maratha Empire. Maratha empire at its peak was stretched from Tamil Nadu (Trichinopoly) in the south to the Afghan border in the north.

In early 1771, Mahadji ,a notable Maratha general, recaptured Delhi and installed Shah Alam II as the puppet ruler on the Mughal throne.In the north India, the Marathas thus regained the territory and the prestige lost as result of the defeat at Panipath in 1761.

Mahadji ruled the Punjab as it used to be a Mughal territory and Sikh sardars and other Rajas of the cis-Sutlej region paid tributes to him. A considerable portion of the Indian subcontinent came under the sway of the British Empire after the Third Anglo-Maratha War, which ended the Maratha Empire completely in 1818.

In northwest India, in the Punjab, Sikhs developed themselves into a powerful force under the authority of twelve Misls. By 1801, Ranjit Singh captured Lahore and threw off the Afghan yoke from North West India. In Afghanistan Zaman Shah Durrani was defeated by powerfulBarakzai chief Fateh Khan who appointed Mahmud Shah Durrani as the new ruler of Afghanistan and appointed himself as Wazir of Afghanistan. Sikhs however were now superior to the Afghans and started to annex Afghan provinces. The biggest victory of theSikh Empire over the Durrani Empire came in the Battle of Attock fought in 1813 between Sikh and Wazir of Afghanistan Fateh Khan and his younger brother Dost Mohammad Khan. The Afghans were routed by the Sikh army and the Afghans lost over 9,000 soldiers in this battle. Dost Mohammad was seriously injured whereas his brother Wazir Fateh Khan fled back to Kabul fearing that his brother was dead. In 1818 they slaughtered Afghans and Muslims in trading city of Multan killing Afghan governor Nawab Muzzafar Khan and five of his sons in the Siege of Multan. In 1819 the last Indian Province of Kashmir was conquered by Sikhs who registered another crushing victory over weak Afghan General Jabbar Khan. The Koh-i-Noor diamond was also taken by Maharaja Ranjit Singh in 1814. In 1823 a Sikh Army routed Dost Mohammad Khan the Sultan of Afghanistan and his brother Azim Khan at Naushera (Near Peshawar). By 1834 the Sikh Empire extended up to the Khyber Pass. Hari Singh Nalwa the Sikh general remained the governor of Khyber Agency till his death in 1837. He consolidated Sikh hold in tribal provinces. The northernmost Indian territories of Gilgit, Baltistan andLadakh was annexed between 1831-1840.

ICONOCLASM

Nalanda

In 1193, the Nalanda University complex was destroyed by Afghan Khilji-Ghilzai Muslims under Bakhtiyar Khalji; this event is seen as the final milestone in the decline of Buddhism in India. He also burned Nalanda's major Buddhist library andVikramshila University, as well as numerous Bhuddhist monasteries in India. When the Tibetan translator, Chag Lotsawa Dharmasvamin (Chag Lo-tsa-ba, 1197–1264), visited northern India in 1235, Nalanda was damaged, looted, and largely deserted, but still standing and functioning with seventy students.

Mahabodhi, Sompura, Vajrasan and other important monasteries were found to be untouched. The Ghuri ravages only afflicted those monasteries that lay in the direct of their advance and were fortified in the manner of defensive forts.

By the end of the 12th century, following the Muslim conquest of the Buddhist stronghold in Bihar, Buddhism, having already declined in the South, declined in the North as well because survivors retreated to Nepal, Sikkim and Tibet or escaped to the South of the Indian sub-continent.

Vijayanagara

The city flourished between the 14th century and 16th century, during the height of the Vijayanagar Empire. During this time, it was often in conflict with the kingdoms which rose in the Northern Deccan, and which are often collectively termed the Deccan Sultanates. The Vijaynagar Empire successfully resisted Muslim invasions for centuries. But in 1565, the empire's armies suffered a massive and catastrophic defeat at the hands of an alliance of the Sultanates, and the capital was taken. The victorious armies then razed, depopulated and destroyed the city over several months. The empire continued its slow decline, but the original capital was not reoccupied or rebuilt.

Somanath

The first temple of Somnath existed before the beginning of the common era.

The second temple, built by the Maitraka kings of Vallabhi in Gujarat, replaced the first one on the same site around 649. In 725 Junayad, the Arabgovernor of Sind, sent his armies to destroy the second temple.

The Pratihara king Nagabhata II constructed the third temple in 815, a large structure of red sandstone. Mahmud of Ghazniattacked this temple in 1026, looted its gems and precious stones, massacred the worshippers and burned it. It was then that the famous Shivalinga of the temple was entirely destroyed.

The fourth temple was built by the Paramara King Bhoj of Malwa and the Solanki king Bhimdev I of Gujarat (Anhilwara) between 1026 and 1042. The temple was razed in 1297 when the Sultanate of Delhi conquered Gujarat, and again in 1394. Mughal Emperor Aurangzeb destroyed the temple again in 1706.

2

The Muslim Community in History

The history of Islam has often been linked to the existence of an Islamic state or empire. From its beginnings, Islam existed and spread as a community-state; it was both a faith and a political order. Within centuries after his death, Muhammad's local Arabian polity became a vast empire, extending from North Africa to Southeast Asia. The development of Islam and state institutions (the caliphate, law, education, the military, social services) were intertwined. Again, the Prophetic period provided the paradigm for later generations. For it was in Medina that the Quranic mandate took on form and substance under the guidance and direction of the Prophet.

The Medinan community formed a total framework for state, society, and culture. It epitomized the Quranic mandate for Muslims as individuals and as a community *(umma)* "to transform the world itself through action in the world." This aspiration and ideal has constituted the challenge for the Islamic community throughout much of its history. It inspired Muhammad to transform a local shiekdom into a transtribal state.

MUHAMMAD AND THE MEDINAN STATE

Seventh-century Arabia was dominated by two great empires: the Byzantine (Christian), or Eastern Roman, empire and the Sasanian Persian (Zoroastrian) empire. In the middle was the Arabian Peninsula, composed of apparently weak and divided tribal societies. Within one hundred years, both empires would fall before the armies of Allah as Arabia united under the umbrella of Islam, which provided a principle of organization and motivation. Under the successors of the Prophet, a vast empire and a commonwealth of Islamic states would come to dominate much of the world. Its missionaries would be soldiers, merchants, and mystics. Islam would provide the basis of community identity and the rationale or legitimacy for rulers and their policies of expansion and conquest. Thus, for example, the wars of conquest were termed *fath*, "opening or victory" of the way for Islam. As Muhammad governed a transtribal state in the name of Islam, so too the Islamic community became associated with an expansive empire. Why and how did this come to pass?

Shortly after the surrender of Mecca, Muhammad turned his attention to the extension and consolidation of his authority over Arabia. Envoys were sent and alliances forged with surrounding tribes and rulers. The fiercely independent Bedouin tribes of Arabia were united behind the Prophet of Islam through a combination of force and diplomacy. As Muhammad was both head of state and messenger of God, so too were the envoys and soldiers of the state the envoys and soldiers of Islam, its first missionaries. Along with their treaties and armies, they brought the Quran and the teachings of their faith. They spread a way of life that affected the political and social order as well as individual life and worship. Islam encompassed both a faith and a sociopolitical system. Ideally, this new order was to be a community of believers, acknowledging the ultimate sovereignty of God, living according to His law, obeying His Prophet, and dedicating their lives to spreading God's rule and law. This was the message and vision that accompanied Arab armies as they burst out of Arabia and established their supremacy throughout the Middle East.

What is most striking about the early expansion of Islam is its rapidity and success. Western scholars have marveled at it, and Muslim tradition has viewed the conquests as a miraculous proof or historic validation of the truth of Islam's claims and a sign of God's guidance. Within a decade, Arab forces overran the Byzantine and Persian armies, exhausted by years of warfare, and conquered

Iraq, Syria, Palestine, Persia, and Egypt. The momentum of these early victories was extended to a series of brilliant battles under great generals like Khalid ibn al-Walid and Amr ibn al-As, which extended the boundaries of the Muslim empire to Morocco and Spain in the west and across Central Asia to India in the east. Driven by the economic rewards from conquest of richer, more developed areas, united and inspired by their new faith, Muslim armies proved to be formidable conquerors and effective rulers, builders rather than destroyers. They replaced the conquered countries, indigenous rulers and armies, but preserved much of their government, bureaucracy, and culture.

For many in the conquered territories, it was no more than an exchange of masters, one that brought peace to peoples demoralized and disaffected by the casualties and heavy taxation that resulted from the years of Byzantine-Persian warfare. Local communities were free to continue to follow their own way of life in internal, domestic affairs. In many ways, local populations found Muslim rule more flexible and tolerant than that of Byzantium and Persia. Religious communities were free to practice their faith to worship and be governed by their religious leaders and laws in such areas as marriage, divorce, and inheritance. In exchange, they were required to pay tribute, a poll tax *(jizya)* that entitled them to Muslim protection from outside aggression and exempted them from military service. Thus, they were called the "protected ones" *(dhimmi).* In effect, this often meant lower taxes, greater local autonomy, rule by fellow Semites with closer linguistic and cultural ties than the hellenized, Greco-Roman élites of Byzantium, and greater religious freedom for Jews and indigenous Christians. Most of the Christian churches, such as the Nestorians, Monophysites, Jacobites, and Copts, were persecuted as heretics and schismatics by Christian orthodoxy. For these reasons, some Jewish and Christian communities aided the invading armies, regarding them as less oppressive than their imperial masters. In many ways, the conquests brought a Pax Islamica to an embattled area:

The conquests destroyed little: what they did suppress were imperial rivalries and sectarian bloodletting among the newly subjected population. The Muslims tolerated Christianity, but they disestablished it; henceforward Christian life and liturgy, its endowments, politics and theology, would be a private and not a public affair. By an exquisite irony, Islam reduced the status of Christians to that which the Christians had earlier thrust upon the Jews, with one difference. The reduction in Christian status was merely judicial; it was unaccompanied by either systematic persecution or a blood lust, and generally, though not everywhere and at all times, unmarred by vexatious behavior.

A common issue associated with the spread of Islam is the role of Jihad, so-called holy war. While Westerners are quick to characterize Islam as a religion spread by the sword, modern Muslim apologists sometimes explain Jihad as simply defensive in nature. In its most general sense, Jihad in the Quran and in Muslim practice refers to the obligation of all Muslims to strive *(Jihad,* self-exertion) or struggle to follow God's will.

This includes both the struggle to lead a virtuous life and the universal mission of the Muslim community to spread God's rule and law through teaching, preaching, and, where necessary, armed conflict. Contrary to popular belief, the early conquests did not seek to spread the faith through forced conversion but to spread Muslim rule.

Many early Muslims regarded Islam as a solely Arab religion. Moreover, from an economic perspective, increase in the size of the community through conversion diminished Arab Muslims' share in the spoils of conquest. As Islam penetrated new areas, people were offered three options: (1) conversion, that is, to become a full member of the Muslim community with its rights and duties; (2) acceptance of Muslim rule as "protected" people and payment of a poll tax *(jizya);* (3) battle or the sword if neither the first nor the second option was accepted. The astonishing expansion of Islam resulted not only from armed conquest but also from the first two peaceful options. Similarly, in later centuries, in many areas of Africa, the Indian subcontinent, and Southeast Asia, the effective spread of Islam would be due primarily to Muslim traders and Sufi (mystic) missionaries who won converts by their example and their preaching.

THE CALIPHATE (632-1258)

Given Muhammad's formative and pivotal role, his death (632) threatened to radically destabilize the community. Who was to lead? What was to happen to the community? The companions of the Prophet moved quickly to steady and reassure the community. Abu Bakr, an early follower of Muhammad, announced the death of the Prophet to the assembled faithful: "Muslims! If any of you has worshipped Muhammad, let me tell you that Muhammad is dead. But if you worship God, then know that God is living and will never die!" Nevertheless, the Prophet's death did plunge the Islamic community into a series of political crises revolving around leadership and authority. Issues of succession and secession were to plague the early community.

The caliphate (632-1258) has traditionally been divided into three periods: the "Rightly Guided Caliphs" (632-661), the Umayyad empire (661-750), and the Abbasid empire (750-1258). During that time, a vast empire was created with successive capitals in Medina, Kufa, Damascus, and Baghdad. Stunning political success was complemented by a cultural florescence in law, theology, philosophy, literature, medicine, mathematics, science, and art.

The Rightly Guided Caliphs

The caliphate began in 632 with the selection of Muhammad's successor. The first four caliphs were all companions of the Prophet: Abu Bakr (reigned 632-634), Umar ibn al-Khattab (634-644), Uthman ibn Affan (644-656), and Ali ibn Abi Talib (656-661). Their rule is especially significant not only for what they actually did, but also because the period of Muhammad and the Rightly Guided Caliphs came to be regarded in Sunni Islam as the normative period. It provides the idealized past to which Muslims have always looked back for inspiration and guidance, a time to be remembered and emulated.

The vast majority of Muslims (Sunni) believe that Muhammad died without designating his replacement or establishing a system for the selection of his successor. After an initial period of uncertainty, the Prophet's companions, the elders or leaders of

Medina, selected or acknowledged Abu Bakr, an early convert and the Prophet's father-in-law, as caliph *(khalifa,* successor or deputy). Abu Bakr's designation as leader was symbolized by the offering of *baya* (oath), a handclasp used by the Arabs to seal a contract, in this case an oath of obedience and allegiance. Abu Bakr had been a close companion and a trusted adviser of Muhammad; he was a man respected for his sagacity and piety. Muhammad had appointed him to lead the Friday community prayer in his absence. As caliph, Abu Bakr was the political and military leader of the community. Although not a prophet, the caliph enjoyed religious prestige as head of the community of believers *(umma).* This was symbolized in later history by the caliph's right to lead the Friday prayer and the inclusion of his name in its prayers.

Having resolved the question of political leadership and succession, Abu Bakr turned to the consolidation of Muslim rule in Arabia. Muhammad's death had precipitated a series of tribal rebellions. Many tribal chiefs claimed that their allegiance had been based on a political pact with Medina that ceased with the Prophet's death. Tribal independence and factionalism, long a part of Arab history, once more threatened the unity and identity of the new Islamic state. Abu Bakr countered that the unity of the community was based on the interconnectedness of faith and politics and undertook a series of battles that later Muslim historians would call the wars of apostasy *(ridda).* Relying on Khalid ibn al-Walid, whom Muhammad had dubbed "the sword of Allah," he crushed the tribal revolt, consolidating Muslim rule over the entire Arabian Peninsula, and thus preserved the unity and solidarity of the Islamic community-state.

Abu Bakr's successor, Umar, initiated the great period of expansion and conquest. One of the great military leaders of his time, he added the title "Commander of the Faithful" *(amir al-muminin)* to that of "Successor" or "Deputy of the Prophet of God." He also introduced a new method for the selection of his successor. On his deathbed, Umar appointed an "election committee" *(shura,* consultation) to select the next caliph. After due consultation, the council of electors chose Uthman ibn Affan from the Umayyad clan, a leading Meccan family. This was accompanied by the traditional sign of allegiance, the clasping of hands. Thus, based on the practice of the first three caliphs, a pattern was established for selecting the caliph from the Quraysh tribe through a process characterized by consultation and an oath of allegiance *(baya).*

Before long, tribal factionalism and the threat of rebellion resurfaced in the community. Uthman's family had been among the strongest foes of the Prophet. Many of the Medinan élite, who had been among the early supporters of Muhammad, resented Uthman's accession to power and the increased prominence and wealth of his family. Although personally pious, Uthman lacked the presence and leadership skills of his predecessors. Accusations that the caliph was weak and guilty of nepotism fueled political intrigue. In 656, Uthman was assassinated by a group of mutineers from Egypt. The caliph's murder was the first in a series of Muslim rebellions and tribal fratricides that would plague the Islamic community's political development.

THE CALIPH ALI AND THE FIRST CIVIL WARS

Ali, the cousin and son-in-law of the Prophet, succeeded Uthman as the fourth caliph. Ali was devoted to Muhammad and among the first to embrace Islam. He had married Fatima, the only surviving child of Muhammad and Khadijah, with whom he had two sons, Hasan and Husayn. Ali was a charismatic figure who inspired fierce loyalty and commitment.

Many of Ali's supporters (Alids) believed that leadership of the Islamic community should remain within the family of the Prophet and that, indeed, Muhammad had designated Ali as his rightful successor and heir. For these partisans of Ali, later to be called Shii *(shiat-u-Ali,* party of Ali), the first three caliphs were interlopers who had denied Ali his rightful inheritance. However, their satisfaction and expectations were to be short-lived. Within the few short years that Ali ruled, the caliphate was racked by two civil wars (*fitna,* trials). Ali's authority was challenged by two opposition movements: first, by a coalition headed by Muhammad's widow, Aisha (the daughter of Abu Bakr), and second, by the forces of Muawiyah, the governor of Syria and a relative of Uthman.

Ali's failure to find and prosecute Uthman's murderers became the pretext for both revolts. In the first, Ali crushed a triumvirate led by Aisha, the youngest wife of Muhammad. The "Battle of the Camel," so named because it took place around the camel on which Aisha was mounted, marked the first time a caliph had led his army against another Muslim army.

Of more long-range significance was Muawiyah's challenge to Ali's authority. Securely established in Damascus with a strong army, Muawiyah, the nephew of Uthman, had refused to step down and accept Ali's appointment of a replacement. In 657, at Siffin (in modern-day Syria), Ali led his army against his rebellious governor.

Faced with defeat, Muawiyah's men raised Qurans on the tips of their spears and called for arbitration according to the Quran, crying out, "Let God decide." Although the arbitration proved inconclusive, it yielded two results that would have lasting effects. A splinter group of Alids, the Kharijites or "seceders," broke with Ali for having failed to subdue Muawiyah; Muawiyah walked away from Siffin and continued to govern Syria, extending his rule to Egypt as well. When Ali was murdered by Kharijites in 662, Muawiyah laid successful claim to the caliphate, moving its capital to Damascus and frustrating Alid belief that leadership of the community should be restricted to Ali's descendants. With the establishment of the Umayyad dynasty, the "golden age" of Muhammad and the Rightly Guided Caliphs came to an end and the caliphate became an absolute monarchy.

Despite the turmoil during the early caliphal years, Muslims regard the period of Muhammad and the first generation of companions or elders *(salaf)* as normative for a variety of reasons. First, God sent down His final and complete revelation in the Quran and the last of His prophets, Muhammad. Second, the Islamic community-state was created, bonded by a common religious identity and purpose. Third, the sources of Islamic law, the Quran and the example of the Prophet, originated at this time. Fourth, this period of the early companions serves as the reference point for all Islamic revival and reform, both traditionalist and modernist. Fifth, the success and power that resulted from the near-miraculous victories and geographic expansion of Islam constitute, in the eyes of believers, historical validation for the message of Islam.

ORGANIZATION AND INSTITUTIONS

The early caliphate established the pattern for the organization and administration of the Islamic state. Islam provided the basic identity and ideology of the state, the source of unity and solidarity. The caliph's authority and leadership were rooted in his claim to be the successor of the Prophet as head of the community. Muhammad's practice provided the model for governance. The caliph exercised direct political, military, judicial, and fiscal control of the Muslim community. He was selected through a process of consultation, nomination, and selection by a small group of electors who, after pledging their allegiance, presented the caliph to the people for acceptance by public acclamation. The caliph was the protector and defender of the faith; he was to assure the following of God's law and spread the rule of God through expansion and conquest. The community *(umma)*was a brotherhood of believers, a society *(jamaa)* based on religious rather than tribal solidarity.

In general, the Arabs did not occupy conquered cities but established nearby garrison towns such as Basra and Kufa in Iraq, Fustat (Cairo) in Egypt, and Qariwiyin in North Africa. [MAP] From these towns, conquered territories were governed and expeditions launched. They were centered around a mosque, which served as the religious and public focal point of the towns. Administratively, conquered territories were divided into provinces, each of which was administered by governor who was usually a military commander. The internal civil and religious administration remained in the hands of local officials. An agent of the caliph oversaw the collection of taxes and other administrative activities. Revenue for the state came from the captured lands and taxes.

The Islamic system of taxes took several forms: the tithe or wealth tax *(zakat)* for the poor and a land tax *(ushr)* paid by Muslims; the poll tax *(jizya)* and tribute *(kharaj)*, later a land tax, paid by non-Muslims. All revenue was owned, collected, and administered by the state. The distribution of revenue was managed by the registry *(diwan)* at Medina through a system of payments and pensions based on priority in accepting Islam. The Muslims at Medina and the family of the Prophet enjoyed a special place of honor because of their closeness to Muhammad and their fidelity to God's call.

Muslim society was divided into four major social classes. The élites of society were the Arab Muslims, with special status given to the companions of the Prophet because of their early support and role in establishing the community. Next came the non-Arab converts *(mawali,* clients) to Islam. Although in theory all Muslims were equal before God, in fact, practice varied. Under the Umayyads, non-Arab Muslims were clearly second-class citizens. They continued to pay taxes even after their conversion. The *dhimmi,* or non-Muslim People of the Book (those who possessed a revealed Scripture, Jews and Christians), constituted communities within and subject to the wider Islamic community-state. In time, this protected status was extended to Hindus and Buddhists. Finally, there were the slaves. As in much of the Near East, slavery had long existed among the Arabs. Although the Quran commanded the just and humane treatment of slaves (16:71) and regarded their emancipation as a meritorious act (90:13; 58:3), the system of slavery was adopted in a modified form. Only captives in battle could be taken as slaves. Neither Muslims nor Jews and Christians could be enslaved in early Islam.

Thus, religion played an important role in the government, law, taxation, and social organization of society.

The Umayyad Empire: Creation of an Arab Kingdom

The advent of Umayyad rule set in motion a process of continued expansion and centralization of authority that would transform the Islamic community from an Arab shaykhdom into an Islamic empire whose rulers were dependent on religion for legitimacy and the military for power and stability.

In 661, Muawiyah (reigned 661-80) laid claim to the caliphate and ushered in the Umayyad era (661-750): imperial, dynastic, and dominated by an Arab military aristocracy. The capital was moved to Damascus, symbolizing the new imperial age with this permanent shift from the less sophisticated Arabian heartland to the established, cosmopolitan Greco-Roman Byzantine city. From this new centre, the Umayyads completed the conquest of the entire Persian and half the Roman (Byzantine) empire. When Muawiyah seized power, Islam had already spread to Egypt, Libya, the Fertile Crescent, Syria, Iraq, and Persia across Armenia to the borders of Afghanistan. Under the Umayyads, Muslims captured the Maghreb (North Africa), Spain, and Portugal, marched across Europe until they were halted in the heart of France by Charles Martel at the Battle of Tours in 732, and extended the empire's borders to the Indian subcontinent. The accomplishments of the Umayyads were indeed remarkable. Damascus became an even greater imperial capital than it had been under Byzantine rule. Umayyad rulers developed a strong centralized dynastic kingdom, an Arab empire. The more advanced government, institutions, and bureaucracy of Byzantium were adopted and adapted to Arab Muslim needs. Native civil servants and ministers were retained to guide and train their Muslim masters. In time, through a process of conversion and assimilation, language and culture, state and society were Arabized and Islamized. Arabic became the language of government as well as the lingua franca of what today constitutes North Africa and much of the Middle East. Islamic belief and values constituted the official norm and reference point for personal and public life.

Umayyad rulers relied on Islam for legitimacy and as a rationale for their conquests. Caliphs were the protectors and defenders of the faith charged with extending the rule of Islam. The basis of Umayyad unity and stability was the establishment of an Arab monarchy and reliance on Arab, in particular Syrian, warriors. Contrary to previous practice, hereditary succession, not selection or election, restricted the caliphate to the Umayyad house. This innovation, or departure from early Islamic practice, became the pretext for later Muslim historians, writing with Abbasid patronage, to denounce Umayyad rule as kingship and thus un-Islamic. In fact, a form of hereditary succession and dynastic rule became standard practice for the remainder of the caliphal period.

Centralization and militarization of the state resulted in an increasingly autocratic and absolutist government supported and protected by its military.

Umayyad society was based on the creation and perpetuation of an Arab military aristocracy that constituted a hereditary social caste. Syrian troops were the heart of the caliphs' powerful military. As the source of caliphal power and security, they were amply rewarded from the booty and tribute that poured into Damascus as a result of the conquests. Arab Muslims enjoyed special tax privileges, exempted from the more substantial taxes levied on non-Arab Muslims and non-Muslims. This preferential treatment became a source of contention, especially among non-Arab Muslims *(mawali)*, who regarded their lesser status as a violation of Islamic egalitarianism. Their alienation eventually contributed to the downfall of the Umayyad dynasty.

DIVISIONS WITHIN THE ISLAMIC COMMUNITY

As had occurred from the time of the Prophet, critics and opponents used an "Islamic yardstick" to judge or condemn the Umayyads and legitimate their own actions and aspirations. Political, social, economic, and religious grievances were viewed through the prism of an Islamic ideal relevant to all areas of life. Thus, Umayyad practice incurred an opposition that ranged from Kharijites, Alids (Shii), and disgruntled non-Arab Muslims to the early legal scholars and mystics of Islam.

The Kharijites. The Kharijites originated in the time of the caliphs Uthman and Ali. They represent the earliest example of radical dissent in Islam and were the first, in a series of movements, to offer a different concept of the nature of the community and its leadership. Combining a rigorous puritanism and religious fundamentalism with an "exclusivist egalitarianism," the Kharijites emerged as revolutionaries who, despite their seeming lack of success in their own times, continue to inspire contemporary radical groups like Egypt's Takfir wal Hijra and Jamaat al-Jihad.

As previously noted, the occasion for the Kharijite secession from the main body of the community was Ali's submission to arbitration in his struggle with Muawiyah. For the Kharijites the situation was simple. Muawiyah had challenged the legitimate authority of the caliph; this grave sin rendered him an apostate or infidel, and thus Ali, and all true Muslims, had an obligation to wage Jihad until Muawiyah desisted or was subdued. When the arbitration was announced, the Kharijites shouted, "Only God can decide." It was not the job of human beings to counter God's command and sit as judge. As a result, the Kharijites believed that Ali too was now guilty of a grave sin and no longer the legitimate head of the community. This early incident contains the basic Khariji beliefs. The Kharijites were extremist. They were very pious believers who interpreted the Quran and Sunna (example) of the Prophet literally and absolutely. Therefore, they believed that the Quranic mandate to "command the good and prohibit evil" must be applied rigorously and without compromise. Acts were either good or bad, permitted or forbidden. Similarly, their world was divided neatly into the realms of belief and un-belief, Muslim (followers of God) and non-Muslim (enemies of God), peace and warfare. Faith must be informed by action; public behavior must rigorously conform to Islamic principles if one was to be a Muslim. Therefore, any action contrary to the letter of the law constituted a grave sin that rendered a person a non-Muslim, subject to excommunication (exclusion), warfare, and death unless the person repented. Sinners were not simply backsliders but apostates who were guilty of treason against the community-state. All true believers were obliged to fight and subdue these nominal or self-styled Muslims.

Within their exclusivist view of the world and the nature of the Muslim community, the Kharijites incorporated an egalitarian spirit that maintained that any good Muslim, even a slave, could be the leader, or imam, of the community, provided he had community support. Their puritan absolutism demanded that an imam, guilty of sin, be deposed.

When the Kharijites broke with Ali, they went about establishing their vision of the true charismatic community based strictly and literally on the Quran and Sunna. Modeling themselves on the example of the Prophet, they first withdrew *(hijra)* to live together in a bonded community. From their encampments, they waged battle (*Jihad*) against their enemies, seeing themselves as the instruments of God's justice. They were the people of God (paradise) fighting against the people of evil (hell). Since they were God's army struggling in a heavenly crusade against the forces of evil, then violence, guerrilla warfare, and revolution were not only legitimate but obligatory in their battle against the sinful usurpers of God's rule.

Defeated by Ali at Nahrawan in 658, they continued to lead uprisings and join in revolts against Muawiyah's Umayyad descendants and engaged in guerrilla warfare against subsequent Abbasid caliphs. A moderate branch of the Kharijites, known as the Ibadiyya, followers of Abd Allah ibn Ibad, founded Ibadi imamates in North (Tripolitania and Tahert) and East (Zanzibar) Africa, Yemen, and Oman. Their descendants still exist in small numbers in North Africa and Oman, where the Ibadi faith is the official state religion.

Shii Islam. The first civil war between Ali and Muawiyah, which had resulted in the secession of the Kharijites and the alienation of Ali's supporters, came back to haunt the Umayyads. During the reign of Muawiyah's son, Yazid, a second round of civil wars broke out. One of these, the revolt of Ali's son Husayn would lead to the division of the Islamic community into its two major branches, Sunni and Shii, and shaped the worldview of Shii Islam.

When Yazid came to power in 680, Husayn, the son of Ali, was persuaded by a group of Alids in Kufa (Iraq) to lead a rebellion. However, when popular support failed to materialize, Husayn and his small band of followers were slaughtered by an Umayyad army at Karbala. The memory of this tragedy, the "martyrdom" of Alid forces, provided the paradigm of suffering and protest that has guided and inspired Shii Islam. For these partisans *(shia)* of Ali, the original injustice that had denied Ali his succession to Muhammad had been repeated, thwarting the rightful rule of the Prophet's family. Thus, the Shii developed their own distinctive vision of leadership and of history, centered on the martyred family of the Prophet and based on a belief that leadership of the Muslim community belonged to the descendants of Ali and Husayn.

The fundamental difference between Sunni and Shii Muslims is the Shii doctrine of the imamate as distinct from the Sunni caliphate. As we have seen, the caliph was the selected and elected successor of the Prophet. He succeeded to political and military leadership but not to Muhammad's religious authority. By contrast, for the Shii, leadership of the Muslim community is vested in the Imam (leader). who, though not a prophet, is the divinely inspired, sinless, infallible, religiopolitical leader of the community. He must be a direct descendant of the Prophet Muhammad and Ali, the first Imam. He is both political leader and religious guide, the final authoritative interpreter of God's will as formulated in Islamic law. Whereas after the death of Muhammad, Sunni Islam came to place final religious authority in interpreting Islam in the consensus (*ijma*) or collective judgment of the community (the consensus of the *ulama),* the Shii believe in continued divine guidance through their divinely inspired guide, the Imam.

Sunni and Shii Muslims also developed differing doctrines concerning the meaning of history. For Sunni historians, early Islamic success and power were signs of God's guidance and the rewards for a faithful community as well as validation of Muslim belief and claims. For the Shii, history was the theater for the struggle of an oppressed and disinherited minority community to restore God's rule on earth over the entire community under the Imam. A righteous remnant was to persist in God's way against the forces of evil (Satan), as had Ali against Muawiyah and Husayn against the army of Yazid, to reestablish the righteous rule of the Imam. The lives of the suffering Imams, like that of Husayn, were seen as embodying the oppression and injustice experienced by a persecuted minority community. Realization of a just social order under the Imam was to remain a frustrated hope and expectation for centuries as the Islamic community remained under Sunni caliphal governments.

Rule of the Imam over the entire Muslim community was frustrated not only by "usurper" Sunni caliphs, but also by disagreements within the Shii community over succession. This led to three major divisions: Zaydi, Ismaili, and Ithna Ashari or Imami. The Zaydis claimed that Zayd ibn Ali, a grandson of

Husayn, was the fifth Imam. The majority of the Shii recognized Muhammad al-Baqir and his son Jafar al-Sadiq as rightful heirs to the imamate. Unlike other Shii, who restricted the imamate to the descendants of Ali by his wife Fatima, the Prophet's daughter, Zaydis believed that any descendant of Ali could become Imam. They were political activists who, like the Kharijites, believed that the duty to enjoin the good and prohibit evil was incumbent on all Muslims at all times. They, too, rebelled against both Umayyad and Abbasid rule. The Zaydis were the first Shii to gain independence when Hasan ibn Zayd founded a Zaydi dynasty in Tabaristan, on the Caspian, in 864. Another Zaydi state was established in Yemen in 893, where it continued to exist until 1963.

In the eighth century, the majority of the Shii community split again into its two major branches over who the sixth Imam, Jafar al-Sadiq (d. 765), actually designated as his heir. While most accepted his younger son, Musa al-Kazim, some followed Ismail, the elder son. This resulted in the two major Shii communities, the Ithna Asharis, or Twelvers, and the Ismailis (sometimes called the Seveners). The numerical designation of both groups stems from a crisis caused by the death or disappearance of their Imam and thus the disruption of hereditary succession. For the Twelvers, or Ithna Asharis, the end of imamate succession occurred in 874 with the disappearance of the twelfth Imam, the child Muhammad al-Muntazar (Muhammad, the awaited one). Shii theology resolved this dilemma with its doctrines of absence or occultation *(ghayba)* of the Imam and his return in the future as the Mahdi (the expected one). Thus, the Imam had not died but had disappeared and gone into hiding or seclusion. However, he would return as a messianic figure, the Mahdi, at the end of the world to vindicate his loyal followers, restore the community to its rightful place, and usher in a perfect Islamic society in which truth and justice shall prevail. During the absence of the hidden Imam, the community was to await*(intizar)* his return and be guided by its religious experts, *mujtahids,* those *ulama* who interpret God's will, Islamic law, for the community. The Ismaili split into a number of subdivisions. For a major group of Ismailis, the line of Imams ended in 760 when Ismail, the designated seventh Imam, died before his father. Another group believed that Ismail had not died but was in seclusion and would return as the Mahdi. Others accepted Ismail's son, Muhammad, as Imam.

The Ismailis. The image of the Ismaili today as a prosperous merchant community, led by the Aga Khan, belies their early revolutionary origins. The early Ismaili were a revolutionary missionary movement. They attacked and assassinated Sunni political and religious leaders, seized power, and at their peak, ruled an area that extended from Egypt to the Sind province of India. For the Ismaili, as for Shii in general, the Quran had two meanings, an exoteric, literal meaning and an esoteric, inner *(batin)* teaching.

This secret knowledge was given to the Imam and through a process of initiation to his representatives and missionaries *(dais,* from *dawa,* "the call," religious propagation). The followers of the Imam, as distinguished from the majority of Muslims, constituted a religious élite who possessed the true guidance necessary for salvation and a mission to spread or propagate, by force if necessary, the message and rule of the Imam. Often functioning as secret organizations to avoid the Abbasid police, Ismaili also used *taqiyya* (to shield or guard), a common Shii practice that permits concealment of one's belief for self-protection or survival as a persecuted minority. The Ismaili consisted of a variety of such missionary communities or movements.

During the early tenth century, one branch, the Qarmatians, attacked Syria, Palestine, and southern Mesopotamia, and set up their own state in Bahrain. Other groups spread to North Africa and India. It was in North Africa and Egypt that the Ismaili Fatimid (named for Fatima, the Prophet's daughter, from whom the ruler claimed descent) dynasty was created. After an abortive attempt to conquer Syria, Ubayd Allah had fled to Qairawan (Tunisia), where he successfully seized power in 909, declaring himself the Mahdi and establishing a line of Fatimid Imams. In 969, Egypt was conquered and a new capital, Cairo (al-Qahiro, the victorious), was built outside the older city of Fustat to celebrate the conquest of Egypt. The Fatimids established an absolute hereditary monarchy. The infallible Imam ruled over a strong, centralized monarchy that relied on its military and religious missionaries *(dais).* From the tenth to the twelfth centuries, the Fatimids successfully competed with a weakened, fragmented Abbasid empire, spreading their influence and rule across North Africa, Egypt, Sicily, Syria, Persia, and Western Arabia to the Sind province of India. Although a Fatimid state, the majority of the population remained Sunni. During this period, the Fatimid caliphate flourished culturally and commercially as well as militarily. Among its most enduring monumemts was its religious centre, the al-Azhar mosque in Cairo, which served as a training centre for its missionary propagandists. Reputed to be one of the world's oldest universities, al-Azhar has remained an internationally recognized (Sunni) centre of Islamic learning, training students from all over the Islamic world and issuing authoritative religious judgments on major issues and questions.

Although the Fatimids even managed to briefly capture Baghdad, their attempt to rule all of the *dar al-Islam* came to an abrupt end in 1171 when Salah al-Din (Saladin) conquered Egypt and restored the Sunni rule of the (Seljuq) Abbasid caliphate. However, the Ismaili persist through several offshoots. The Nizari Ismaili began as a Persian-based sect under Hasan al-Sabah that broke away from the Fatimids in 1094.

Called the assassins, from the Arabic *hashishi,* and guided by a series of Grand Masters who ruled from a stronghold on Mt. Alamut in northern Persia (thus each becoming known as the Old Man of the Mountain), they were particularly effective in murdering Abbasid princes, generals, and leading *ulama* in the name of their hidden Imam. They struck such terror in the hearts of their Muslim and Crusader enemies that their exploits in Persia and Syria earned them a name and memory in history long after they were overrun and driven underground by the Mongols in 1258. A descendant of Hasan al-Sabah, Hasan Ali Shah, received the honorary title Aga Khan through marriage to the daughter of the shah. He fled to India in 1840 after a failed revolt in Persia. Centered in Bombay, these Nizari (Khoja) Ismailis were led by a series of Imams, known as the Aga Khan, whose personal fortunes have been matched by the wealth of remarkably successful and thriving Ismaili communities in East Africa, South Asia, Britain, and Canada. Currently, the Aga Khan oversees the spiritual and cultural life of the community. As its living Imam, he has been able to reinterpret Islam to respond to modern life. At the same time, he oversees extensive commercial and industrial Ismaili investments and supervises the many educational, medical, and social welfare projects of its philanthropic foundation.

The Druze. Among the sectarian offshoots of Ismailism were the Druze of Lebanon. The Druze date back to Fatimid missionaries named Darazi (d. 1019) and Hamza ibn Ali, who had been encouraged by the Fatimid caliph al-Hakim (reigned 996-1021) to spread the Ismaili faith in southern Lebanon. Al-Hakim was an eccentric ruler who had taken the title Imam and progressively came to believe that he was not only the divinely appointed religiopolitical leader but also the cosmic intellect, linking God with creation. Darazi and Hamza became leaders of a movement centered on recognition of al-Hakim as a divine incarnation, the highest or first cosmic intellect *(aql al-kulli).* This supernatural status became the excuse for his erratic, authoritarian behavior, which, at times, included the persecution of Ismaili, Sunni, and Christian leaders alike. When al-Hakim disappeared or was killed, they maintained that he had gone into seclusion to test the faith of his followers and would return to restore justice in the world. After Darazi's death, Hamza, now claiming to be the leader (imam) in Hakim's absence, organized and developed Hakim's cult into what became a separate religion. Hamza then disappeared, to return as the Mahdi at a later date with al-Hakim. In the interim, Baha al-Din al-Muktana served as the earthly link between Hamza and the community.

The Druze call themselves the unitarians *(muwahhidun),* followers of al-Hakim who embodied and revealed the one true God. Forming a distinct religion, the Druze possess their own Scripture, the *Risail al-Hikma* (the Book of Wisdom), and law. The Book of Wisdom is a collection of letters from al-Muktana, al-Hamza, and al-Hakim. The Sharia, mosque, and *ulama* were replaced by Druze law, places of prayer *(khalwah,* secluded), and religious leadership. The community is hierarchically organized.

The two major divisions are the majority of ordinary members, the so-called ignorant *(jahili),* and the wise *(uqqal),* those men and women who are initiated and as such can read the Scriptures and are expected to lead an exemplary life of regular prayer and abstention from wine, tobacco, and other stimulants. They can be recognized by the quality of their lives and their special dress and white turbans. Among the wise are a group of religious leaders called shaykhs, noted for their learning and piety, who preside over meetings, weddings, and funerals. The head of the community is the*rais* (chief), who is selected from one of the leading families.

Historically, the Druze have been a secret and closed community. They have steadfastly kept their texts, beliefs, and practices secret, carefully guarding them from outsiders. Regarded by both Sunni and Shii as heretics and living in a Sunni-dominated world, they too have followed the Shii doctrine of *taqiyya,* with its double meaning of caution and dissimulation for survival in a hostile world.

Thus, although they do not observe the fast of Ramadan or pilgrimage to Mecca, when necessary they have outwardly followed the prevailing Sunni faith and a modified form of Hanafi (Islamic) law. Druze beliefs and practices emphasize solidarity; they neither accept converts nor marry outside the faith. They practice monogamy and endogamy and discourage divorce. The seven pillars or basic religious obligations reinforce a strong sense of community. They include speaking the truth to other members (though not necessarily to nonbelievers), mutual defense, and living separately from unbelievers. Unlike other monotheistic faiths, the Druze believe in the transmigration of souls until perfected souls cease to be reborn and ascend to the stars. At the end of time, when Hakim and Hamza return to establish a reign of justice, the faithful will be rewarded by being placed close to God. The Druze have survived in Syria, Israel, and especially Lebanon, where they number several hundred thousand.

LAW AND MYSTICISM

Dissatisfaction with Umayyad rule also led to the development of nonrevolutionary reform movements within society. The rapid geographic expansion and conquests brought the rise of new centers of power and wealth, the influx of "foreign" ways, and greater social stratification.

The very success of the Umayyad empire contained the seeds of its downfall. With wealth and power came corruption and abuse of power, symbolized by the new lifestyle of its flourishing, cosmopolitan capital and the growth of new cities. This was accompanied by the infiltration of new ideas and practices. The strengths that came with acculturation were offset, in the eyes of some, by innovations that were seen as undermining the older Arab way of life. Alongside the disaffected Kharijites and Alids, a host of other critics sprang up who contrasted an idealized Medinan Islamic community with the realities of Umayyad life. This gave rise, in particular, to the growth of two Islamic movements or institutions, the *ulama* (religious scholars) and the Sufis (mystics).

For a growing number of pious Muslims, who would become a religious and social class in the Muslim community known as the *ulama* (plural of *alim*, "learned" or scholar), Umayyad practice seemed more indebted to foreign innovations than to the practice of the Prophet and the early community. Arab power and wealth, not Islamic commitment and ideals, inspired and unified the empire. The behavior of many caliphs, the intrigues of court life, and the privileged status of new élites were regarded as having little to do with Islam. Though the Umayyads had done what was pragmatically necessary, since the Arabs had not had the institutions and trained personnel required for empire building, their critics believed that the Umayyad system of incorporating the indigenous bureaucracy of the conquered lands inevitably produced an un-Islamic society based more on the command of the caliph than the command of God. The problem was epitomized by the application of Islamic law. God's law, they argued, should provide the blueprint for Muslim society. Yet, conquest and empire had introduced a diversity of cultures, lifestyles, and customs. The differing customary laws of Medina, Damascus, Kufa, and Basra, coupled with the caliph's decision and his judges' ability to settle disputes on the basis of their own discretion, resulted in a confused and often contradictory body of laws. Many asked, "Can God's will be discerned through so subjective a process; can His law for Muslims in Medina be so different from that in Kufa?" They responded that if all Muslims were bound to submit to and carry out God's law, then Islamic law ought to be defined clearly and with more uniformity. Maintaining that Islam offered a self-sufficient, comprehensive way of life based on the Quran and *sunna,* or custom, they argued that Islam must permeate every area of life. Umayyad practice and law should be brought into line with Islamic principles, and the institutions of the state should have as their source Islam and not the precedents of Byzantium. The outcome of this movement was a burst of activity that would result in the development of Islamic religious sciences. Pious Muslims from all walks of life devoted themselves to the study of the Quran, Arabic language and linguistics, and the collection and examination of Prophetic traditions. In particular, in order to safeguard their beliefs and limit the power of the caliph, many devoted themselves to the formulation and explication of Islamic law. By the late Umayyad period, centers of law could be found in many cities of the empire.

Reaction to the excesses of empire contributed to the development of mysticism as well as law. Luxury, the pursuit of conquest and wealth, the transformation of the caliphate into a dynastic monarchy with the trappings of imperial court life, and the moral character of some Umayyad caliphs struck some pious Muslims as standing in sharp contrast with the early example of Muhammad and the Rightly Guided Caliphs and the relative simplicity of life in Medina. They believed that Umayyad goals of power and wealth conflicted with and distracted from the true centre and goal of Muslim life, Allah. Therefore, the early mystics preached a message stressing renunciation and detachment from worldly concerns and attachments for the pursuit of the "real" God. As we shall see, mysticism or Sufism became a major popular force within Islam that swept across the Muslim world, spreading its spirit of love and devotion.

GROWTH OF "ISLAMIC" REVOLT

Despite the accomplishments of Umayyad rule, by the eighth century (720) anti-Umayyad sentiment spread and intensified. It included a variety of disaffected factions: non-Arab Muslims *(mawali)* who denounced their second-class status vis-a-vis Arab Muslims as contrary to Islamic egalitarianism; Kharijites and Shii who continued to regard the Umayyads as usurpers; Arab Muslims in Mecca, Medina, and Iraq who resented the privileged status of Syrian families; and, finally, pious Muslims, Arab and non-Arab alike, who viewed the new cosmopolitan lifestyle of luxury and social privilege as foreign and an unwarranted innovation or departure from their established, Islamic way of life.

Opposition forces shared a discontent with Umayyad rule as well as a tendency to legitimate their own claims and agenda Islamically; they condemned Umayyad practice and policies as un-Islamic innovations and called for a return to the Quran and the practices of the Prophet and the early Medinan community:

The ideology of a restoration of primitive Islam, with variants reflecting different trends, had conquered the masses, and, with the support of the majority of the learned men, became part of the programme of all, or nearly all, the leaders of parties. It triumphed when the Abbasids adopted it as their slogan.

By 747, an opposition movement, with substantial Shii support, rallied behind Abu Muslim, a freed Abbasid slave. In 750, the Umayyads fell, and Abu al-Abbas, a descendant of the Prophet's uncle al-Abbas, was proclaimed caliph. Islam's capital was moved from Damascus to the newly created Baghdad, known in Arabic as the City of Peace. Under Abbasid rule, the Islamic community would become an empire remembered not only for its wealth and political power, but also for its extraordinary cultural activity and accomplishments.

The Abbasid Caliphate: The Flowering of Islamic Civilization

Abbasid rule of the Islamic community ushered in an era of strong centralized government, great economic prosperity, and a remarkable civilization. Abbasid caliphs could be as autocratic and ruthless as many of their Umayyad predecessors. Indeed, Abu al-Abbas did not hesitate to take the title "the blood shedder" *(al-saffah)*; he came to be remembered as Abu Abbas al-Saffah. The Abbasid caliphs consolidated their power by first crushing their opponents as well as their Shii supporters. This betrayal further alienated the Shii from the Sunni majority. The name Sunni comes from their self-designation as *ahl al-sunna wal jamaa,* those who follow the Prophet's example and thus belong to his society or community.

The Abbasids came to power under the banner of Islam. Their seizure of power and continued dynastic reign were Islamically legitimated. However, the Abbasids took great care to publicly align their government with Islam. They became the great patrons of an emerging religious class, the *ulama* (religious scholars). They supported the development of Islamic scholarship and disciplines, built mosques, and established schools.

The Abbasids refined Umayyad practice, borrowing heavily from Persian culture, with its divinely ordained system of government. The caliph's claim to rule by divine mandate was symbolized by the transformation of his title from Successor or Deputy of the Prophet to Deputy of God and by the appropriation of the Persian-inspired title, Shadow of God on Earth. The ruler's exalted status was further reinforced by his magnificent palace, his retinue of attendants, and the introduction of a court etiquette appropriate for an emperor. Thus, subjects were required to bow before the caliph, kissing the ground, a symbol of the caliph's absolute power. Persian influence was especially evident in the government and military. Preempting critics of the previous regime, the Arab Syrian-dominated military aristocracy was replaced by a salaried army and bureaucracy in which non-Arab Muslims, especially Persians, played a major role. The Abbasids attributed this change to their espousal of Islamic egalitarianism. More often than not, it was royal favor and fear, symbolized by the royal executioner who stood by the side of the caliph, that brought him prestige and motivated obedience.

The early centuries of Abbasid rule were marked by an unparalleled splendor and economic prosperity whose magnificence came to be immortalized in the *Arabian Nights (The Thousand and One Nights),* with its legendary exploits of the exemplary caliph, Harun al-Rashid (reigned 786-809). In a departure from the past, Abbasid success was based not on conquest, but on trade, commerce, industry, and agriculture. The enormous wealth and resources of the caliphs enabled them to become great patrons of art and culture, and thus provide the more significant and lasting legacy of the Abbasid period, Islamic civilization. The development of Islamic law, the Sharia, constitutes their greatest contribution to Islam. Since part of the indictment of the Umayyads had been their failure to implement an effective Islamic legal system, the Abbasids gave substantial support to legal development. The early law schools, which had begun only during the late Umayyad period (ca. 720), flourished under caliphal patronage of the *ulama.* Although Islam has no clergy or priesthood, by the eighth century the *ulama* had become a professional elite of religious leaders, a social class within Muslim society. Their prestige and authority rested on a reputation for learning in Islamic studies: the Quran, traditions of the Prophet, law. Because of their expertise, they became the jurists, theologians, and educators in Muslim society, the interpreters and guardians of Islamic law and tradition. The judge *(qadi)* administered the law as it was developed by the early jurists, firmly establishing the Islamic court system.

In addition to law, the Abbasids were committed patrons of culture and the arts. The process of Arabization, begun during the late Umayyad period, was completed by the end of the ninth century. Arabic language and tradition penetrated and modified the cultures of conquered territories. Arabic displaced local languages — Syriac, Aramaic, Coptic, and Greek — becoming the language of common discourse, government, and culture throughout much of the empire. Arabic was no longer solely the language of Muslims from Arabia but the language of literature and public discourse for the multiethnic group of new Arabic-speaking peoples, especially the large number of non-Arab converts, many of whom were Persian. Translation centers were created. From the seventh to the ninth centuries, manuscripts were obtained from the far reaches of the empire and beyond and translated from their original languages (Sanskrit, Greek, Latin, Syriac, Coptic, and Persian) into Arabic. Thus, the best works of literature, philosophy, and the sciences from other cultures was made accessible: Aristotle, Plato, Galen, Hippocrates, Euclid, and

Ptolemy. The genesis of Islamic civilization was indeed a collaborative effort, incorporating the learning and wisdom of many other cultures and languages. As in government administration, Christians and Jews, who had been the intellectual and bureaucratic backbone of the Persian and Byzantine empires, participated in the process as well as Muslims. This "ecumenical" effort was evident at the Caliph al-Mamun's (reigned 813-833) House of Wisdom and at the translation centre headed by the renowned scholar Hunayn ibn Ishaq, a Nestorian Christian. This period of translation and assimilation was followed by one of Muslim intellectual and artistic creativity as Muslims ceased to be merely disciples and became masters, in the process producing Islamic civilization, dominated by the Arabic language and Islam's view of life: "It was these two things, their language and their faith, which were the great contribution of the Arab invaders to the new and original civilization which developed under their aegis." Major contributions were made in many fields: literature and philosophy, algebra and geometry, science and medicine, art and architecture. Towering intellectual giants dominated this period: al-Razi (865-925), al-Farabi (d. 950), ibn Sina (known as Avicenna, 980-1037), ibn Rushd (known as Averroes, d. 1198), al-Biruni (973-1048), and al-Ghazali (d. 1111). Islam had challenged the world politically; it now did so culturally. Great urban cultural centers in Cordova, Baghdad, Cairo, Nishapur, and Palermo emerged and eclipsed Christian Europe, mired in the Dark Ages. During the Abbasid period, the comprehensiveness of Islam was clearly manifested and delineated:

> Islam — the offspring of Arabia and the Arabian Prophet — was not only a system of belief and cult. It was also a system of state, society, law, thought and art — a civilization with religion as its unifying, eventually dominating factor.

Thus, for Muslim and non-Muslim alike, the political and cultural life of a vast empire, consisting of many tribal, ethnic, and religious groups, was brought within the framework of the Arabic language and Islamic faith. Islamic civilization was the result of a dynamic, creative process as Muslims borrowed freely from other cultures. It proceeded from a sense of mission, power, and superiority. Muslims were the dominant force — masters not victims, colonizers not the colonized. The new ideas and practices were Arabized and Islamized. It was a process of change characterized by continuity with the faith and practice of Muhammad. Unlike the modern period, Muslims controlled the process of assimilation and acculturation. Their autonomy and identity were not seriously threatened by the specter of political and cultural domination. As with the early conquests and expansion of Islam, Muslims then (and now) regarded this brilliant period as a sign of God's favor and a validation of Islam's message and the Muslim community's universal mission.

The extraordinary spread and development of Islam was not without its religious conflicts. That same concern that had motivated the attempt by the *ulama* to preserve Islam in the face of caliphal whim and uncritical adoption of foreign, un-Islamic practices, led to conflicts between the *ulama* and those whom they sometimes regarded as their competitors, the Sufis and the philosophers.

The *ulama* delineation of law as the embodiment of the straight path of Islam set the criteria for belief and behavior in intellectual, social, and moral life and the pattern for orthodoxy (correct belief) or, perhaps more accurately, orthopraxy (correct practice). This vision of Muslim life as the observance of God's law did not always coincide comfortably with the Sufi emphasis on the interior path *(tariqa)* of contemplation and personal religious experience or the tendency of philosophy*(falsafa)* to give primacy to reason over the unquestioned acceptance of revelation.

The tension between religious scholars on the one hand and philosophers and Sufis on the other was reflected in the life and work of a towering giant in the history of Islam, indeed in the history of religions, Abu Hamid al-Ghazali.

Ironically, the golden age of Islamic civilization paralleled the progressive political fragmentation of the universal caliphate. The relative peace, prosperity, and unity of the Islamic community, epitomized during the rule of Harun al-Rashid, was challenged internally by competing groups and externally by the Fatimids and the Crusades.

Governing a vast empire extending from the Atlantic to central Asia proved impossible. Abbasid political unity deteriorated rapidly from 861 to 945 as religious (Khariji and Shii) and regional differences, and particularly competing political aspirations, precipitated a series of revolts and secessionist movements. In Morocco, Tunisia, Iran, Syria, and Iraq itself, local governors, who were often army commanders, asserted their independence as heads of semiautonomous states.

These regional rulers (amirs, or commanders), while continuing to give formal, nominal allegiance to the caliph, exercised actual rule over their territories, establishing their own hereditary dynasties. By 945, the disintegration of a universal caliphate was evident when the Buyids (Buwayhids), a Shii dynasty from Western Persia, invaded Baghdad and seized power, and their leader assumed the title commander-in-chief or commander of the commanders. Although Shii, they did not change the Sunni orientation of the empire and left the caliph on his throne as a titular leader of a fictionally unified empire. The Abbasids continued to reign but not rule. With an Abbasid on the throne as a symbol of legitimate government and Muslim unity, real power passed to a series of Persian (Buyid) and Turkic (Seljuq) military dynasties or sultanates. The sultan ("power," ruler), as chief of the commanders, governed a politically fragmented empire as the caliph helplessly stood by.

Sunni Islam was also threatened by two other developments during the Abbasid caliphate — the rise of the Fatimid dynasty and the Crusades. The Ismaili rebellion in Tunisia and subsequent establishment of a Shii imamate in Egypt constituted a serious religiopolitical challenge. The Fatimids claimed to be Imams and were not content to simply govern Egypt, but, as we have seen, followed other Ismaili groups in sending their missionaries to spread their Shii doctrine. This Shii challenge elicited a religious as well as a military response as Sunni *ulama* moved to protect their version of orthodoxy in the face of Shii innovations. They were supported in their endeavors by the royal court, wishing to counter Shii anticaliphal sentiments. This contributed to a growing tendency among the Sunni *ulama* to preserve the unity of Islam through greater self-definition and standardization. In the face of the internal breakup of the central empire, this meant achieving a consensus on the corpus of Islamic law in order to protect and maintain the sociopolitical order.

ISLAM AND THE WEST: THE CRUSADES AND MUSLIM RESPONSE TO MILITANT CHRISTIANITY

Despite their common monotheistic roots, the history of Christianity and Islam has been more often than not marked by confrontation rather than peaceful coexistence and dialogue. For the Christian West, Islam is the religion of the sword; for Muslims, the Christian West is epitomized by the armies of the Crusades. From the earliest decades of Islamic history, Christianity and Islam have been locked in a political and theological struggle, because Islam, in contrast to other world religions, has threatened the political and religious ascendancy of Christianity.

Muslim armies overran the Eastern Roman empire, Spain, and the Mediterranean from Sicily to Anatolia. At the same time, Islam challenged Christian religious claims and authority. Coming after Christianity, Islam claimed to supersede Christian revelation. While acknowledging God's revelation and revering God's messengers, from Adam through Jesus, as prophets, Islam rejected the doctrine of Christ's divinity, the finality of Christian revelation, and the authority of the church. Instead, it called on all, Jews and Christians as well, to accept finality of revelation and prophecy in Islam, to join the Islamic community, and to live under Islamic rule. Islam's universal mission had resulted in the spread of Muslim rule over Christian territories and Christian hearts. While conversions were initially slow, by the eleventh century large numbers of Christians, living under Muslim rule, were converting to Islam. Even those who had remained Christian were becoming Arabized, adopting Arabic language and manners. The European Christian response was, with few exceptions, hostile, intolerant, and belligerent. Muhammad was vilified as an imposter and identified as the anti-Christ. Islam was dismissed as a religion of the sword led by an infidel driven by a lust for power and women. This attitude was preserved and perpetuated in literature such as the *Divine Comedy,* where Dante consigned Muhammad to the lowest level of hell. Christian fears were fully realized as Islam became a world power and civilization while Christianity staggered and stagnated in its Dark Ages.

By the eleventh century, Christendom's response to Islam took two forms: the struggle to reconquer (the *Reconquista)* Spain (1000-1492) and Italy and Sicily (1061), and the undertaking of another series of Christian holy wars, the Crusades (1095-1453).

Two myths surround Western perceptions of the Crusades: first, that the Crusades were simply motivated by a religious desire to liberate Jerusalem, and second, that Christendom ultimately triumphed.

Jerusalem was a sacred city for all three Abrahamic faiths. When the Arab armies took Jerusalem in 638, they occupied a centre whose shrines had made it a major pilgrimage site in Christendom. Churches and the Christian population were left unmolested. Jews, long banned from living there by Christian rulers, were permitted to return, live, and worship in the city of Solomon and David. Muslims proceeded to build a shrine, the Dome of the Rock, and a mosque, the al-Aqsa, near the area formerly occupied by Herod's Temple and close by the Wailing Wall, the last remnant of Solomon's temple.

Five centuries of peaceful coexistence elapsed before political events and an imperial-papal power play led to centuries-long series of so-called holy wars that pitted Christendom against Islam and left an enduring legacy of misunderstanding and distrust.

In 1071, the Byzantine army was decisively defeated by a Seljuq (Abbasid) army. The Byzantine emperor, Alexius I, fearing that all Asia Minor would be overrun, called on fellow Christian rulers and the pope to come to the aid of Constantinople by undertaking a "pilgrimage" or crusade to free Jerusalem and its environs from Muslim rule.

For Pope Urban II, the "defense" of Jerusalem provided an opportunity to gain recognition of the authority of the papacy and its role in legitimating the actions of temporal rulers. A divided Christendom rallied as warriors from France and other parts of

Western Europe (called "Franks" by Muslims) united against the "infidel" in a holy war whose ostensible goal was the holy city. This was ironic because, as one scholar has observed, "God may indeed have wished it, but there is certainly no evidence that the Christians of Jerusalem did, or that anything extraordinary was occurring to pilgrims there to prompt such a response at that moment in history." In fact, Christian rulers, knights, and merchants were driven primarily by political and military ambitions and the promise of the economic and commercial (trade and banking) rewards that would accompany the establishment of a Latin kingdom in the Middle East. However, the appeal to religion captured the popular mind and gained its support.

The contrast in the behavior of the Christian and Muslim armies in the First Crusade has been etched deeply in the collective memory of Muslims. In 1099, the Crusaders stormed Jerusalem and established Christian sovereignty over the Holy Land.

They left no Muslim survivors; women and children were massacred. The Noble Sanctuary, the Haram al-Sharif, was desecrated as the Dome of the Rock was converted into a church and the al-Aqsa mosque, renamed the Temple of Solomon, became a residence for the king.

Latin principalities were established in Antioch, Edessa, Tripoli, and Tyre. The Latin Kingdom of Jerusalem lasted less than a century. In 1187, Salah al-Din (Saladin), having reestablished Abbasid rule over Fatimid Egypt, led his army in a fierce battle and recaptured Jerusalem. The Muslim army was as magnanimous in victory as it had been tenacious in battle. Civilians were spared; churches and shrines were generally left untouched. The striking differences in military conduct were epitomized by the two dominant figures of the Crusades: Saladin and Richard the Lion-Hearted. The chivalrous Saladin was faithful to his word and compassionate toward noncombatants. Richard accepted the surrender of Acre and then proceeded to massacre all its inhabitants, including women and children, despite promises to the contrary.

The Crusades degenerated by the thirteenth century into intra-Christian wars, papal wars against its Christian enemies who were denounced as heretics and schismatics. The result was a weakening, rather than a strengthening, of Christendom. As Roger Savory has observed:

An ironical but undeniable result of the Crusades was the deterioration of the position of Christian minorities in the Holy Land. Formerly these minorities had been accorded rights and privileges under Muslim rule, but, after the establishment of the Latin Kingdom, they found themselves treated as "loathsome schismatics." In an effort to obtain relief from persecution by their fellow Christians, many abandoned their Nestorian or Monophysite beliefs, and adopted either Roman Catholicism, or the supreme irony — Islam.

By the fifteenth century, the Crusades had spent their force. Although initially launched to unite Christendom and turn back the Muslim armies, the opposite had occurred. Amid a bitterly divided Christendom, Constantinople fell in 1453 before Turkish Muslim conquerors. This Byzantine capital was renamed Istanbul, and became the seat of the Ottoman empire.

GROWTH OF MUSLIM POPULATION

A study of the preceding pages clearly shows that the rise in Muslim population was due mainly to conversions of Hindus to Islam. It also needs no reiteration that it was part of the state policy to establish Islam as the religion of the whole land. It would again be a truism to say that Islam is essentially a missionary religion and every Muslim is a propagandist of his faith; and as they settled in India, they must have entered upon proselytizing efforts. Thus Muslim rulers, nobles, Mashaikh, Maulvis, traders and merchants were all in one way or the other Muslim missionaries.

Conversions

Islam has spread in many parts of the world through wars and campaigns. In the medieval Indian chronicles the sovereign is always mentioned as the king of Islam, the territories of his empire are referred to as the land of Islam, its armies as soldiers of Islam, and its religious and Judicial head as Shaikh-ul-Islam. The monarch was committed to make Islam the true basis of private and public life through the enforcement of the Shariat and to convert the people to the true faith. In India the Muslim rulers keenness to obtain converts in war is vouched by many chroniclers. The *Tarikh-i-Muhammadi* gives a clear idea of the psychology of the rulers in this regard. Its author was a contemporary of Sultan Nasiruddin Mahmud, the son of Firoz Tughlaq. He says that while fighting Rai Subir (Sumer) in the vicinity of Iraj, the Sultan thought: If I will give orders to the army to fight (outright), they will not leave even a trace of the Kafirs in the region, but if I shall advance slowly, then probably these people will agree to embrace Islam. What professor Mohammad Habib writes concerning the Mongol applies equally to Turkish expeditions. In 1330 the country was invaded by the Mongols who indulged in arson, rape and murder throughout the Valley (of Kashmir). The king and the Brahmans fled away but among the inhabitants who remained Muslim ways of life were gradually adopted by the people as the only alternative Thus warfare brought captives, and captives were made Musalmans. Such was not the situation only in the North; in South also such methods of conversion prevailed, especially during wars between Bahmani and Vijayanagar kingdoms. Throughout the medieval period such wars were common, and forcible conversions helped in the rapid growth of Muslim population.

The rulers used force and persuasion in equal measure. Their resources were great. They could give jobs, honours, and titles and many other economic concessions and status benefits as inducements to conversion, and many people would have taken advantage of these facilities. We have referred to Mubarak Khaljis encouragement to Hindus to accept Islam by presenting the convert with a robe and a gold ornament. People used to be converted in this fashion right up to the reign of Aurangzeb and perhaps even thereafter. There were other methods too. The Banshasmriti of Satya Krishna Biswas states that in Bengal the Rajas and Zamindars who could not deposit land revenue by a certain date had to convert to Muhammadanism. The *Banshasmriti* narrates an isolated incident, but as this regulation of the thirteenth century had been revived by Murshid Quli Khan, or had continued right up to his times, many local Rajas and Zamindars would have been converted in the course of four centuries, for full payment of land tax by due date was not always possible. Firoz Tughlaq (1351-88) instructed his revenue collectors to convert Hindus to Islam. He rescinded the Jiziyah to lure people to become Muhammadans, and this measure brought large additions to Muslim population. In his *Fatuhat-i-Firoz Shahi,* Sultan Firoz Tughlaq candidly writes: I encouraged my infidel subjects to embrace the religion of the prophet and I proclaimed that everyone who repeated the *Kalima of tauhid* and became Musalman should be exempt from Jiziyah Information of this came to the ears of the people at large, and great number of Hindus presented themselves, and were admitted to the honour of Islam. Thus they came forward day by day from every quarter, go on coming to this day, and adopting the faith, are exonerated from the Jiziyah, and are favoured with Khilats and presents.

Side by side the governments efforts was the proselytizing activity of the Muslim Sufis. It is however not clear how far Sufi and other Mashaikh were interested in the work of conversion and what amount of success they achieved in this regard. Following in the footsteps of T.W. Amold, Titus, Aziz Ahmad and Mujeeb assert that conversions to Islam were mainly a result of the labours of the mystics. Perhaps the idea is to prove that the conversions were voluntary. On the other hand Mohammad Habib and S.A.A. Rizvi say that Sufi Mashaikh were not engaged in effecting conversions. Prof. Habib says, The Musalmans have no missionary labours to record *We find no trace of any missionary movement for converting non-Muslims* (italics by the author himself). Medieval Islam was a converting creed, but it failed to develop any missionary activity So far as our country is concerned we have to confess frankly that no trace of a missionary movement for the conversion of non-Muslims has yet been discovered. In a footnote he adds: Some cheap mystic books now current attribute conversions to Muslim mystics on the basis of miracles they performed. So in order to believe in the conversions one has to believe in the miracles also. But all such books will be found on examination to be latter-day fabrications. Prof. Rizvi arrives at the same conclusion. He simply says that the early mystic records (*Malfuzat and Maktubat*), contain no mention of conversion of the people to Islam by these Saints.

From the hagiological literature also it is evident that Sufi Mashaikh were not organized for propaganda work in any modern way. Sufi Shaikhs and scholars are not known to have preceded but always followed the armies of invasion. They mostly lived in metropolitan cities, in their respective Khanqahs or monasteries, basking in the sunshine of royal favour, and do not appear to have moved about in the countryside for propaganda work. The whole atmosphere in the Khanqah was Muslim: not many, if any, Hindus ever visited them, not to speak of their coming in large numbers for being converted. The two greatest Chishti Mashaikh of the medieval period were Muin-ud-din Chishti and Nizam-ud-din Auliya Rizvi rightly says that Shaikh Muin-ud-din Chishti was neither a missionary nor a miracle monger.

He did not work among the masses In the *Fawaid-ul-Fuad*, a biographical memoir on Shaikh Nizam-ud-din Auliya, there is mention of conversion of only two Hindu curd-sellers. Similarly during the reign of Iltutmish, Khwaja Qutubuddin Bakhtiyar Kaki and Qazi Hamid-ud-din Nagori were two prominent saints in Delhi but no proselytizing activity is attributed to them. Indeed the Mashaikh sometimes resented governments appeals to do proselytizing work; and Muhammad bin Tughlaq, who wanted to employ this class on missionary work, met with lot of opposition from them.

In brief, while it would not be safe to declare that hardly any conversions through peaceful methods were effected by the Sufi Mashaikh in India, it has also to be admitted that not many reliable references to their proselytizing activity are available in genuine hagiological works. They may have helped those who showed an inclination to become Muslim. Occasionally they restored to force also to convert people. But the Mashaikh were probably responsible only for stray and individual conversions and their contribution to the growth of Muslim population may not have been much. Saiyyad Muhammad bin Nasiruddin Jafar Makki al-Husaini , the Khalifa of Nasiruddin Chiragh-i-Delhi held that there were five reasons which led the people to embrace Islam:

(1) Fear of death,

(2) fear of their families being enslaved,

(3) propagation (of Islam) on the part of Muslims,
(4) the lust for obtaining *mawajib* (pensions or rewards) *ghanaim* (booty), and
(5) Tassub (bigotry or superstition?).

Thus according to Saiyyad Muhammad, propagation of Islam by Muslims did not necessarily involve missionary activity of Sufi Mashaikh. Prior to its introduction in India, Islam had spread in many other countries like Arabia, Persia and Syria. No names of missionaries or Sufi saints have come down to us as having been instrumental in spreading Islam in those countries. It is only about India that such a theory is put forward.

Today many classes or groups of people who were originally Hindu are found to belong to the Muhammadan faith, and their conversion can be traced to medieval times. An oft-repeated reason for such conversions is said to be the tyranny of the Hindu caste system. Arnold, Titus and Aziz Ahmad give credit to the democratic social system of Islam for the conversion of low caste Hindus to win a degree of social freedom because for the lower Hindu castes acceptance of Islam meant an escape from the degraded status they had in the Hindu society. Dr. Wise thinks that the Muhammadan Julaha (Jolha or Momin) weaver class of Bengal and Bihar belonged to a despised Hindu caste who in a body became converts to Muhammedanism. Ruben Levy also talks of the coarse rabble or Ajlaf in Bengal, who formed the functional groups such as weavers, cotton carders, oil pressers, barbers, tailors etc., as well as converts of originally humble castes in Bengal.

However, contemporary writings of Persian chroniclers nowhere mention caste as a factor leading to conversions. Muslim historians of medieval India were surely aware of the existence of the caste system in Hindu society; Alberuni, Abul Fazl and emperor Jahangir, to mention a few. And yet no one mentions even once tyranny on the low caste people as cause for conversion. Their evidence shows beyond doubt that conversions in India were brought about by the same methods and processes as seen in Arabia, Persia, Central Asia, etc. India was not the first country where Islam was introduced in medieval times. It had spread in Persia, Central Asia, Afghanistan, and North Africa before it came to India. There was no caste system in these countries and yet there were large-scale conversions there.

Therefore, a little reflection off the beaten track would show that the reason behind the conversion of some groups *en masse* was not due to the assumed oppression of the caste system but to escape oppressive taxes and other disabilities. Conversion also provided new avenues of employment and economic advancement in the Muslim regime and society. Naturally large numbers of poor people were attracted to Islam as the following Table, prepared on the basis of U.P. Census Report of 1931, indicates.

Table : Showing Some Muslim Low Castes of U.P.

	Per cent of caste Members adhering to Hindu Religion	*Per cent of each caste in Total Religious Membership*
Julaha	95.5	14.7
Faqir	93.0	12.9
Dhunia	93.5	5.4
Teli	25.1	3.4
Nai (Hajjam)	26.9	3.3
Darzi	69.5	2.3
Qassab	100.0	2.2
Dhobi	14.0	1.5
Manihar	96.4	1.4

Like U.P. functional groups many occupational groups in other parts of the country, especially in northern India, too went over to Islam in large numbers in medieval times. Now, did the ancestors of the above Muslim castes convert in medieval times because of the tyranny of the caste system? Let us take the Faqirs first. In Hindu society there is no caste of beggars. But any number of beggars would be born if they could get free food without doing any work. It is stated in almost every chronicle that in medieval times food was very cheap, even then, many idlers would have avoided to do work if they could get free food just for a change of name - religion of the poor being the proverbial bread. Muslim regime provided it and Faqirs flocked to it and to Islam. The number of Faqirs had grown so large by the time of Ghayasuddin

Tughlaq (1320-25) that the sultan wanted to put a stop to a free treat to them and wanted them to take up some work, but his attitude was resented and the sultan maligned. According to Ahmad Abbas 40, 000 beggars used to be fed by Ghayass successor Muhammad Tughlaq. Muhammad Tughlaq sometimes even attended the funeral of Faqirs. The Faqirs were so well paid under Firoz Tughlaq that some nobles, who used to recommend them to the liberality of the sultan, did not fail to take a bribe out of their gains. Generosity of kings and nobles towards Faqirs never slackened even during the Mughal period. A good number of people would have converted in medieval times to become Muslim Faqirs to form a caste in the Muslim social order in modern times.

Similar was the position with regard to the Qassab. Arab geographers of the ninth to twelfth centuries found most Indians vegetarians. Some Hindus ate hunted game but not flesh of animals and animals were not slaughtered for providing meat. By many Hindus meat is still called shikar (game). The Hindu Gorkhas call it only by this name. Therefore, while it could be difficult to categorically state that Hindus in the pre-Muslim period did not do the work of meat-selling, there does not seem to have been a caste of Hindu butchers which went over to Islam because of the oppression of caste system. The few Hindu butchers might have become Musalmans because their vocation found a flourishing and sympathetic clientele among Muhammadans but many others who were not butchers by profession would have found in cutting and selling of meat a new avenue of employment in a new society and joined it to form a Muslim caste of hundred per cent Qassab.

In the case of *darzis* or tailors, their employment chances lay more with the Muslim community. Muslims dressed elaborately, and the sartorial habits of Arabs and Turks would point to even some tailors having come from abroad, and converted Hindu tailors joining their ranks.

The requirements of the Sultan, the elite, and even the common Muslims would have needed the services of a whole tribe of tailors, who, passing the whole day in the palace workshops or catering to the needs of the patronizing Muslim society would have found it profitable and convenient to become Muslim. The interdependence of cotton-carders, weavers, (*dhunia, julaha*) and tailors would have induced the former to embrace Islam, and once some people of this class converted to Muhammadanism, others followed suit because of class affiliation and vocational compulsions. Cotton-carders, weavers, and tailors were there both in the urban and the rural areas; only in the urban they were more skilled and produced fine quality stuffs required by the Muslim nobility and elite, and conversions seem to have occurred mostly in the urban areas; and many village *julahas* have remained Hindu. A Hajjam does not enjoy a better status in Muslim society than a Nai in Hindu, but the Hajjams profession provided greater avenues of economic betterment in Muslim society; he did the work of circumcision and other minor surgical operations.

Such instances need not be multiplied, but some other cases not included in the above Table may also be mentioned in passing. Many elephant drivers (mahauts) are today Muslims. It is on record that Muslim rulers were extremely fond of elephants. Mahmud of Ghazni had an *elephant corps of 2,500 all collected from India*. Minhaj Siraj affirms that during Bakhtiyars Bengal campaign, many elephants were captured with their drivers. He also writes that Sultan Ruknuddin Firoz Shah (son of Iltutmish), was very fond of elephants, *and all the elephant drivers were much benefited by his bounty* (italics mine). Ferishtah says that by the time of Bahram Shah (C.E. 1240), the sultans had monopolised the privilege of keeping elephants. Being in the employment of Muslim rulers and nobles, living in the palace or Sultans forts all the time, and benefiting from their bounty, it was but profitable for them to convert to a faith in which advantages of service and profession lay. On the contrary those professional groups, which had a mixed Hindu-Muslim clientele, but whose business would have been adversely affected by losing the Hindu customers if they had converted to Islam, like the *panwaris* (betel sellers), *halwais* (sweetmeat sellers), *banias*, goldsmiths etc., did not convert and have remained Hindu through the ages.

Besides, not all low-caste Muslims have converted from low caste Hindus. Many foreign Muslims also would have been relegated to low caste on marrying low-caste women. The sultans and Amirs usually married in the families of the Rajas and Zamindars they defeated. But the common soldiers or common Musalmans would have married either in their own religious group, that is among the newly converted, or among the low-caste Hindus. And as class distinctions crystallized in medieval Indian Muslim society, these people would have been given only a low caste status, having obtained it through their wives.

Needless to say that such Muslims, originally of foreign extraction, would have swelled the ranks of low-caste Muhammadans. Thus the few low-caste groups which converted to Islam did so not to escape from the tyranny of the caste system because they have remained at as lower a rung in Muslim society as they were in Hindu, but because of new professional and vocational opportunities in a changed society. Such conversions took place mostly in urban areas.

Artisans, mechanics, handicraftsmen were loyal to their guilds and their castes. Where guilds were loosely knit or contained many occupational groups, chances of conversions were more. There was a greater possibility of such a situation in the urban areas and port-towns where there was concentration of Muslim clientele and influences of Muslim religious, political and economic leadership. In the conversions at port-towns, for example, foreign Muslim merchants played a great part. From what we know of their contribution in the conversion of South-East Asia, it stands to reason that their propagandism for Islam in India too would have been very effective.

The Zamorin of Calicut, for instance, encouraged the fishermen of Malabar to become Musalmans in order to man his warships; and to this end ordered that, in every family of fishermen in his dominions, one or more of the male members should be brought up as Muhammadans. Either in deference to the wishes or specific condition of his Arab or other Muslim captains and crew, or to see that the men working on the ships under Muslims should have no caste inhibitions, the Zamorin may have issued such orders. But the fact is that today many boatmen and fishermen in Bengal and other parts of the Indian seacoast are Muhammadans. Similarly some mercantile groups like Khojas and Bohras also converted to

Islam under the influence of foreign merchants, although legendary accounts attribute their conversion to saints.

Immigration

It was thus mainly conversions that were responsible for the rise and growth of Muslim population in medieval India. This component of growth went on extending with Muslim territorial expansion. Immigration of foreign Muslims too helped in its growth. As has been seen at many places earlier, from the inception of Muslim rule right up to the eighteenth century foreign Muslims, especially from Persia, Central Asia and Abyssinia used to arrive in India and settle down here. Hindustan was a paradise for Muslim merchants, scholars and adventures. Muslim regime of Hindustan promised and provided excellent jobs to all and sundry foreign Muslims. No wonder that the latter came here in large numbers to settle down and make fortunes. Hazards of journey were there no doubt, but these were reduced with passing of time and minimised by migrant adventurers and merchants travelling in groups. Throughout the medieval period they came in droves, like ants and locusts, and were given here important and influential positions. It was naturally a one way traffic; Muslims only came, nobody migrated from here. By the seventeenth century they formed many pressure groups - like Irani and Turani - in the Mughal empires politics and society. Many Muslims even today take pride in asserting their extra-territorial identity by adding suffixes like Iraqi and Bukhari to their names.

Polygamy

The most efficacious generator of the quick growth of Muslim population was their practice of polygamy. Marriage is enjoined on every Muslim. It is related in the Traditions that Muhammad said: When the servant of God marries, he perfects half his religion Consequently in Islam, even the ascetic orders are rather married than single. In Islam there is provision for temporary marriages (Mutas), multi-marriages, divorce, remarriage of widows, concubinage - in short there is freedom from all inhibitions and reservations in matters of matrimony. The insistence is on everybody marrying. Naturally celibacy is frowned upon. One of

Muhammads companions wanted to live in celibacy Muhammad forbade him to do so. According to a tradition derived from Ibn Abbas and quoted by Ibn Sad, popularly known as Katib al-Waqidi, the prophets biographer, Muhammad said: In my *ummah,* he is the best who has the largest number of wives.

Practice excelled the precept. Muslim kings and commoners, nobles and soldiers, merchants and Ulema, Sufis and Qazis were all known for maintaining large or small harems according to finances and circumstances. There used to be four regular wives, and numberless concubines. The result was prodigious progeny. And so the scriptures desired. Muhammad said: Marry women who will love their husbands and be very prolific, *for I wish you to be more numerous than any other people.* (italics ours). It is not surprising therefore that all Muslims ever desire to be more numerous than any other people. Polygamy, multi-marriages, etc. sometimes reached ridiculous limits so that often the mothers of the sultans sons could not be identified, nor perhaps even the children as shown by the frantic enquiries made after the death of Alauddin, Mubarak Khalji and Muhammad bin Tughlaq whether any of their sons were alive so that the throne could be offered to them. And what is true of the sultans is also true of the elite. Among Muhammadans the widows, even widows of sultans, remarried. But a Hindu widow, even if she did not immolate herself, did not remarry. Sati and jauhar had a noble motivation and yet had a demographic aspect; these decimated Hindu numbers. Above all in India, as elsewhere, the growth of population is regulated to a large extent by the material condition of the people. In the medieval period the Muslims - but for the very poor sections - had better lands, more nutritious diet, and, as ruling classes everywhere, were in happier circumstances.

Higher Fecundity

In the Hindu-Muslim mixed marriages the couple and the progeny invariably became Muslim. This practice formed another important component of growth of Muslim population in India. There is also higher fecundity among Muslims. Kingsley Davis rightly remarks that in six decades (1881-1941) at no census have the Muslims failed to improve their percentage and the Hindus failed to lose It is due not only to the proportion of Muslim women married, but those who are married also have a higher fertility. Today every seventh man in the world is a Muslim, and in this great rise of Muslim population their high fertility should have contributed its share. Dudley Kirk, after a detailed study of fertility among various nationalities and religious groups, too, has arrived at the conclusion that birth rate among Muslims is the highest.

Lesser Losses

While Muslim population rose through conversion, immigration, and polygamy, and possibly high rate of fertility, its losses in wars and famines were lesser than those of the Hindus, and its natural growth was high. We have referred at many places to the losses of Muslims in war. But a major portion of Muslim armies consisted of Hindus. Even Mahmud of Gaznis forces had Hindu contingents. During the Sultanate period Muslims, especially foreign Muslims, belonged to the officer cadre and were mostly cavalrymen; Hindus are often mentioned as Paiks or footsoldiers. The Paiks formed the rank and file and probably the bulk of the Muslim armies. There were large armies in India, both in the North and the South, of Bahmani, Vijayanagar, Mughal. The second volume of Abul Fazls *Ain-i-Akbari* gives lists of the large number of Hindu contingents that could be called to duty under Akbar. Naturally it is these who were killed in large numbers in wars being placed, as infantry was then placed, in a vulnerable position. The Hindus thus died not only for defending their kings and kingdoms during the unending process of Muslims territorial expansion; they also died in large numbers for their Muslim masters as soldiers in the latters armies. Compared with theirs, the loss of the Muslim numbers was small. Muslim population at least was not affected by these wars, because any loss in battles was more than made up by the number of captives, who used to be converted and also by replenishment through immigration.

Whenever famines occurred Muslim rulers took necessary steps to provide relief to the people. But from the narrative of the chroniclers it is evident that these relief measures were mostly confined to urban areas. And Muslims were mostly concentrated in urban areas. Even in the cities sometimes the mission of mercy was marred by bigotry.

Between 1387 and 1395 the Deccan was visited by a severe famine, and Muhammads measures for the relief of his subjects displayed a combination of administrative ability, enlightened compassion, and religious bigotry. A thousand bullocks belonging to the transport establishment maintained for the court were placed at the disposal of. those in charge of relief measures, and travelled incessantly to and fro between his dominions and Gujarat and Malwa, which had escaped the visitation bringing thence grain which was sold at low rates in the Deccan, but to Muslims only. And Muhammad Bahmani was not the only orthodox sultan in medieval India. It may not be proper to generalize, but probably in famines and such like calamities the Muslims suffered less loss than the Hindus.

3

The Earliest Muslim Indians

CHERAMAN JUMA MASJID

Even before the life of Prophet Muhammad (Peace Be Upon Him) in the 600s, Arab traders were in contact with India. Merchants would regularly sail to the west coast of India to trade goods such as spices, gold, and African goods.

Naturally, when the Arabs began to convert to Islam, they carried their new religion to the shores of India. The first mosque of India, the Cheraman Juma Masjid, was built in 629 (during the life of Prophet Muhammad) in Kerala, by the first Muslim from India, Cheraman Perumal Bhaskara Ravi Varma. Through continued trade between Arab Muslims and Indians, Islam continued to spread in coastal Indian cities and towns, both through immigration and conversion.

Muhammad bin Qasim

The first great expansion of Islam into India came during the Umayyad Dynasty of caliphs, who were based in Damascus. In 711, the Umayyads appointed a young 17 year old man from Ta'if to extend Umayyad control into Sindh: Muhammad bin Qasim. Sindh is the land around the Indus River in the Northwestern part of the subcontinent, in present-day Pakistan.

Muhammad bin Qasim led his army of 6,000 soldiers to the far eastern reaches of Persia, Makran. He encountered little resistance as he made his way into India. When he reached the city of Nerun, on the banks of the Indus River, he was welcomed into the city by the Buddhist monks that controlled it. Most cities along the Indus thus voluntarily came under Muslim control, with no fighting. In some cases, oppressed Buddhist minorities reached out to the Muslim armies for protection against Hindu governors.

Despite the support and approval of much of the population, the Raja of Sindh, Dahir, opposed the Muslim expansion and mobilized his army against Muhammad bin Qasim. In 712, the two armies met, with a decisive victory for the Muslims. With the victory, all of Sindh came under Muslim control.

It is important to note, however, that the population of Sindh was not forced to convert to Islam at all. In fact, for almost everyone, there was no change in day-to-day life. Muhammad bin Qasim promised security and religious freedom to all Hindus and Buddhists under his control.

For example, the Brahman caste continued their jobs as tax collectors and Buddhists monks continued to maintain their monastaries. Due to his religious tolerance and justice, many cities regularly greeted him and his armies with people dancing and music.

Patterns of Conversion

The successive waves of Muslim armies penetrating into India followed much the same pattern. Leaders such as Mahmud of Ghazni and Muhammad Tughluq expanded Muslim political domains without altering the religious or social fabric of Indian society.

Because pre-Islamic India was entirely based on a caste system in which society was broken into separate parts, conversion to Islam happened in a step-by-step process. Often, entire castes would convert to Islam at a time. This would happen for many different reasons. Often, however, the equality Islam provided was more attractive than the caste system's organized racism. In the caste system, who you are born to determines your position in society. There was no opportunity for social mobility or to achieve greater than what your parents achieved. By converting to Islam, people had the opportunity to move up in society, and no longer were subservient to the Brahman caste.

The Jama Masjid in Delhi, India

Buddhism, which was once very popular in the subcontinent, slowly died out under Muslim rule. Traditionally, when people wanted to escape the caste system, they would move to the major population centers and convert to Buddhism. When Islam became an option, however, people began to convert to Islam instead of Buddhism, while still leaving the caste system. The myths of Islam violently destroying Buddhism in India are simply false. Buddhists were tolerated under Muslim rule and no evidence exists that shows forced conversions or violence against them.

Wandering teachers also had a major role in bringing Islam to the masses. Muslim scholars traveled throughout India, making it their goal to educate people about Islam. Many of them preached Sufi ideas, a more mystical approach to Islam that appealed to the people. These teachers had a major role in bringing Islam to the masses in the countryside, not just the upper classes around the Muslim rulers.

Did Islam Spread by Force?

While some claim that Islam's huge population in India is a result of violence and forced conversion, the evidence does not back up this idea at all. Although Muslim leaders replaced Hindu kings in most areas, society was left as is. Stories of forced conversion are very few and often not credible enough to warrant academic discussion.

If Islam spread through violence and warfare, the Muslim community today in India would exist only in the areas closest to the rest of the Muslim world. Thus only the western part of the subcontinent would have any Muslim population at all. What we see instead is pockets of Islam throughout the subcontinent. For example, Bangladesh and its 150 million Muslims are in the far east, separated from other Muslim-majority areas by Hindu lands in India. Isolated communities of Muslims exist also exist in western Myanmar, central India, and eastern Sri Lanka. These communities of Muslims are proof of Islam spreading peacefully throughout India, regardless of whether or not a Muslim government existed there. If Islam spread by force as some claim, these communities of Muslims would not exist.

EARLY HISTORY OF ISLAM IN INDIA

Trade relations have existed between Arabia and the Indian subcontinent from ancient times. Even in the pre-Islamic era, Arab traders used to visit the Malabar region, which linked them with the ports of South East Asia. Newly Islamised Arabs were Islam's first contact with India. According to Historians Elliot and Dowson in their book *The History of India as told by its own Historians*, the first ship bearing Muslim travellers was seen on the Indian coast as early as 630 AD. H.G. Rawlinson, in his book: *Ancient and Medieval History of India* claims the first Arab Muslims settled on the Indian coast in the last part of the 7th century AD. Shaykh Zainuddin Makhdum's "Tuhfat al-Mujahidin" is also a reliable work.

This fact is corroborated, by J. Sturrock in his *South Kanara and Madras Districts Manuals*, and also by Haridas Bhattacharya in *Cultural Heritage of India Vol. IV*. It was with the advent of Islam that the Arabs became a prominent cultural force in the world. The Arab merchants and traders became the carriers of the new religion and they propagated it wherever they went.The first Indian mosque is thought to have been built in 629 A.D, purportedly at the behest of Rama Varma Kulashekhara, who is considered the first Indian Muslim, during the lifetime of Muhammad (c. 571–632) in Kodungallur, Kerala by Malik Bin Deenar. In Malabar, the Mappilas may have been the first community to convert to Islam as they were more closely connected with the Arabs than others. Intensive missionary activities were carried out along the coast and a number of natives also embraced Islam.

These new converts were now added to the Mappila community. Thus among the Mappilas, we find, both the descendants of the Arabs through local women and the converts from among the local people. In the 8th century, the province of Sindh (in present day Pakistan) was conquered by an Arab army led by Muhammad bin Qasim. Sindh became the easternmost province of the Umayyad Caliphate. In the first half of the 10th century, Mahmud of Ghazni added the Punjab to the Ghaznavid Empire and conducted several raids deeper into modern day India. In 11th century, Ghazi Saiyyad Salar Masud played significant role. A more successful invasion came at the end of the 12th century by Muhammad of Ghor. This eventually led to the formation of the Delhi Sultanate.

Arab-Indian interactions

There is much evidence in history to show that Arabs and Muslims interacted with India and Indians from the very early days of Islam, if not before the arrival of Islam in Arabia. Arab traders transmitted the numeral system developed by Indians to the Middle East and Europe. Many Sanskrit books were translated into Arabic as early as the Eighth century. George Saliba writes in his book 'Islamic Science and the Making of the European Renaissance' that "some major Sanskrit texts began to be translated during the reign of the second Abbasid caliph al-Mansur [754–775], if not before; some texts on logic even before that, and it has been generally accepted that the Persian and Sanskrit texts, few as they were, were indeed the first to be translated."

THE COMING OF ISLAM TO INDIA (711-C.1800)

Until 711 C.E., India had faced many invaders, but no substantial challenges on both a military and cultural level. The Persians and Greeks had confronted India with highly developed civilizations, but also had reached the limits of their expansion by the time they arrived there.

The various nomadic peoples who entered India between the second century B.C.E. and eighth century C.E. may have been more potent military threats, but their cultures were thoroughly absorbed by India. However, in 711 C.E., India faced for the first time a vital people with a culture and religion both as sophisticated and powerful as its own: Islam.

Much of the relationship between Islam and Hinduism hinged on a battle that took place at the Talas River in Central Asia in 751 C.E. between the expanding empires of the Arab Muslims and T'ang China. The Arab victory in that battle not only stopped the T'ang dynasty's expansion to the West; it also led to the triumph of Islam over Buddhism as the prevailing religion in Central Asia. As a result, although India continued to face a succession of invaders from the North, all those invaders had Islam as the common defining element of their cultures, a religion that in its own way was as appealing as Hinduism.

Pattern of Development

For 1000 years following the entry of the Arab Muslims into India, a basic pattern of development emerged. Muslims would come into North-western India and expand to the south and east. Eventually, India's environment would slow them down, as Islamic and Indian civilizations would leave their marks on each other. Then another group of Muslims would come in and repeat the process. This pattern repeated itself in three successive waves: the Arabs in the eighth century, various Turkish peoples starting around 1000 C.E., and the Mughal dynasty that entered India in 1526. This cycle may have continued repeating itself except for the intrusion of the British who would present India with a new cultural challenge.

Arabs and Rajputs (711-c.1000 C.E.)

The Arab Muslims entered India in 711, the same year their religious compatriots in the West entered Spain. They conquered the area known as Sind in the Indus River valley (modern Pakistan). It is hard to imagine two religions and civilizations so different in their outlooks as Islam and Hinduism. Whereas Islam saw all people as equal before God, India's rigid caste system presented a highly stratified social structure sanctioned by religion. On the other hand, while Hinduism was incredibly tolerant of a multitude of gods, Islam was strictly monotheistic. For better or worse, the two cultures have co-existed, though not always peacefully, since the Arabs arrived until the present day.

Arab expansion was stopped by various feudal Indian princes known as the Rajputs who themselves may have been descended from invading Huns two centuries earlier. While theoretically loyal to a king, they functioned as virtually independent rulers. As trade increased, so did competition for the control of that trade.

As a result, the Rajputs often spent as much time fighting each other as they did resisting foreign invaders. Their warfare was highly ritualized and regulated by an elaborate code of behavior, much like the codes of chivalry and Buhsido regulated the fighting of elite nobles in medieval Europe and Japan.

Our modern game of chess, originating in India, reflects this ceremonial way of fighting wars. Unfortunately for the Rajputs, this also kept them from adapting to changes in warfare and hampering the Muslim advance across Northern India.

Arab rule was fairly tolerant of Hinduism. They even preserved the temple of a Hindu sun god in Multan, which also prevented Hindu attacks on the city that might damage this holy spot. Although the Arabs only conquered the northwestern part of India, their tolerant rule won many converts to Islam in that region which remains Muslim to this day. This provided a solid base for further Muslim expansion into India.

TURKISH INVADERS AND THE SULTANATE OF DELHI (C.1000-1526)

By 1000 C.E., the Abbasid Caliphate and Arabs' grip on their empire were in decline because of the empire's vast size, weak caliphs, and the split between Sunni and Shiite Muslims. Like the caliphs in Baghdad, the Arabs in Afghanistan relied increasingly on slave bodyguards drawn chiefly from neighboring Turkish tribes.

Eventually these Turkish warriors asserted their independence and took over from the Arabs. From this base in Afghanistan, they launched raids into India, thus resuming Muslim expansion in the subcontinent.

Compared to the Arabs, Turkish raids into India were much more ruthless and destructive. The first of these raiders, Mahmud of Ghazni, earned the title of "the Idol Smasher" for the damage he did to Hindu Temples, while the ruler, Ala al-Din, similarly came to be called "the World Burner." These raids and invasions especially hurt Buddhism, as kings in East India were no longer able or willing to patronize Buddhist monasteries. This led many

Buddhists either to convert to Islam or flee to Tibet and Southeast Asia. As a result, Buddhism virtually died out as a religion in India although its influence elsewhere continued to spread.

The Mongol invasions in the twelfth and thirteenth centuries seriously disrupted Muslim civilization, especially in Central Asia. As a result, Muslims left on their own in India built an independent kingdom, the Sultanate of Delhi (1206-c.1500). Also, many Muslim scholars fleeing the Mongol onslaught came to India. This, along with an active sea-borne trade with Southeast Asia, East Africa, and the Middle East led to a flowering of Muslim culture in India. The Sultanate of Delhi witnessed a gradual blending of Muslim and Hindu cultures. Many Hindus learned Persian and Muslim bureaucratic procedures. Helping this process was the introduction of paper, which made record keeping easier, thus, enhancing the Sultan's control over his realm. Islam gained a number of converts from lower castes, especially from such castes as elephant trainers, weavers, and butchers who worked for the Muslims and saw this as a way to improve their station in life.

Muslims also absorbed Indian Culture, with caste distinctions starting to appear among them, Muslim men marrying Hindu women, and a mystical branch of Islam, Sufism, developing that used Hindu techniques such as meditation. Altogether, these developments paved the way for the next wave of invaders: the Mughals.

The Mughal Dynasty (1526-c.1700) was founded by Babur the Tiger, an Afghan leader claiming descent from both Genghis Khan and Timur the Lame. His original intention was the reconquest of Timur's Central Asian empire. However, when the Safavid Dynasty in Persia thwarted this plan, he turned toward India. Using a combination of firearms, artillery, and nomadic cavalry, he defeated the Sultan of Delhi's much larger army at Panipat in 1526 and beat an even larger army of Rajputs the next year. By his death in 1530, Babur had established the basis for over a century and a half of Mughal expansion that would encompass all but the southern tip of India.

The greatest of the Mughal rulers was Akbar the Great (1656-1605). Coming to the throne at the age of thirteen, he soon proved himself a firm and shrewd ruler who quickly crushed any revolts in his inherited lands and expanded Mughal power into the Deccan. However, it was Akbar's talents as a ruler, not a conqueror that earned him the title, "the Great."

Instead of trying to rule the stubborn Rajputs by force, he allied with them, using them as his officers and government officials to keep his unruly Muslim nobles in line. He tolerated Hinduism, married Hindu princesses, and held scholarly discussions on any and all religions each Friday. He even founded his own religion, Din Ilahi, a simple monotheistic faith that would not survive its founder's death.

Akbar looked out for his peoples' welfare by holding a land survey to ensure fair taxes. He would even over-rule his own Muslim judges, the ulema, in order to secure justice and prosperity for his subjects. Akbar was also a patron of the arts, encouraging both Hindu and Muslim artists, poets, and musicians.

Akbar established a strong and stable state that allowed his three successors, Jahangir (1605-27), Shah Jahan (1628-58), and Aurangzeb (1658-1707), to keep expanding the Mughal realm. During this time, India experienced another flourishing of the arts with the fusion of Persian and Hindu styles. In painting, Mughal artists combined the Persian tradition of colorful painting with the looser and more natural style of Indian artists. Architecture especially reflected Muslim influence as seen in the Taj Mahal, a mausoleum for Shah Jahan's wife and still considered one of the world's most beautiful buildings. In music, the sultan, Aurangzeb's ban on music caused Muslim musicians to flee to the countryside where they blended their style of music with Hindu folk music to create a style of music still known as Mughal music.

Decline of the Mughals

It was during the reign of Aurangzeb that two major seeds of Mughal decline were sown. One was the over-extension of his empire in the conquest of all but the southern tip of India. The other was his persecution of Hindus, a reversal of the traditional Mughal policy of tolerance. Together, these bred disaffection among the people and drained the empire's resources. After Aurangzeb's death in 1707, the Mughal Empire went into rapid decline, allowing a new people with a new culture, the British, to take over.

MUSLIM WOMEN AND THE POST- INDEPENDENCE WOMEN'S MOVEMENT

Independent India's Constitution redefined the relationship between the state and its citisens. The notion of the individual as citisen with fundamental rights, including the right to universal adult suffrage, was a break with past authoritarian structures.The secular discourse of a multilayered past and a common future for all Indians in the wake of partition's bitterness evoked a powerful appeal. Yet, for most uneducated, economically deprived Muslim communities it was difficult, even painful, to identify with a secular Indian identity while their religious identity was still suspect; while they remained targets of communal violence; when it meant learning Hindi instead of Urdu; or when Hindu right-wing discourse posited Muslims as major impediments to national integration, casting thinly veiled aspersions on Muslim cultural identity.

Furthermore, Muslim women faced the additional disadvantage of being women within a minority community. Like most Indian women, Muslim women were yet to benefit from the gains of the women's movement made at the turn of the century.

Practices like polygamy and seclusion of women were common to both Hindu and Muslim women; so was the lack of education and economic independence. Muslim women joined other Indian women in the struggle for access to economic resources, education and employment. The impetus of the women's movement lay somewhat diffused in the aftermath of partition. Its communal solidarity was commendable, yet the transition was particularly difficult for Muslim women. Devoid of a national or visionary leadership, the voices and experiences of Muslim women came to be usurped by male Muslims claiming to represent the community.

The political opportunism of the latter, combined with the failure of state programmes to alleviate women's socio-economic status, left the majority of Muslim women economically and educationally impoverished. The restricted agendas of organisations like Jamiat-e-ulema-e-Hind, which focus on the retention of Muslim personal law; the Jamaat-e- Islami, wishing to preserve the Shari'a; together with the revivalist and missionary activities of the Tablighi Jamaat, which propagates a particularly rigid and puritanical Islamic doctrine, do not offer any hope of initiating debate within Muslim communities or of taking up problems with central government.

Personal Law

Personal law (*i.e.,* laws covering family relations, marriage, divorce, inheritance, custody rights, etc.,) is a contested arena for the women's movement as well as for Hindu and Muslim conservatives.

It not only defines the relationship between men and women in marriage and family relations but also marks the relationship between women and the state. While civil and criminal laws in post-independent India are secular, personal laws are governed by the respective religious laws. Accordingly, Muslim women came under the purview of Muslim personal (family) law. The passage of the Hindu Code Bill and the Shah Bano controversy brought Muslim personal law - which had not been subject to any legislative changes since, the 1937 Shariat Act and the 1939 Dissolution of Muslim Marriages Act - back into focus.

Legislation on women in post-independence India faced stiff opposition from Hindu and Muslim conservatives. The Assembly debates preceding the passage of the Hindu Code Bill - which gave Hindu women the right to divorce and allowed for inter-caste marriage and monogamy - symbolised the cross-communal patriarchal collusion in opposing any pro-women legislation. The Special Marriages Act, 1952, which allowed two Indians to marry without renouncing their religion provoked strong opposition from Hindu and Muslim Members of Parliament (MPs).

The debates also highlighted the transformation of a women's rights debate into a discourse where personal codes merged with perceptions of communal 'identity'. At another level, the debate also translated into a set of competing concessions between Hindu and Muslim men.

As Dr Mookerjee and Pandit Govind Malviya asserted: 'Hindus would accept monogamy only when Muslims did, that divorce could not take place in "Ram Rajya" and that they were against a daughter's share in her father's property since, that would be imitating Muslims.'

In 1973, in an amendment relating to the rights of divorced women to maintenance under the Criminal Procedure Code, the word 'wife' in Section 125 was amended to include a 'divorced wife'. This provoked protests from the Muslim League whose members argued that the amendment violated Muslim personal law. The amendment went on to exclude Muslim women from the provisions of Section 125 if they had already received payment due to them under Muslim law.

However, in a subsequent judgement (Bai Tahira vs Ali Hussain) the Supreme Court held that: 'The payment of illusory amounts by way of customary or Personal Law requirement will be considered in the reduction of maintenance rate but cannot annihilate the rate unless it is a reasonable substitute'.

The provision of triple talaq (unilateral divorce by saying the word talaq [divorce] three times in one sitting) is another area within Muslim law where women face discrimination. The threat of verbal divorce (invested with men) acts as a perpetual legal and psychological threat against Muslim women. This was acknowledged by National Commission of Women (NCW) member Syeda Saiyedain Hameed at a recent seminar on Muslim women in Bombay, when she called for personal laws to be amended 'so as to help ease the sufferings of Muslim women'. In 1986, Shah Bano, a 73-year-old Muslim woman was thrown out of her house by her husband after 43 years of marriage after he used the triple talaq.

In 1977 Shah Bano's husband stopped the payment of ₹200 as maintenance, upon which she filed an application for maintenance of ₹500 under Section 125 of the Criminal Procedure Code. Her husband subsequently divorced her, paying ₹3,000 as final settlement. A judicial magistrate, however, ordered him to pay a sum of ₹25 (approximately US $0.50), which was later raised to ₹179.20 by the Madhya Pradesh High Court. Shah Bano's former husband appealed to the Supreme Court of India and argued that Muslim personal law did not oblige ex-husbands to provide maintenance for their former wives.

The Supreme Court dismissed his appeal and upheld the maintenance order under Section 125 of the Criminal Procedure Code. Subsequently, Parliament passed the Muslim Women Protection of Rights on Divorce Bill - which denied Muslim women the right to maintenance under constitutional law.

The judgement and subsequent Muslim Women's Bill generated much debate and led to widescale mobilisation by women's groups on the issue of personal law. It also highlighted the disjunction between constitutional law premised on the principle of sexual equality and religious laws which discriminate on the basis of this very category.

Parties like the Jamaat-e-Islami have argued that Muslim personal law is divine, beyond human intervention and that any attempt to change it would represent an erosion of Muslim cultural identity.

Reactions from the Muslim Personal Law Board were equally intolerant. It declared its intention to set up 'Islamic courts' in order to dispense justice according to the Qur'an. The BJP appropriated the women's rights debate by aggressively campaigning for a Uniform Civil Code, which would replace Muslim personal law. Equating nationalism with the adoption of a Uniform Civil Code, the Hindu right-wing portrayed Muslim reluctance towards reform in personal law as 'minority appeasement' and an impediment to national progress. The fact that many Muslims wanted reform within personal law without being considered culturally inferior or unpatriotic was completely overlooked.

As Mr M.Y. Kazi wrote: 'It is such a pity that the issue of Muslim personal law has been politicised by motivated people who have thus vitiated the atmosphere for a serious debate. As a Muslim, I am only too well aware of where the shoe pinches and what needs to be done. But let me make it very plain, I won't oblige those who regard any identity except their own as inferior, alien and unpatriotic, and who would shed copious tears on the "plight" of Muslim women but have no sympathy to spare when those very women are made widows and orphans in the streets of Bhiwandi, Ahmedabad, Baroda, Meerut and other innumerable places... As a Muslim, I would not mind having a common code provided that code incorporate the good points of all the existing codes'.

Despite its commitment to the principle of gender-just laws for all Indian women, the women's movement, in the case of this divorce Bill, faced the unhappy predicament of sharing the same platform with the right-wing, albeit for very different reasons.

The movement's genuine concern at women's subordination within personal laws could not entirely obliterate Muslim fears of the imposition of a 'Hindu' code under the guise of national integration. The women's movement has since, then moved away from a pro- or anti-Uniform Civil Code position to more nuanced positions which combine the options of reform within personal law, with the formulation of a gender-just law deriving from the concept of a common civil code.

There is no definitive conclusion to the debate, which continues, but as a researcher comments: 'Their [the women's movement] first task is to reclaim the debate, take it back from the fundamentalist forces, debunk the false choices that they are advocating, and expose the electoral gimmicks of the BJP and the Congress.'

Since independence, successive Indian governments have avoided taking any legislative measures to end discrimination in personal laws. Such a policy contradicts India's commitment to the Convention on the Elimination of All Forms of Discrimination Against Women (CEDAW) which upholds the principle of equality among men and women in the family.

India has also entered the following reservations on Articles 5a and 16 of CEDAW:

- With regard to Articles 5(a) and 16(I) of the Convention on the Elimination of All Forms of Discrimination Against Women, the Government of the Republic of India declared that it shall abide by and ensure these provisions in conformity with its policy of non-interference in the personal affairs of any community without its initiative and consent.

- With regard to Article 16(2) of the Convention on the Elimination of All Forms of Discrimination Against Women, the Government of the Republic of India declares that though in principle it fully supports the principle of compulsory registration of marriages, it is not practical in a vast country like India with its variety of customs, religions and levels of literacy.
- With regard to Article 29 of the Convention on the Elimination of All Forms of Discrimination Against Women, the Government of the Republic of India declares it does not consider itself bound by Paragraph 1 of this Article.'

The Indian government's rejection of the clauses with reference to personal laws highlights its lack of commitment to promoting women's rights in the family and society, and a violation of women's constitutional rights to equality.

Government positions notwithstanding, Muslim fundamentalist parties have appropriated the debate for their own ends, while the lesser vocal Muslim majority has been unable to voice its demands at a national level. Reform of Muslim personal law remains an urgent necessity.

As an eminent Muslim lawyer remarked: 'It is futile to argue that where a certain rule of law, as applied by courts in India, needs a change, we are interfering with an immutable rule of divine law. Such an argument is used for personal, polemical or political ends, and not with any spiritual motives... it is for us Muslims of India, to find a solution and to bring our law into line with every other system of jurisprudence, giving justice to whom it is denied.'

Law by itself, however, cannot be the sole determinant of Muslim women's status in Indian society.

Nor can their status be ascribed to some essential Islamic feature. The socio-economic status of Indian Muslim women mandates attention not only because it is a marker of women's progress, but also because it is difficult to institute legal reforms without simultaneous progress in Muslim women's educational status and economic autonomy.

DIVERSITY OF ISLAM IN INDIA

Spread of Sufi Islam

Sufis (Islamic mystics) played an important role in the spread of Islam in India. They were very successful in spreading Islam, as many aspects of Sufi belief systems and practices had their parallels in Indian philosophical literature, in particular nonviolence and monism. The Sufis' orthodox approach towards Islam made it easier for Hindus to practice. Hazrat Khawaja Muin-ud-din Chishti, Qutbuddin Bakhtiar Kaki, Nizam-ud-din Auliya, Shah Jalal, Amir Khusro, Sarkar Sabir Pak, Shekh Alla-ul-Haq Pandwi, Ashraf Jahangir Semnani, Sarkar Waris Pak, Ata Hussain Fani Chishti trained Sufis for the propagation of Islam in different parts of India.

Once the Islamic Empire was established in India, Sufis invariably provided a touch of colour and beauty to what might have otherwise been rather cold and stark reigns.

The Sufi movement also attracted followers from the artisan and untouchable communities; they played a crucial role in bridging the distance between Islam and the indigenous traditions. Ahmad Sirhindi, a prominent member of the Naqshbandi Sufi advocated the peaceful conversion of Hindus to Islam. Ahmed Rida Khan contributed much in defending traditional and orthodox Islam in India through his work *Fatawa Razvia*.

Dawoodi Bohra in India

Dawoodi Bohra' Ismailli shia whose belief system originates in Yemen, evolved from the Fatimid were persecuted due to their adherence to Fatimid Shia Islam - leading the shift of Dawoodi Bohra to India. After occultation of their 21st Imam Tayyib, they follow Dai as representative of Imam which are continued till date. This community was established in Gujarat in the second half of the 11th century. Per legend, two travellers (Moulai Abadullah (formerly known as Baalam Nath) and Maulai Nuruddin (Rupnath)) from India went to the court of Imam Mustansir. They were so impressed that they converted and went back to preach in India. Abadullah was first Wali-ul-Hind. He came across a married couple named Kaka Akela and Kaki Akela who became his first converts.

One Dai succeeded another until the 23rd Dai in Yemen. In India also Wali-ul-Hind were appointed by them one after another until Wali-ul-Hind Moulai Qasim Khan bin Hasan (11th and last Wali-ul-Hind, d.950AH, Ahmedabad). Due to persecution by the local Zaydi Shi'a ruler in Yemen, the 24th Dai, Yusuf Najmuddin ibn Sulaiman (d.1567 AD), shifted the whole administration of the *Dawat* (mission) to India. The 25th Dai Jalal Shamshuddin (d.1567 AD) was first dai to die in India; his mausoleum is in Ahmedabad, India. The Dawat subsequently shifted from Ahmedabad to Jamnagar Mandvi, Burhanpur, Surat and finally to Mumbai and continues there to the present day, currently headed by 52nd Dai Mohammad Burhanuddin.

Ahmadiyya Islam

India has a significant Ahmadiyya population. Most of them live in Rajasthan, Orissa, Haryana, Bihar, Delhi, Uttar Pradesh, and a few in Punjab in the area of Qadian. In India, Ahmadis are considered to be Muslims by the Government of India. This recognition is supported by a court verdict (Shihabuddin Koya vs. Ahammed Koya, A.I.R. 1971 Ker 206). There is no legislation that declares Ahmadis non-Muslims or limits their activities, but they are not allowed to sit on the All India Muslim Personal Law Board, a body of religious leaders India's government recognises as representative of Indian Muslims.

ROLE IN INDIAN INDEPENDENCE MOVEMENT

The Freedom Movement, as popularly conceived of, was not the sole agenda of a particular political party but it had moved the masses to revolt against the British Raj and even aam aadmi in his or her own capacity contributed in this movement. It may be borne in mind that even littérateurs like Sir Sayyad Ahmad and poets like Hasrat Mohani with their creative writings spread the message of this movement far and wide. The papers that were presented provide scholarly treatments to the genesis of the movement. Naseem Ahmad, former Vice Chanecellor , Aligarh

Muslim University in his inaugural address justified the timing of the seminar since the attempts to underplay the role of leaders of minorities in freedom movement is playing havoc with the social fabric of our country. Though there is no denial of the fact that the country has a majority of Hindus, nevertheless the Muslims and other minorities never conceived India as an adopted land. Instead they consider themselves as an integral part of constituents of population aggregates of this country. Naseem Ahmad spoke that Muslims have not come from outside but are the converts to Islam and hence have a deep sense of belonging to this country and therefore contributed in country's economic, cultural, intellectual and spiritual progress through the ages. Those who happened to visit the Cellular Jail in Port Blair and moved along with local residents would hear names like Pir Ali, Ali Karim, Mahdi Ali, Sher Ali etc. who are legends and icons in the freedom movement.

Naseem Ahmad gave example of Sir Syed Ahmad Khan who dared to publish a book under the tile of Asbab Baghawat-e-Hind wherein he squarely blamed the British rulers for the outbreak of 1857 revolt. The objectives with which Aligarh Muslim University was established envisaged that students from various communities would not only pursue higher education, develop scientific temper but also imbibe the secular traditions of India and thus would be impediment in growing gulf between the Hindu and the Muslims engineered by the British Raj officials to continue their subjugation through pursuing the policy of "divide and rule".

The contribution of Muslim revolutionaries, poets and writers is documented in India's struggle against the British. Titu Mir raised a revolt against British. Abul Kalam Azad, Hakim Ajmal Khan and Rafi Ahmed Kidwai are Muslims who engaged in this purpose. Muhammad Ashfaq Ullah Khan of Shahjehanpur conspired to loot the British treasury at Kakori (Lucknow). Khan Abdul Gaffar Khan (popularly known as Frontier Gandhi), was a great nationalist who spent 45 of his 95 years of life in jail; Barakatullah of Bhopal was one of the founders of the *Ghadar party* which created a network of anti-British organisations; Syed Rahmat Shah of the Ghadar party worked as an underground revolutionary in France and was hanged for his part in the unsuccessful Ghadar (mutiny) uprising in 1915; Ali Ahmad Siddiqui of Faizabad (UP) planned the Indian Mutiny in Malaya and Burma along with Syed Mujtaba Hussain of Jaunpur and was hanged in 1917; Vakkom Abdul Khadir of Kerala participated in the "Quit India" struggle in 1942 and was hanged; Umar Subhani, an industrialist and millionaire of Bombay provided Gandhi with congress expenses and ultimately died for the cause of independence. Among Muslim women, Hazrat Mahal, Asghari Begum, Bi Amma contributed in the struggle of freedom from the British. The first ever Indian rebellion against the British saw itself in the Vellore Mutiny of 10 July 1806 which left around 200 British Officers and troops dead or injured. But it was subdued by the British and the mutineers and the family of Tippu Sultan who were incarcerated in the Vellore Fort at that time had to pay a heavy price.

It predates the First war of Independence, which is British imperialists called the Sepoy Mutiny of 1857. And as a result of the Sepoy Mutiny, mostly the upper class Muslims were targeted by the Britishers, as under their leadership the war was mostly fought in and around Delhi. Thousands of kith and kins were shot or hanged near the gate of Red Fort, Delhi, which is now known as 'Khooni Darwaza'(the bloody gate). The renowned Urdu poet Mirza Ghalib(1797–1869) has given a vivid description of such massacre in his letters now published by the Oxford University Press 'Ghalib his life and letters' compiled and translated by Ralph Russel and Khurshidul Islam(1994).

As the Muslim power waned with the gradual demise of the Mughal Empire, the Muslims of India faced a new challenge – that of protecting their culture and interests, yet interacting with the alien, technologically advantaged power. In this period, the Ulama of Firangi Mahal, based first at Sehali in District Barabanki, and since, 1690s based in Lucknow, educated and guided the Muslims. The Firangi Mahal led and steered the Muslims of India. The moulanas and moulvis (religious teachers) of Darul-uloom, Deoband (UP) also played significant role in freedom struggle of India declaring subjugation of an unjust rule is against Islamic tenets.

Other famous Muslims who fought for freedom against the British rule: Abul Kalam Azad, Mehmud Hasan of Darul Uloom Deoband who was implicated in the famous Silk Letter Conspiracy to overthrow the British through an armed struggle, Husain Ahmed Madani, former Shaikhul Hadith of Darul Uloom Deoband, Ubaidullah Sindhi, Hakeem Ajmal Khan, Hasrat Mohani, Syed Mahmud, Professor Maulavi Barkatullah, Zakir Husain, Saifuddin Kichlu, Vakkom Abdul Khadir, Manzoor Abdul Wahab, Bahadur Shah Zafar, Hakeem Nusrat Husain, Khan Abdul Gaffar Khan, Abdul Samad Khan Achakzai, Colonel Shahnawaz, M.A.Ansari, Rafi Ahmad Kidwai, Fakhruddin Ali Ahmad, Ansar Harwani, Tak Sherwani, Nawab Viqarul Mulk, Nawab Mohsinul Mulk, Mustsafa Husain, VM Ubaidullah, SR Rahim, Badaruddin Taiyabji, and Moulvi Abdul Hamid. Until the 1930s, Muhammad Ali Jinnah was a member of the Indian National Congress and was part of the freedom struggle.

Allama Muhammad Iqbal, poet and philosopher, was a strong proponent of Hindu – Muslim unity and an undivdided India until the 1920s.Huseyn Shaheed Suhrawardy was also active in Indian National Congress in Bengal during his early political career. Muhammad Ali Jauhar and Shaukat Ali struggled for the emancipation of the Muslims in the overall Indian context, and struggled for freedom alongside Mahatama Gandhi and Abdul Bari of Firangi Mahal. Until the 1930s, the Muslims of India broadly conducted their politics alongside their countrymen, in the overall context of an undivided India.

PROMINENT MUSLIMS IN INDIA

India is home to several eminent Muslims who have made their mark in several fields and have played a constructive role in India's economic rise and cultural influence across the world. Out of the twelve Presidents of independent India, three were Muslims – Zakir Hussain, Fakhruddin Ali Ahmed and A.P.J. Abdul Kalam. Additionally, Mohammad Hidayatullah, A. M. Ahmadi and Mirza Hameedullah Beg held the office of the Chief Justice of India on various occasions since, independence. Mohammad Hidayatullah also served as the acting President of India on two separate occasions;

and holds the distinct honour of being the only person to have served in all three offices of the President of India, the Vice President of India and the Chief Justice of India.

The current Vice President of India, Mohammad Hamid Ansari, and the current Chief Election Commissioner of India, S. Y. Quraishi are both Muslims. Prominent Indian bureaucrats and diplomats include Abid Hussain and Asaf Ali. Zafar Saifullah was Cabinet Secretary of the Government of India from 1993 to 1994. Salman Haidar was Indian Foreign Secretary from 1995 to 1997 and Deputy Permanent Representative of India to the United Nations. Influential Muslim politicians in India include Sheikh Abdullah, Farooq Abdullah and his son Omar Abdullah (the current Chief Minister of Jammu and Kashmir), Mufti Mohammad Sayeed, Sikander Bakht, A R Antulay, C. H. Mohammed Koya, A.B.A. Ghani Khan Choudhury, Mukhtar Abbas Naqvi, Salman Khurshid, Saifuddin Soz, E. Ahamed, Ghulam Nabi Azad, Syed Shahnawaz Hussain and Asaduddin Owaisi. Some of the most popular and influential actors and actresses in Mumbai-based Bollywood are Muslims.

These include Yusuf Khan (stage name Dilip Kumar), Shahrukh Khan, Aamir Khan, Salman Khan, Saif Ali Khan, Madhubala, and Emraan Hashmi. India is also home to several critically acclaimed Muslim actors such as Naseeruddin Shah, Johnny Walker, Shabana Azmi, Waheeda Rehman, Amjad Khan, Parveen Babi, Feroz Khan, Meena Kumari, Prem Nazir, Mammootty, Nargis Dutt, Irrfan Khan, Farida Jalal, Arshad Warsi, Mehmood, Zeenat Aman, Farooq Sheikh and Tabu. Some of the best known film-directors of Indian cinema include Mehboob Khan, K. A. Abbas, Kamal Amrohi, K. Asif and the Abbas-Mustan duo. Indian Muslims also play pivotal roles in other forms of performing arts in India, particularly in music, modern art and theater. M. F. Husain is one of India's best known contemporary artists. Academy Awards winners Resul Pookutty and A. R. Rahman, Naushad, Salim-Sulaiman and Nadeem Akhtar of the Nadeem-Shravan duo are some of India's celebrated musicians.

Abrar Alvi penned many of the greatest classics of Indian cinema. Prominent poets and lyricists include Shakeel Badayuni,

Sahir Ludhianvi and Majrooh Sultanpuri. Popular Indian singers of Muslim faith include Mohammed Rafi, Anu Malik, Lucky Ali, Talat Mahmood and Shamshad Begum. Another famous personality is the tabla maestro Zakir Hussian. Sania Mirza, from Hyderabad, is the highest-ranked Indian woman tennis player. In cricket (the most popular game in India), there are many Muslim players who have made their mark. Iftikhar Ali Khan Pataudi, Mansoor Ali Khan Pataudi and Mohammad Azharuddin captained the Indian cricket team on various occasions. Other prominent Muslim cricketers in India are Mushtaq Ali, Syed Kirmani, Arshad Ayub, Mohammad Kaif,[Munaf Patel], Zaheer Khan, Irfan Pathan, Yusuf Pathan and Wasim Jaffer. India is home to several influential Muslim businessmen. Some of India's most prominent firms, such as Wipro, Wockhardt, Himalaya Health Care, Hamdard Laboratories, Cipla and Mirza Tanners were founded by Muslims.

The only two South Asian Muslim billionaires named by Forbes Magazine, Yusuf Hamied and Azim Premji, are from India. Though Muslims are under-represented in the Indian Armed Forces compared to Hindus and Sikhs, several Indian military Muslim personnel have earned gallantry awards and high ranks for exceptional service to the nation. Air Chief Marshal Idris Hasan Latif was Deputy Chief of the Air Staff during the Indo-Pakistani War of 1971 and later served as Chief of the Air Staff of the Indian Air Force from 1973 to 1976. Indian Army's Abdul Hamid was posthumously awarded India's highest military decoration, the Param Vir Chakra, for knocking-out seven Pakistani tanks with a recoilless gun during the Battle of Asal Uttar in 1965. Two other Muslims – Brigadier Mohammed Usman and Mohammed Ismail – were awarded Mahavir Chakra for their actions during the Indo-Pakistani War of 1947.

High ranking Muslims in the Indian Armed Forces include Lieutenant General Jameel Mahmood (former GOC-in-C Eastern Command of the Indian Army) and Major General Mohammed Amin Naik. Abdul Kalam, one of India's most well respected scientists and the father of the Integrated Guided Missile Development Program (IGMDP) of India was honoured through his appointment as the 11th President of India.

His extensive contribution to India's defence industry lead him to being nicknamed as the *Missile Man of India* and during his tenure as the President of India, he was affectionately known as *People's President*. Zahoor Qasim, former Director of the National Institute of Oceanography, led India's first scientific expedition to Antarctica and played a crucial role in the establishment of Dakshin Gangotri. He was also the former Vice Chancellor of Jamia Millia Islamia, Secretary of the Department of Ocean Development and the founder of Polar Research in India. Other prominent Muslim scientists and engineers include C. M. Habibullah, a stem cell scientist and director of Deccan College of Medical Sciences and Allied Hospitals and Center for Liver Research and Diagnostics, Hyderabad.

In the field of Unani medicine, one can name Hakim Ajmal Khan, Hakim Abdul Hameed and Hakim Syed Zillur Rahman. Zakir Naik is one of the most influential spiritual leader of India as noted by The Indian Express in 2009. Ahle Sunnat Sufi leader Hazrat Syed Muhammad Ameen Mian Qaudri and Aboobacker Ahmad Musliyar have been included in the list of most influential Muslims list by Georgetown University. Mahmood Madani, leader of Jamiat Ulema-e-Hind and MP was ranked at 36 for initiating a movement against terrorism in South Asia. Syed Ameen Mian has been ranked 44th in the list.

Conversion Controversy

Considerable controversy exists both in scholarly and public opinion about the conversions to Islam typically represented by the following schools of thought:

- The bulk of Muslims are descendants of migrants from the Iranian plateau or Arabs.
- Conversions occurred for non-religious reasons of pragmatism and patronage such as social mobility among the Muslim ruling elite or for relief from taxes
- Conversion was a result of the actions of Sunni Sufi saints and involved a genuine change of heart.
- Conversion came from Buddhists and the en masse conversions of lower castes for social liberation and as a rejection of the oppressive Hindu caste strictures.

- A combination, initially made under duress followed by a genuine change of heart.
- As a socio-cultural process of diffusion and integration over an extended period of time into the sphere of the dominant Muslim civilization and global polity at large.

Embedded within this lies the concept of Islam as a foreign imposition and Hinduism being a natural condition of the natives who resisted, resulting in the failure of the project to Islamicise the Indian subcontinent and is highly embroiled within the politics of the partition and communalism in India. An estimate of the number of people killed, based on the Muslim chronicles and demographic calculations, was done by K.S. Lal in his book *Growth of Muslim Population in Medieval India*, who claimed that between 1000 CE and 1500 CE, the population of Hindus decreased by 80 million. His work has come under criticism by historians such as Simon Digby (School of Oriental and African Studies) and Irfan Habib for its agenda and lack of accurate data in pre-census times. Lal has responded to these criticisms in later works.

Historians such as Will Durant contend that Islam was spread through violence. Sir Jadunath Sarkar contends that several Muslim invaders were waging a systematic jihad against Hindus in India to the effect that "Every device short of massacre in cold blood was resorted to in order to convert heathen subjects".

Hindus who converted to Islam were not immune to persecution due to the Muslim Caste System in India established by Ziauddin al-Barani in the *Fatawa-i Jahandari*, where they were regarded as an "Ajlaf" caste and subjected to discrimination by the "Ashraf" castes. Disputers of the "Conversion by the Sword Theory" point to the presence of the large Muslim communities found in Southern India, Sri Lanka, Western Burma, Bangladesh, Southern Thailand, Indonesia and Malaysia coupled with the distinctive lack of equivalent Muslim communities around the heartland of historical Muslim Empires in the Indian Sub-Continent as refutation to the "Conversion by the Sword Theory".

The legacy of the Muslim conquest of South Asia is a hotly debated issue and argued even today. Different population estimates by economics historian Angus Maddison and by Jean-

Noël Biraben also indicate that India's population did not decrease between 1000 and 1500, but increased by about 35 million during that time. Not all Muslim invaders were simply raiders. Later rulers fought on to win kingdoms and stayed to create new ruling dynasties. The practices of these new rulers and their subsequent heirs (some of whom were borne of Hindu wives) varied considerably.

While some were uniformly hated, others developed a popular following. According to the memoirs of Ibn Batuta who travelled through Delhi in the 14th century, one of the previous sultans had been especially brutal and was deeply hated by Delhi's population, Batuta's memoirs also indicate that Muslims from the Arab world, Persia and Anatolia were often favored with important posts at the royal courts suggesting that locals may have played a somewhat subordinate role in the Delhi administration. The term "Turk" was commonly used to refer to their higher social status. S.A.A. Rizvi (*The Wonder That Was India – II*), however points to Muhammad bin Tughlaq as not only encouraging locals but promoting artisan groups such as cooks, barbers and gardeners to high administrative posts. In his reign, it is likely that conversions to Islam took place as a means of seeking greater social mobility and improved social standing.

The Sufis of India and Pakistan

In the words of Muhammed Iqbal, the philosopher-poet of India-Pakistan, Islam is like a balloon. When it is squeezed in one direction, it bulges out in another. Within a hundred years after Genghis Khan, Islam conquered the conquerors. The Mongols who had destroyed Bukhara and Baghdad themselves became the standard bearers of the new faith. The westward thrust of Islam carried it into Europe. To the east, it put down new roots in India and Indonesia. The center of gravity of the Islamic world shifted from Cairo and Damascus to Lahore and Kuala Lumpur.

After the conquest of Sindh by Muhammed bin Qasim in 711, the borders between the Baghdad Caliphate and India were relatively stable for 500 years. Islam made limited inroads into the subcontinent along the coast of Malabar in southern India and in southern Pakistan. Political Islam had reached equilibrium and was preoccupied as much with internal debates as with external threats. For almost 200 years, Fatimid chieftains controlled Multan and Sindh. Propagation of the faith took second place to the global struggle between the Sunnis and the Fatimids and later between the Muslims and the Crusaders. This situation changed towards the end of the 12th century with the dissolution of the Fatimid Caliphate in Cairo (1171), the defeat of the Crusaders at the Battle of Hittin (1186) and the conquest of Delhi by Muhammed Ghori (1192).

The Islamic penetration of the subcontinent accelerated in the 13th century. Several reasons may be cited for this change. First, the establishment of the Delhi sultanate enabled Muslim scholars and traders to travel freely throughout India under the protection of the political authorities. Second, India was a beneficiary of the Mongol invasions (1219-1261) that devastated Central Asia and Persia. Many noted scholars fled the Mongols into the security of Hindustan. Third and perhaps the most important element, was the establishment of Sufi orders throughout the vast subcontinent. Indeed, Islam spread in India and Pakistan not by the force of conquest or the elaborate arguments of *mullahs* and *kadis* but through the work of the great Sufi shaykhs. In this respect, Muslim India is different from the Arab countries where Islam was introduced during the classical period (665-1258) through the work of the *muhaddithin* and the *mujahideen*.

The process by which a faith enters the hearts of the believers has a profound impact on the way religion is felt and followed by them. In the Arab experience, the solidification of Islamic life took place during the imperial days of the Baghdad Caliphate and was tilted heavily in favor of the exoteric aspects of religion. By contrast, the Indo-Pakistanis, Indonesians and Africans were exposed more to the esoteric and spiritual dimension of Islam.

The Sufi shaykhs of the 13th century were not missionaries. They were not merchants of faith peddling their religion. They were men drunk with the love of God, giving of themselves for no gain but the prospect of divine pleasure, serving humanity irrespective of creed or nationality and sharing their spiritual bounty with whoever would partake of it. Proselytizing was not their goal; it was a byproduct of their selfless service. The Sufi way strove to mend human behavior and to open up human vistas to the sublime peace that comes from proximity to God. Their "miracles" were the transformations of human hearts. The Muslims needed this spirituality as much as did the Hindus and the Buddhists. When a Muslim experienced a spiritual rebirth through a Sufi, it was called an awakening. When a non-Muslim was similarly transformed, it was called conversion.

India, whose social structure was fossilized by the caste system, was ready to accept a universal religion like Islam. In a predominantly Hindu society, the position of a person was determined at birth. The Brahmans reserved for themselves the exclusive privilege to recite the *mantras* and propitiate the gods. The warrior Rajput class whose princely privileges were also guaranteed by birth backed the status quo. The *vyasyas* tilled the toil and paid the taxes. At the bottom of the social ladder were the *shudras* or the untouchables. To quote a well-known Indian writer V.T. Rajshekar: "These untouchables were denied the use of public wells and were condemned to drink any filthy water they could find. Their children were not admitted to schools attended by the caste Hindu children. Though they worshiped the gods of Hindus and observed the same festivals, the Hindu temples were closed to them. Barbers and washer men refused to render them service. Caste Hindus, who fondly threw sugar to ants and reared dogs and other pets and welcomed persons of other religions to their houses, refused to give a drop of water to the untouchables or to show them one iota of sympathy. These untouchable Hindus were treated by the caste Hindus as sub-human, less then men, worse than beasts . . ." In this social matrix, the message of Islam with its emphasis on the brotherhood of man and the transcendence of God found a ready reception.

But the most important reason for the success of the Sufis lay in the spiritual bent of the Indian mind. Every culture produces an archetype that personifies the ethos of that culture. For instance, in contemporary America, it is the businessman who personifies the ethos of the American culture. During the industrial revolution in Europe it was the empiricist and the inventor. During the Dark Ages in Europe it was the monk. In medieval Japan it was the Samurai. In the Muslim Middle East it was the traditionalist. In India, it was the *sadhu* and the *rishi*. Gautama Buddha personified this archetype; so did Shankara Acharya and Tulsi Das. These men of faith enjoyed and continue to enjoy an honor and respect that is the envy of kings and emperors. As Islam entered the subcontinent, it adapted its mode to fit the spiritual paradigm. The Sufi could intuitively and immediately relate to the Indian psyche in a manner that the learned doctors of law could not. Thus it was the great Sufis who not only succeeded in introducing millions of Indians to Islam but also contributed to the evolution of a unique Hindustani language, culture, poetry and music which amalgamated the ancient inheritance of India with the vibrancy of Islam.

In the subcontinent, by far the most outstanding among the great Sufi shaykhs was Khwaja Moeenuddin Chishti of Ajmer. Indeed, he is generally accepted as the fountainhead of Islamic spiritual movements in India and Pakistan. The Khwaja was born in Sajistan in Central Asia in the year 1139. Orphaned at the young age of twelve, he traveled to Samarqand and received his early education in that great center of learning. He was a *Hafiz*e Qur'an at age fifteen and had mastered the Arabic, Farsi and Turkic languages. He then traveled to Neshapur where he became a disciple of Khwaja Uthman Chisti. After receiving his training in the methodology of the Chistiya Order for seven years, Khwaja Moeenuddin was inducted into that Order. From Neshapur, he traveled to Baghdad where he met the towering personages of the age including Shaykh Abdul Qader Jeelani, Shaykh Ziauddin Suhrawardi, Khwaja Awhaduddin Kirmani and Khwaja Abu Saeed Tabrizi. In Isfahan, he met Khwaja Qutbuddin, who became his disciple and later his successor in Delhi. From Isfahan, Khwaja Moeenuddin traveled to Ghazna, Lahore and Multan where he mastered Sanskrit and Hindi so that he could communicate with the local people.

It was about this time that Muhammed Ghori defeated Prithvi Raj Chauhan at the Battle of Tarain (1192) and added Delhi and Ajmer to the Ghorid Sultanate. Khwaja Moeenuddin moved from Multan to Delhi and then to Ajmer, which had been the capital of the Chauhan dynasty. This town in the Rajasthan desert became the fountainhead of a Sufi movement that touched every corner of India and Pakistan. Thousands embraced Islam through his efforts. Millions did so through the efforts of his disciples. Three of his disciples themselves became towering personages of renown and occupy an important place in the hierarchy of the great Sufis. These were Khwaja Qutbuddin Bakhtiar Khaki (after whom the *Qutub Minar* of Delhi is named), Shaykh Hameeduddin Naguri and Baba Fareed Ganj of Lahore. Only once did the Khwaja of Ajmer return to Delhi. Sultan Shamsuddin Altumish was the Sultan of Delhi. When the Khwaja approached the capital, the Sultan presented himself in person with enormous presents of gold, silver and jewels. The presents were politely declined. This pattern of solicitation on the part of the ruling monarchs and a rebuff by the great Sufis was to be repeated countless times in Muslim history. The vision of the Sufis was fixed on a far higher goal than the gold of the world. They scorned the world; so the world chased them. Theirs was the kingdom of heaven, eternal, transcendent, unscathed and untouched by the rise and fall of dynasties. It was this selflessness that made them the beloved of the masses, something the rulers wanted but could not attain.

Khwaja Moeenuddin was a poet of renown. Over 10,000 couplets in Farsi are ascribed to him. He was a prolific writer, but most of his writings have been lost. He died in 1236, adored, venerated and extolled. If there is one person to whom belongs the credit for introducing Islam to India and Pakistan and of building the largest Islamic community in the world today, it was Khwaja Moeenuddin Chisti of Ajmer.

The Sufis were eminently successful not just because they recited the *dhikr,* chanted devotional songs and practiced charity, but because they established effective institutions to do their work in their own lifetime and to continue it after they departed. At the center of the Sufi approach is the belief that only a learned and pious teacher can impart true knowledge to a discipline. The structure of a Sufic order is pyramidal. At the apex of the pyramid is the *Qutub* (the pole) or the *Wali* (master, protector), *Khalifa* (representative) or *Sujjuduh Nishin* (one who resides in the sanctuary). For instance, the *Qutub* of the Qadariya School is Shaykh Abdul Qader Jeelani of Baghdad.

The methodology or approach of a Sufic order is called the *tareeqah*. Initiation into a Sufi order is voluntary. Upon initiation, a person becomes a *murid*. The word *murid* derives from the Arabic word *iradah,* meaning desire or will. A *murid* is one who desires and craves for proximity to God and is inclined towards Divine Love. In this journey, he is guided by a Shaykh. The *murid's* progression in the ranks of the *tareeqah* takes him (her) through the following stages: *Mubtadi* (student); *Mutadarrij* (practitioner);

Shaykh (teacher) and finally the *Qutub* (the pillar or pole). The exact terms may vary between the *tareeqas*. Obedience to the teacher and an extraordinary degree of discipline is required of the *murid*. There is no conflict between the various Sufi orders. A person may belong to several orders at the same time, although attachment to a single teacher is preferred.

The progress of a murid is measured in *darajat* (degrees) or *maqamat* (stages) *tawbah* (repentance), *zuhd* (avoidance of impure actions), *faqr* (humility, renunciation of worldly goods), *sabr* (patience), *tawakkul*(reliance on God alone for one's needs) and *rada* (earning Divine pleasure). Thus a Sufi order establishes an organizational structure, provides a methodology for instruction, measures progress of the initiates and takes them step-by-step towards certain knowledge (*ilm al yaqin*).

The principal place where adherents of a Sufi order meet is called a *zawiyah*. Secondary places of meeting for *dhikr* and study are referred to as *halqah* (circle). *Zawiyahs* and *halqahs* grew up throughout the Muslim world. The Sufi orders and their organizations provided continuity through their *silsilah* (spiritual connectivity relating a Sufi through his teachers to the Prophet). Ascension to the highest position in the organization was by appointment of the *Qutub*, who, as he approached the end of his life, would nominate and confirm his heir. Syed Mohammed Ghouse of Sindh introduced the *silsilah* of Abdul Qader Jeelani into India and Pakistan in the 15th century (1482). Although the Qadariya *silsilah* had less of an impact on Indian soil than the Chishtiya order, the name of Abdul Qader Jeelani is revered throughout the subcontinent. He is commonly referred to as*Peeran-e-pir Dastagir* or *Ghouse-ul-Azam Dastagir*. One of the most famous shaykhs of the Qadariya *silsilah* was Miyan Pir who passed away in Lahore in 1635. Miyan Pir was a teacher to Dara Shikoh, the eldest son of Moghul Emperor Shah Jehan. Dara Shikoh, a scholar of repute who was well versed in several languages, wrote a biography of Miyan Pir, who is widely credited with introducing Islam to the rural areas of Punjab and Kashmir.

From Ajmer the Chishtiya order spread to Delhi, Punjab, Bengal and the Deccan. Khwaja Moeenuddin Chisti trained and dispatched to the far-flung corners of the subcontinent men who stand out as spiritual giants in the region. These include Khwaja Qutbuddin Bakhtiar Khaki (Delhi, d. 1236), Baba Farid of Punjab (Pak Patan, d. 1265), Nizamuddin Awliya (Delhi, d. 1325) who was a disciple of Baba Farid, Hazrat Maqdum, another disciple of Baba Farid (Rourki, Bihar, d. 1291), Nasiruddin Muhammed, commonly referred to as *Chirag-e-Dehli* (a disciple of Nizamuddin Awliya, Delhi, d. 1356) and Hazrat Gaysu Daraz (a disciple of *Chirage-e-Dehli*, Gulbarga, d.1422). Together, these men transformed a continent, molded it in an Islamic crucible, lit the candle of faith in the hearts of millions and laid the spiritual foundation for one of the richest and most powerful dynasties the world has ever known, namely the great Moghuls of India.

The history of the Chishtiya order is so intricately woven into the politics of the Delhi court that no survey of Indian history is complete without an acknowledgment of the profound impact made by the Chishtiya order. The first Moghul emperor Babur was himself a Sufi mystic. Emperor Akbar was a *murid* of Shaykh Salim Chishti (Fatehpur Sikri, d. 1572). He made annual pilgrimages on foot to the tomb of Shaykh Salim as well as to the tomb of Khwaja Moeenuddin of Ajmer. Emperors Jehangir, Shah Jehan and his son Dara Shikoh were ardent believers in these shaykhs. Since the methods and processes of the Sufis have changed little over the last thousand years, the Chishtiya order, together with its sister Qadariya and Suhrwardi orders, provide a cultural link between modern Islam with the Middle Ages. Their history helps us understand the condition of the Muslims in the world today.

Khwaja Khutbuddin Bakhtiar Khaki was the designee of Khwaja Moeenuddin for the Delhi region. Born in Turkistan, he was educated in Baghdad where he met Khwaja Moeenuddin and became his *murid*. When Khwaja Moeenuddin migrated to Ajmer, Bakhtiar Khaki followed him and was sent to Delhi as the Chishtiya representative. Delhi was the seat of political power and a caldron of political intrigue. Sultan Altumish offered the post of the Kadi of Delhi to Shaykh Bakhtiar but the Shaykh declined, preferring the independence of the spiritual pursuit to the constraint of official power. The sultan was an avid supporter of *tasawwuf*. Sufi practices received official protection and common acceptance. Shaykh Bakhtiar himself was a well-known *khawwal* (reciter of mystic poetry) and often led *qawwali* gatherings (called *sama'a* by the Sufis). Thousands in the Delhi area accepted Islam through the radiance of this great mystic. Shaykh Bakhtiar passed away in 1236 and the mantle of the Chishtiya order passed on to Baba Fareed Ganj Shakr.

The emergence of *tasawwuf* as a powerful force in the Indian milieu did not go unchallenged by competing ideas. In the 14th century, the courts of Delhi witnessed a tug-of-war between the Sufis, the reformers, the kadis, the philosophers and the ruling elite. The geopolitics of the times presents a colorful backdrop for the war of ideas in the Delhi courts.

By the middle of the 14th century, trade routes between Africa, Europe, the Middle East, Central Asia, India and China, which had been cut by the Mongol invasions, had been restored. With the conversion of Ghazan the Great (1295), Persia was back in the fold of Islam. This removed the impediment to travel by land from India to west Asia and from there to Africa and Spain. A resilient Islam welded together a world order wherein people and ideas traveled freely from one continent to another.

There emerged three centers of political power in the Muslim world. The first was the rich Mali Kingdom in Africa, which attained its zenith under Mansa Musa (d. 1332). The second was the Mamluke Empire embracing Egypt and Syria. The third, and by far the most powerful, was the Sultanate of Delhi. (Yuan China was a global power but we will refer to it only in the context of diplomatic relations between Delhi and Beijing). The Khiljis (1296-1316) conquered all of India and Pakistan, from Peshawar to Malabar, an area covering more than a million and half square miles. The Tughlaqs (1316-1451), who followed the Khiljis, inherited this vast empire. We shall focus on the court of Muhammed bin Tughlaq (d. 1351), primarily because we know a great deal about his court through the writings of Ibn Batuta. So rich was the Delhi Sultanate that Ibn Batuta, who was a*kadi* in Delhi from 1335-1341, records that whenever the Emperor passed through the streets of Delhi, the courtiers following him threw coins of gold and silver in the streets for the *amah* (common folk) to pick up. It was in this magnificent Delhi court that the final resolution of the tug-of-war between the Sufis, the anti-Sufis, the philosophers, the doctors of law and the ruling elite took place. It is a fascinating story because the outcome of the events in the 14th century directly affected the course of further historical developments down to our own times.

The Mongol devastations resulted in a substantial migration of men of learning from Central Asia and Persia into India. The influx of the Sufis provided the spiritual momentum for the spread of Islam in India and Pakistan. However, the migration was not confined to dervishes and Sufis. A large number of *ulema* and *kadis* also fled and sought employment in Hindustan. Others migrated further east to the Indonesian islands.

The Delhi sultans, eager to show that they were defenders of the faith, made every effort to employ these scholars. They also sent out emissaries to the far-flung corners of the Islamic world to hire renowned *kadis*, *ulema*and philosophers for official service in the Indian empire. The simultaneous presence of the Sufis who pursued the intuitive and spiritual approach to Islam and the *kadis* who sought strict adherence to the rules of *Fiqh*provided the first element of tension in the Delhi courts. The doctors of law sought to influence the empire in the direction of strict adherence to the Shariah. They found some Sufi practices, such as *sama'a* (a forerunner of modern day *qawwali*) objectionable and sought to influence the Delhi court to declare a ban on them.

A second element of tension was introduced by the reform movements of the era. In the 13th century, as it is today, there were reformers who saw in *tasawwuf* the possibility of social stagnation. One of the best-known reformers of the age was Ibn Taymiyah of Damascus (d. 1326). Ibn Taymiyah was one of the last of the scholars of the classical age of Islam and he saw in the other-worldliness of *tasawwuf* the seeds of social decadence. Through his writings and his speeches he sought to energize a defeated community, which was reeling from the Mongol onslaught. His model was the activist model of the early Companions of the Prophet. As a young man, he aroused the Mamlukes to take a stand against the Mongols. Ibn Taymiyah's ideas traveled to Delhi where they were pitted against the powerful Sufi movement of the Chishtiya Order.

A third element of tension was the presence of the Mu'tazilites (philosophers). The Mu'tazilites emerged in the eight century as a result of the impact of Greek ideas on Islam. They won the patronage of the Abbasids and their dogma became the court dogma at the court of Harun al Rashid. Taking advantage of official patronage, the Mu'tazilites overextended themselves, applied the philosophical approach to the Qur'an, incurred the wrath of the conservative *ulema* and were finally dethroned from power towards the beginning of the 9th century. But philosophy was by no means dead among the Muslims. The Islamic intellectual world rediscovered the empirical method within its own ethos and became the originators of the scientific method. The Islamic world continued to produce a galaxy of philosopher-scientists right up to the time of the Mongol invasions. Among the more renowned were Al Khwarizmi (d. 863), Al Farabi (d. 950), Abu Ali Sina (d. 1037), Omar Khayyam (d. 1132) and Al Tusi (d. 1274). The great philosopher of the Maghrib, Ibn Rushd (d. 1198) wrote his commentaries on Aristotle in the 12th century. During the 13th and 14th centuries, some of the philosopher-scholars migrated to India and found a receptive environment in the Delhi courts. Amongst the more notable of the philosophers in Delhi was Shaykh Ilmuddin. The philosophers, too, were pitted against the popular Sufi movement of the Chishtiya Order.

It was under the Tughlaq emperors that the Sufi movement ran headlong into the combined opposition of the *ulema*, the philosophers and the monarchs. The *kadis* and the *ulema* sought a ban on *sama'a*, declaring it to be against the injunctions of the Shariah. To sort out these controversies, Gayasuddin Tughlaq, Sultan of Delhi, convened a conference of the leading *ulema*, *kadis* and philosophers in Delhi at his court in 1320. Nizamuddin Awliya was also invited. What started as a conference turned into a court martial of the Chishtiya Sufis. Kadi Jalaluddin, chief *kadi* of Delhi and Shaykh Zadajam argued against *sama'a*. Nizamuddin Awliya defended the practice, basing his arguments on certain *Hadith*. The opposition argued that the supporting *Hadith* were weak. The discussion became heated, so the Sultan turned to Shaykh Ilmuddin, who was a philosopher (Mu'tazilite) and had traveled extensively through Persia, Iraq, Syria and Egypt. Shaykh Ilmuddin answered that sama'a was halal for those who listened to it with their hearts and was *haram* for those who heard it with their *nafs*. Nonetheless, he too sided with Kadi Jalaluddin and asked the Emperor to forbid *sama'a*. The Emperor deliberated and, not to be drawn into a religious controversy, gave a split decision permitting *sama'a*gatherings for the Chishtiya Order but forbidding it to the followers of the Qalandariya and Haidari Orders. (The Qalandariya and Haidari orders had not yet made major inroads into India at that time so the Emperor had nothing to lose in taking a position against the practices of these two orders).

Gayasuddin Tughlaq died in 1325. The tug-of-war between the Sufis, the kadis and the philosophers, continued in the court of Muhammed bin Tughlaq (d. 1351). One of the most capable monarchs of the age, Muhammed bin Tughlaq is an enigma to students of history. He was a scholar, a *hafiz-e-Qur'an*, well versed in *Fiqh* and was punctual in his prayers, fasting and *zakat*. Like the first four caliphs, he treated the non-Muslims with dignity and ensured that taxation was fair to all of his subjects. Yet, he was impetuous, intolerant of dissent and punished, with a vengeance, those who stood in his way. He was the first monarch who realized that ruling the vast subcontinent from far-away Delhi was hopeless and sought to establish his capital near the center of gravity of Hindustan, namely at Daulatabad, located about a hundred miles inland from the modern city of Bombay. When the entrenched bureaucrats, comfortable in their luxurious villas in the capital, dragged their feet, he forced them to move. Then, as fate would have it, the monsoons failed for five consecutive years and India was hit with a terrible famine. Daulatabad was without water. Tughlaq had the entire court trek back to Delhi, causing untold misery for everyone.

It was during the Tughlaq period and the preceding Khilji period that Islam was introduced into the Deccan and the Dakhni language, the parent of modern Urdu, was born. Borrowing an idea from Kublai Khan of China (d. 1294), Tughlaq introduced leather currency. This was a far-sighted move designed to further trade, which was constrained by the availability of gold and silver. But the wily Indians, Muslims and Hindus alike, frustrated this move by creating counterfeit currency. Tughlaq had to withdraw the currency at an enormous cost to the treasury. However, it is his interactions with the *ulema, kadis*, philosophers and Sufis of the age that concern us here because these interactions determined the shape of Islam for centuries to come.

Returning to the powerful Chishtiya movement, Shaykh Baba Fareed Ganj succeeded Khwaja Qutbuddin in 1235. His forefathers had migrated from Kabul during the Mongol devastations. As directed by Moeenuddin Chishti of Ajmer, Baba Fareed migrated to western Punjab. If there was one person who may be given credit for the introduction of Islam into Punjab (and hence into today's Pakistan), it was Baba Fareed.

Impressed with his piety, sincerity and dedication, thousands, including some of the powerful Rajput clans, accepted Islam. Baba Fareed was a doctor of *Fiqh* and was a noted poet in Arabic and Farsi. Both the Sabiriya and Nizamiya branches of the Chishti Order within the subcontinent originated from him. He trained and sent teachers to the far corners of India and Pakistan. Notable among them were Shaykh Jamal of Hanswi, Imamul Haq of Sialkot, Mawzum Alauddin Sabir of Sahranpur, Shaykh Muntaqaddin of Deccan and most importantly, Nizamuddin Awliya of Delhi. Baba Fareed was the author of *Israr ul Awliya* (secrets of the sages), which contains encyclopedic information about Sufi thought and practices.

The mantle of leadership of the Chishtiya Order passed on to Nizamuddin Awliya in 1257. No other Sufi master achieved the acceptance of the Indian masses and the Sultans of Delhi, as did Nizamuddin Awliya. Indeed, his was the zenith of the Sufi movement in Hindustan. He was a scholar of *Hadith*, a fountain of spirituality, a powerful debater and a dedicated teacher. It is related that at any given time, over 3,000 students and two hundred *qawwals* attended his *zawiyah* at the outskirts of Delhi. Chief among his students were Shaykh Hishamuddin of Multan, Shaykh Burhanuddin Gareeb of Deccan, Shaykh Yaqub Patni of Gujrat,

Sirajuddin Uthmani and Bu Ali Qalandar of Panipat. The great poet Emir Khusro was a *murid* of Nizamuddin Awliya.

The relationship between the Chishtiya Order and the Delhi Sultanate had been cordial until that time. The Sultans, aware of the hold that the Sufis had over the masses, sought to cultivate the blessings of the Sufi masters. The advent of the Khilji dynasty (1296-1316) saw the armies of the Delhi Sultans conquer the entire subcontinent, all the way to the southern tip of the peninsula. The architect of these conquests, the mighty Alauddin Khilji, was of a secular bent. But he was aware of the power of the Sufis and sought cordial relations with them. It was Alauddin who sent word to Nizamuddin Awliya expressing his desire to meet the Master. The message elicited the famous riposte from the Shaykh: "My hut has two doors. If the Emperor enters it through one door, I go out the other". After Alauddin, there was a brief period of turbulence in Delhi, followed by the establishment of the Tughlaq dynasty (1316-1351).

Nizamuddin Awliya passed away in 1325 and designated Maqdum Nasiruddin Mahmud (commonly known as *Chirag-e-Dehli*, the light of Delhi) as his successor. It was the same year that Muhammed bin Tughlaq ascended the throne of Hindustan. To break the hold of the Sufis and to keep them busy with superfluous work, Muhammed bin Tughlaq forced them into his service. *Chirag-e-Dehli* was asked to assist the king with royal robes, a ceremony that signified obedience and submission to the crown. When the Master refused, he was thrown into jail. Others were forced out of the capital. For instance, Shaykh Shamsuddin Yahya was forced to retire to Kashmir. Shaykh Shahabuddin was told to serve the king. When the learned Shaykh refused, his beard was pulled out, a *fatwa* was passed against him by Kadi Kamaluddin of Delhi and he was finally killed. Delhi was depleted of the Sufi masters, except for those who could not leave because of age or official constraint.

Muhammed bin Tughlaq had spent his youth in the company of philosophers and he was a Mu'tazilite by training. He was particularly influenced by Shaykh Ilmuddin, the renowned philosopher of the times, who lived in Delhi. Shaykh Ilmuddin had traveled through Syria and had met Ibn Taymiyah of Damascus (d. 1326) and had absorbed his reformist and counter-Sufi thoughts. Tughlaq, in his Mu'tazilite thinking, was similar to Harun al Rashid, but he lacked the sagacity and statesmanship of Harun. Just as the successors of Harun punished those who opposed the Mu'tazilite doctrines, so did Muhammed bin Tughlaq.

It is an irony of Islamic history that those who should have been the most liberal in their tolerance of dissident thought, namely the philosophers, turned out to be the most intolerant. Twice they had the opportunity to influence history-once during the early years of the Abbasids (circa 800) and the second time during the powerful Tughlaq dynasty of India (circa 1330). Both times they failed miserably and embarked on a tyrannical suppression of those who disagreed with them. Islamic history, in turn, rejected them. Their role was relegated to the periphery of the Islamic body politic, to the detriment of both philosophy and the Muslim *ummah*. Muhammed bin Tughlaq died in 1335, classified a maverick sultan by history.

The Sufis survived and prospered because theirs was the kingdom of God, untouched by the vagaries of time. They sang of the love of God and people resonated to their tune. They gave of themselves for the love of mankind and fought for what was right, often laying down their lives in the struggle. The *ulema* and *kadis* were defeated, because they were employees of the kings and could be fired from their jobs at will.

Despite their independence, they were construed to be an arm of the ruling classes. The philosophers lost because of their tyrannical approach. They were bogged down in endless argumentation and they over-extended their approach to the Qur'an, a subject that was clearly beyond the scope of their methodology. The Islam that survived was a Sufic Islam, inward-looking, spiritual, amalgamating within its folds the cultures of the lands where it flourished. It was different in color and character from classical Islam (up to the destruction of Baghdad in 1258), which was empirical, vibrant, extrovert. It was this Sufic Islam that was destined to shape the history of Muslim peoples after the 13th century.

BENGALI SUFIS AND HINDU THOUGHT

From the beginning of the Indo-Turkish encounter with Bengal, one section of Muslims sought to integrate into their religious lives elements of the esoteric practices of local yogis, together with the cosmologies that underpinned those practices. Contemporary Muslims perceived northern Bengal generally, and especially Kamrup, lying between the Brahmaputra River and the hills of Bhutan, as a fabulous and mysterious place inhabited by expert practitioners of the occult, of yoga, and of magic. During his visit to Sylhet, Ibn Battuta noted that "the inhabitants of these mountains are noted for their devotion to and practice of magic and witchcraft." Around 1595 the great Mughal administrative manual *Ain-i Akbari* described the inhabitants of Kamrup as "addicted to the practice of magic [*jadugari*]." Some twenty-five years later a Mughal officer serving in northern Bengal described the Khuntaghat region, in western Kamrup, as "notorious for magic and sorcery." And in 1662–63 another Mughal chronicler, referring to the entire Assam region, of which Kamrup is the western part, remarked that "the people of India have come to look upon the Assamese as sorcerers, and use the word 'Assam' in such formulas as dispel witchcraft."

Since Sufis were especially concerned with apprehending transcendent reality unmediated by priests or other worldly institutions, it is not surprising that they, among Muslims, were most attracted to the yogi traditions of Kamrup. Within the very first decade of the Turkish conquest, there began to circulate in the delta Persian and Arabic translations of a Sanskrit manual on tantric yoga entitled *Amritakunda* ("The Pool of Nectar"). According to the translated versions, the Sanskrit text had been composed by a Brahman yogi of Kamrup who had converted to Islam and presented the work to the chief, or judge, of Lakhnauti, Rukn al-Din Samarqandi (d. 1218). The latter, in turn, is said to have made the first translations of the work into Arabic and Persian. While this last point is uncertain, there is no doubt that for the following five hundred years the *Amritakunda*, through its repeated translations into Arabic and Persian, circulated widely among Sufis of Bengal, and even throughout India. The North Indian Sufi Shaikh 'Abd al-Quddus Gangohi (d. 1537) is known to have absorbed the yogic ideas of the *Amritakunda* and to have taught them to his own disciples. In the mid seventeenth century, the Kashmiri author Muhsin Fani recorded that he had seen a Persian translation of the *Amritakunda,* and in the same century the Anatolian Sufi scholar Mohammad al-Misri (d. 1694) cited the *Amritakunda* as an important book for the study of yogic practices, noting that in India such practices had become partly integrated with Sufism. In both its Persian and Arabic translations, the *Amritakunda* survives as a manual of tantric yoga, with the first of its ten chapters affirming the characteristically tantric correspondence between parts of the human body and parts of the macrocosm, "where all that is large in the world discovers itself in the small." In the mid sixteenth century, there appeared in Gujarat a Persian recension of the *Amritakunda* under the title, attributed to the great Shattari Shaikh Mohammad Ghauth of Gwalior (d. 1563). A prologue to this version, written by a disciple of the Shaikh, records how these yogic ideas were thought to have entered the Bengali Sufi tradition:

This wonderful and strange book is named in the Indian language [i.e., Sanskrit]. This means "Water of Life," and the reason for the appearance of this book among the Muslims is as follows. When Sultan 'Ala al-Din [i.e., 'Ali Mardan] conquered Bengal and Islam became manifest there, news of these events reached the ears of a certain gentleman of the esteemed learned class in Kamrup. His name was Kama, and he was a master of the science of yoga.

In order to debate with the Muslim [scholars] he arrived in the city of Lakhnauti, and on a Friday he entered the Congregational Mosque. A number of Muslims showed him to a group of, and they in turn pointed him to the assembly of Qazi Rukn al-Din Samarqandi. So he went to this group and asked: "Whom do you worship?" They replied, "We worship the Faultless God." To his question "Who is your leader?" they replied, "Mohammad, the Messenger of Allah." He said, "What has your leader said about the Spirit" They replied, "God the All-nourishing has commanded (that there be) the Spirit." He said, "In truth, I too have found this same thing in books that are subtle and committed to memory."

Then that man converted to Islam and busied himself in acquiring religious knowledge, and he soon thereafter became a scholar (*mufti*). After that he wrote and presented this book to Qazi Rukn al-Din Tamami [Samarqandi]. The latter translated it from the Indian language into Arabic in a book of thirty chapters, and somebody else translated it into Persian in a book of ten chapters....And when Hazrat Ghauth al-Din himself went to Kamrup he necessarily spent several years in studying this science....The name of this book is *Bahar al-hayat.*

The exchange between the yogi and the *ghazi* cited here appears to have been modelled on a passage in the Qur'an (17:85), in which God tells the Prophet Mohammad: "They [the Jews] will ask thee concerning the Spirit. Say: the Spirit is by command of my Lord." By putting into the mouth of a yogi words that in the Qur'an were those of the Jews of Mohammad's day, the author of this recension apparently intended to make the yogi's exchange comprehensible to a Muslim audience.

A second prologue to the *Bahar al-hayat* established a framework within which a text on yoga could be accommodated within the rich body of classical Sufi lore. In it, the translator tells of once being in a country whose king summoned him and ordered that he undertake a great journey to a distant but fabulous realm. The king reminded the traveller that they were joined together by a covenant and that they would meet again at the end of the traveller's voyage. Then the translator/traveller describes the hardships he endured while on his journey: the two seas (the soul and nature), the seven mountains, the four passes, the three stations filled with dangers, and the path narrower than the eye of an ant. Ultimately, he reached the promised land, where he found a Shaikh who mirrored or echoed each of his own moves and words. Realizing that the man was but his own reflection, the traveller remembered his covenant with his master, to whom he was now led. The story's climax is reached in the traveller's epiphanic self-discovery: "I found the king and minister in myself." The dominant motifs of this second prologue—the traveller, the arduous path with its temptations and dangers, and the ultimate realization that the goal is identified with the seeker—all show the influence of Sufi notions current in the thirteenth-century Perso-Islamic world. The placement of the yogic text immediately after this prologue suggests that the esoteric practices described therein constitute, in effect, the means to achieving the mystical goals stated in the second prologue.

Although some scholars have regarded the *Bahar* as a work of religious syncretism, this judgment is difficult to sustain if by syncretism one means the production of a new synthesis out of two or more antithetical elements. Rather, the work consists of two independent and self-contained worldviews placed alongside one another—a technical manual of yoga preceded by a Sufi allegory—with later editors or translators going to some lengths to stress their points of coincidence. Although Islamic terms and superhuman agencies are generously sprinkled through the main text, allusions to Islamic lore serve ultimately to buttress or illustrate thoroughly Indian concepts. Here, at least, yoga and Sufi ideas resisted true fusion.

Nonetheless the book's popularity illustrates the Sufis' considerable fascination with the esoteric practices of Bengal's indigenous culture. The renowned Shattari saint Shaikh Mohammad Ghauth even travelled from Gwalior in Upper India to Kamrup in order to study the esoteric knowledge that Muslims had identified with that region. In doing so he was following a tradition of Sufis of the Shattari order, whose founder, Shah 'Abd Allah Shattari (d. 1485), included Bengal on his journey from Central Asia through India. Although one cannot establish a continuous intellectual tradition between Bengali Muslims of the thirteenth century and the Shattari Sufis of the fifteenth and sixteenth centuries, the association of the *Bahar al-hayat* both with Rukn al-Din Samarqandi in the former century and with Shaikh Mohammad Ghauth in the latter century suggests the likelihood of its continued use in Bengal during the intervening period.

SUFIS OF THE CAPITAL

The principal carriers of the Islamic literary and intellectual tradition in the Bengal sultanate were groups of distinguished and influential Sufis who resided in the successive capital cities of

Lakhnauti (from 1204), Pandua (from ca. 1342), and Gaur (from ca. 1432). Most of these men belonged to organized Sufi brotherhoods—especially the Suhrawardi, the Firdausi, and the Chishti orders—and what we know of them can be ascertained mainly from their extant letters and biographical accounts.

The urban Sufis about whom we have the most information are clustered in the early sultanate period, from the founding of the independent Ilyas Shahi dynasty at Pandua in 1342 to the end of the Raja Ganesh revolution in 1415. The political roles played by Sufis in Bengal's capital were shaped by ideas of Sufi authority that had already evolved in the contemporary Persian-speaking world.

We have already referred to the central place that Sufi traditions assigned to powerful saints, a sentiment captured in 'Ali Hujwiri's statement that God had "made the Saints the governors of the universe." Being in theory closer to God than warring princes could ever hope to be, Muslim saints staked a moral claim as God's representatives on earth. In this view, princely rulers possessed no natural right to earthly power, but had only been entrusted with a temporary lease on such power through the grace of some Muslim saint.

This perspective perhaps explains why in Indo-Muslim history we so often find Sufis predicting who would attain political office, and for how long they would hold it. For behind the explicit act of "prediction" lay the implicit act of appointment—that is, of a Sufi's entrusting his *wilayat*, or earthly domain, to a prince. For example, the fourteenth-century historian Shams-i Siraj 'Afif recorded that before his rise to royal stature, the future Sultan Ghiyath al-Din Tughluq, founder of the Tughluq dynasty of Delhi (1321–1398), had been one of many local notables attracted to the spiritual power of the grandson of the famous Chishti Sufi Shaikh Farid al-Din Ganj-i Shakar (d. 1265).

The governor made frequent visits to the holy man's lodge in the Punjab, and on one occasion brought along his son and nephew, the future sultans Mohammad bin Tughluq and Firuz Tughluq. All three were given turbans by the saint and told that each was destined to rule India. The length of each turban, moreover, exactly corresponded to the number of years each would reign. In this anecdote one may discern the seeds of the complex pattern of mutual patronage between Shaikhs of the Chishti order and one of the mightiest empires in India's history.

Similar traditions circulated in Bengal concerning the foundation of independent Muslim rule there. In 1243–44 the historian Minhaj al-Siraj visited Lakhnauti, where he recorded the following anecdote. Before embarking for India, the future sultan of Bengal Ghiyath al-Din 'Iwaz (1213–27) was once travelling with his laden donkey along a dusty road in Afghanistan. There he came upon two dervishes clothed in ragged cloaks. When the two asked the future ruler whether he had any food, the latter replied that he did and took the load down from the donkey's back. Spreading his garments on the ground, he offered the dervishes whatever victuals he had. After they had eaten, the grateful dervishes remarked to each other that such kindness should not go unrewarded. Turning to their benefactor, they said, "Go thou to Hindustan, for that place, which is the extreme (point) of Muhammadanism, we have given unto thee." At once the future sultan gathered together his family and set out for India "in accord with the intimation of those two Darweshes." In the Perso-Islamic cultural universe of the thirteenth and fourteenth centuries, Bengal really did in some sense "belong" to those two dervishes, that they might "entrust" it to a kind stranger.

In Bengal as in North India, the connection between political fortune and spiritual blessing is most evident in the early history of the Chishti order, the order to which the most ascendant Shaikhs of early-fourteenth-century Delhi belonged. "Anybody who was anyone," as Simon Digby puts it, visited the lodge of Delhi's most eminent Shaikh of the time, Nizam al-Din Auliya (d. 1325). Indeed, the two principal Persian poets of the early fourteenth century, Amir Khusrau and Amir Hasan, together with the sultanate's leading contemporary historian, Zia al-Din Barani, were all spiritual disciples of this Shaikh. Since Delhi at this time happened to be the capital of a vital and expanding empire, it is not surprising that the literary, cultural, and institutional traditions of that city—together with the Shaikhs and institutions of its dominant Sufi order—expanded along with Khalaji and Tughluq arms to the far corners of India, including Bengal.

But there was a deeper reason why Indo-Muslim courts patronized Chishti Shaikhs. By the fourteenth century, when other Sufi orders in India still looked to Central Asia or the Middle East as their spiritual home, the Chishtis, with their major shrines located within the Indian subcontinent, had become thoroughly indigenized. Seeking to establish their legitimacy both as Muslims and as Indians, Indo-Muslim rulers therefore turned to prominent Shaikhs of this order for blessings and support. For the same reason, leading Chishti Shaikhs dispersed from Shaikh Nizam al-Din's lodge to all parts of the empire and often enjoyed the patronage of provincial rulers. Conversely, many young Indian-born Muslims journeyed from all over India to live in or near that Shaikh's lodge, later to return to their native lands, where they would establish daughter Chishti lodges and enjoy the patronage of local rulers. The first Bengal-born Muslim known to have studied with Shaikh Nizam al-Din was Akhi Siraj al-Din (d. 1357), who journeyed to Delhi as a young man. Having distinguished himself at the Sufi lodge of the renowned Shaikh, Siraj al-Din received a certificate of succession and so thoroughly associated himself with the North Indian Chishti tradition that he was given the epithet "âyina-yi Hindûstân," or "Mirror of Hindustan." Returning to Bengal some time before 1325, when his master died, he inducted others into the Chishti discipline, his foremost pupil being another Bengal-born Muslim, Shaikh 'Ala al-Haq (d. 1398). But unlike his own teacher, who had no known dealings with royalty, Shaikh 'Ala al-Haq was destined to play a special role in the political history of Muslim Bengal. In fact, the earliest-known monument built by the founder of Bengal's longest-lived dynasty, the Ilyas Shahi line of kings (1342–1486), was dedicated to this Shaikh. On a mosque built in 1342 in what is now part of Calcutta, Shams al-Din Ilyas Shah praised the Sufi as "the benevolent and revered saint (Shaikh) whose acts of virtue are attractive and sublime, inspired by Allah, may He illuminate his heart with the light of divine perception and faith, and he is the guide to the religion of the Glorious, 'Alaul-Haqqmay...his piety last long."

The importance of this inscription derives from its political context. Shams al-Din Ilyas Shah, an ambitious and politically astute newcomer to the delta, was just then launching a bid for independence from Delhi, evidently using southwestern Bengal as his power base. The imperial governor of nearby Satgaon having recently died, Shams al-Din, aware that Delhi was convulsed by the various crises provoked by the eccentric Sultan Mohammad bin Tughluq, seized the moment to attain provincewide power. As his earliest-known coin was minted at Pandua in A.D. 1342–43 (A.H. 743), Shams al-Din's ascendancy exactly synchronizes with the dedication of this mosque and his patronage of Shaikh 'Ala al-Haq. Moreover, the patronage of the two men was mutual, since Shaikh 'Ala al-Haq, attaching himself to this rising political star, adopted Shams al-Din as a recipient of his teachings and blessings. This early connection cemented an alliance between government and prominent Chishti Shaikhs that would last for the duration of Muslim rule in Bengal.

Not all alliances between Sufis and sultans were initiated by would-be rulers seeking to broaden their political bases. Some Sufis were drawn to the court out of a fervent desire to advance the cause of Islam as they understood it, and to augment the welfare of Muslims in the realm. We see this in the correspondence between Muzaffar Shams Balkhi (d. 1400) and Sultan Ghiyath al-Din Azam Shah (r. 1389–1410). An immigrant from Central Asia, Muzaffar had left his native Balkh for Delhi, where he taught at the college of Firuz Shah Tughluq. But the man's restless spirit led him to Bihar city, where, after meeting and becoming the disciple of the great Firdausi Shaikh Sharaf al-Din Maneri (d. 1381), he experienced a major change in life-orientation. Abandoning his pride in scholarship, Muzaffar subjected himself to various austerities and distributed all his worldly possessions in charity. He also made several pilgrimages to Mecca, where he once stayed for four years, teaching lessons in *hadith* scholarship. His extant letters reveal him not as an ecstatic, quiescent, or contemplative sort, but as committed to imposing his understanding of the Prophet's religious vision on the here-and-now world, a man inclined to scrutinize human society by scriptural standards and, finding it wanting, to transform it so as to meet those standards. In the sultan of Bengal, the Sufi found an outlet for these impulses.

Muzaffar Shams first seems to have become concerned about tutoring Sultan Ghiyath al-Din while waiting in Pandua for official permission to embark on a trip from Chittagong to Mecca. "The four months of the ship season are ahead of us," he wrote; "there are eight months still left; during all this while I have spent my life as a guest in the auspicious threshold of your majesty, may not your exaltation lessen." Although the Sufi politely described himself as a mere "guest" of the sultan, it is evident that he felt himself entrusted with a higher calling. "In my opinion," he wrote the king, by the gifts of God, the cherisher of mankind, you have developed a capacity of looking at the inside of things of the pure faith and the understanding of things of manifold signification. It appears that my heart would be opened out to you. A pious inspired man, Abdul Malik, has been a recipient of my letters[,] which might form a volume. It may be at Pandua or at Muazzamabad, but I don't remember where it exactly is. Oh, my son, get the permission and go through its contents. Something of my inward part may be opened out to you. You are the second person on whom I have poured out my secret (mystic) thoughts. It behooves you not to disclose these to anyone else.

Who, here, is patronizing whom? The Sufi's reference to the sultan as his "son" signals a clear inversion of the usual relationship between a patrimonial king and his subjects. Nor would the Sufi give the king privileged access to his personal correspondence; to see it the monarch had first to secure permission from a third party. Muzaffar Balkhi also reminded the king that although Sultan Firuz Tughluq of Delhi had repeatedly requested letters and spiritual guidance from Muzaffar's own master, Shaikh Sharaf al-Din Maneri, the latter had refused to oblige him, choosing instead to correspond with Sultan Sikandar of Bengal, Ghiyath al-Din's father. "You," he noted pointedly, "have had the effects and legacy of those blessings on yourself." In short, Muzaffar felt that he and his own master had been doing the Bengal sultans a favour by bestowing their blessings and advice on them instead of on the sultans of Delhi.

In addition to his recommendations concerning Islamic piety—for example, on the need to suppress innovation not prescribed by the Sharia, or to enforce the payment of alms by Muslims — Muzaffar cautioned the king against placing non-Muslims in positions of authority. "The substance of what has come in the tradition and commentaries," wrote the Shaikh, "is this":

"Oh believers, don't make strangers, that is infidels, your confidential favourites and ministers of state." They say that they don't allow any to approach or come near to them and become favourite courtiers; but it was done evidently and for expedience and worldly exigency of the Sultanate that they are entrusted with some affairs. To this the reply is that according to God it is neither expediency nor exigency but the reverse of it, that is an evil and pernicious thing....Don't entrust a work into the hands of infidels by reason of which they would become a *wali* (Governor-ruler or superior) over the Musalmans, exercise their authority in their affairs, and impose their command over them. As God says in the Quran, "It is not proper for a believer to trust an infidel as his friend and *wali*, and those who do so have no place in the estimation of God." Hear God and be devout and pious; very severe warnings have come in the Kitab (holy book) and traditions against the appointment of infidels as a ruler over the believers.

The Sufi thus saw in Islamic Law a clear course of action the sultan should take in order to avert certain disaster. For in Bengal's affairs Muzaffar Shams discerned more than just a political crisis. Referring to Timur's recent sacking of Delhi (A.D. 1398, or A.H. 801), which marked the eclipse of the once-mighty Tughluq empire, he wrote: "The eighth century has passed out, and the signs of the coming Resurrection are increasingly visible. An Empire like that of Delhi with all its expanse and abundance, spiritual and physical comfort, peace and tranquility, has turned upside down (is in a topsy-turvy condition). Infidelity has now come to hold the field; the condition of other countries is no better. Now is the time, and this is the opportunity." His gaze riveted on scripture, Muzaffar saw a palpable link between worldly decay and the Day of Judgment, heralded by that decay. Only by removing infidelity could Muslims forestall an otherwise inevitable cosmic process.

And since the sultan had the power to stamp out infidelity by suppressing non-Muslims in a kingdom originally established by Muslims, the Sufi saw the sultan as capable of playing a pivotal role in implementing what he understood as God's will in that process.

It was Shaikhs of the Chishti order, however, who by the early fifteenth century had emerged as the principal spokesmen for a Muslim communal perspective in Bengal. If Shaikh 'Ala al-Haq had risen to prominence with the ascending fortunes of the founder of the Ilyas Shahi dynasty, his son and successor, Nur Qutb-i 'Alam (d. 1459), presided over Bengal's Chishti tradition when Ilyas Shahi fortunes had sunk to their lowest point—the period of Raja Ganesh's domination over the Ilyas Shahi throne.

According to Sufi sources, Raja Ganesh even persecuted Chishti Shaikhs, banishing Nur Qutb-i 'Alam's own son, Shaikh Anwar, to Sonargaon, and plotting the death of the son of another Chishti Shaikh, Husain Dhukkarposh. In these circumstances, the Shaikh implored Sultan Ibrahim Sharqi of Jaunpur to invade Bengal and remove the "menace" of Raja Ganesh.

The following passage shows the extent to which the Chishtis of Bengal had come to identify the fortunes of Islam with the political fortunes of the Ilyas Shahi dynasty. "After a period of three hundred years," wrote the Sufi, "the Islamic land of Bengal—the place of mortals, the kingdom of the end of the seven heavens—has been overwhelmed and put to the run by the darkness of infidels and the power of unbelievers." The Shaikh elaborated this point using the Sufi and Qur'anic metaphor of light:

The lamp of the Islamic religion and of true guidance
Which had [formerly] brightened every corner with its light,
Has been extinguished by the wind of unbelief blown by Raja Ganesh.
Splendor from envy of the victorious news,
The lamp of [the celebrated preacher, Abul-Husain] Nuri, and the candle of [the Shia martyr] Husain
Have all been extinguished by the might of swords and the power of this thing in view.

What does one call the lamp and candle of men
Whose nature is devoid of virility [lit., has eaten camphor]?
When the abode of faith and Islam has fallen into such a fate,
Why are you sitting happily on your throne?
Arise, come and defend the religion,
For it is incumbent upon you,
O king, possessed of power and capacity.

While publicly clamoring for military intervention, privately, in a letter to his exiled son, Nur Qutb-i 'Alam brooded over the theological implications of Raja Ganesh's appearance in Bengali history. To the anguished Sufi, it seemed that God had not been heeding the supplication of the very people to whom the Qur'an had promised divine favour and protection. "Infidelity," he wrote;

> *Has gained predominance and the kingdom of Islam has been spoiled....Neither the devotion and the worship of the votaries of God proved helpful to them nor the unbelief of the infidels fettered their steps. Neither worship and devotion does any good to His Holy Divine Majesty, nor does infidelity do any harm to Him. Alas! Alas! O, how painful! With one gesture and freak of independence he caused the consumption of so many souls, the destruction of so many lives, and shedding of so much of bitter tears. Alas, woe to me, the sun of Islam has become obscured and the moon of religion has become eclipsed.*

But the fortunes of Bengali Muslims did not ebb as the Shaikh had feared. Once the stormy period of Raja Ganesh had subsided, his converted son resumed the patronage of the Chishti establishment, re-confirming the Chishti-court alliance that had been established between Nur Qutb-i 'Alam's father and the dynasty's founder. Both Sultan Jalal al-Din and his son and successor Ahmad (r. 1432–33) became disciples of Nur Qutb-i 'Alam himself, and twelve succeeding sultans down to the year 1532 enlisted themselves as disciples of the descendants of Shaikh 'Ala al-Haq. By the end of the fifteenth century, the tomb of Shaikh Nur Qutb-i 'Alam in Pandua had become in effect a state shrine to which Sultan 'Ala al-Din Husain Shah (r. 1493–1519) made annual pilgrimages. Despite the mutual patronage and even dependency between Bengal's Sufis and its rulers, one also detects an undercurrent of friction between the two. Occasionally erupting into open hostility, this friction derived from the radical distinction made in Islam between *din* and *dunya,* "religion" and "the world." Withdrawn from worldly affairs and living in a state of poverty, self-denial, and remembrance of God, the Sufi recluse was in theory dramatically opposed by the ruler-administrator, glittering in his wealth and utterly immersed in worldly affairs. Sufis who rejected the world made much of their refusal to consort with "worldly" people—including above all royalty. Conversely, rulers sometimes suspected their Sufi allies, or even feared having around them such popular, charismatic leaders who might conceivably stir up the mob to riot or rebellion.

Here we may consider an inscription of Sultan Sikandar Ilyas Shah, dated 1363, in which the king dedicated a dome he had built for the shrine of a saint named Maulana 'Ata. Although the Shaikh may have been the king's contemporary, Maulana 'Ata was more likely an earlier holy man whose shrine had become the focus of an important cult by the time the inscription was recorded. "In this dome," the inscription reads,

> *Which has been founded by 'Ata, may the sanctuary of both worlds remain. May the angels recite for its durability, till the day of resurrection:* "We have built over you seven solid heavens" *[Qur'an 78:12].*

By the grace of (the builder of) the seven wonderful porticos *"who hath created seven heavens, one above another"* [Qur'an 67:3], may His names be glorified; the building of this lofty dome was completed. (Verily it) is the copy of a vault (lit., shell) of the roof of Glory, (referred in this verse) *"And we have adorned the heaven of the world"* (lit., lamps) [Qur'an 67:5]. (This lofty dome) in the sacred shrine of the chief of the saints, the unequaled among enquirers, the lamp of Truth, Law and Faith, Maulana 'Ata, may the High Allah bless him with His favours in both worlds; (was built) by order of the lord of the age and the time, the causer of justice and benevolence, the defender of towns, the pastor of people, the just, learned and great monarch, the shadow of Allah on the world, distinguished by the grace of the Merciful, Abul Mujahid Sikandar Shah, son of Ilyas Shah, the Sultan, may Allah perpetuate his kingdom. The king of the world Sikandar Shah, in whose name the pearls of prayer have been strung; regarding him they have said, "May Allah illuminate his rank," and regarding him they have prayed "May Allah perpetuate his kingdom."

While outwardly acclaiming the greatness of Maulana 'Ata, Sultan Sikandar was also asserting his own claims to closeness to God, styling himself the one in whose name "the pearls of prayer have been strung," and "the Shadow of God on Earth."

And by referring to this shrine as a copy (*nuskha*) of the heavens, the sultan drew attention to parallels between God's creative activity and his own. For if it had been God's creative act to adorn the seven heavens with lamps, that is, stars, it was Sultan Sikandar's creative act to adorn the earth with a tomb for the lamp (*Siraj*) of Truth, Law, and Faith, that is, Maulana 'Ata. Implicitly, then, had it not been for the munificence of Sultan Sikandar, Maulana 'Ata would have remained shrouded in obscurity.

Royal distrust of or aversion to Sufis, even those of the Chishti order, is seen in other ways. Although Shams al-Din Ilyas Shah had patronized a prominent Chishti Shaikh while establishing a new dynasty, the king's son and successor, Sultan Sikandar, was suspicious of the disciples of his father's saintly patron.

He was especially suspicious of the most eminent of these, Shaikh 'Ala al-Haq, whose shrine complex had become in Sikandar's day a major nexus for economic transactions, redistributing amongst the city's poor large sums of money received in the form of pious donations. Alarmed at the Sufi's substantial expenditure on the urban populace, Sikandar declared: "My treasure is in the hands of your father [the kingdom's Treasurer]; [yet] you are giving away as much as he spends." Evidently jealous of the Shaikh's wealth and influence, the king banished the Sufi to Sonargaon.

Bengal's Sufis and sultans, then, were fatefully connected by ties of mutual attraction and repulsion. Generally, when they were first establishing themselves politically, and especially when launching new dynasties, rulers actively sought the legitimacy powerful saints might lend them. Sultan Ghiyath al-Din 'Iwaz's earliest chronicler situated the launching of Bengal's first independent dynasty (1213) in the context of the grace, or *baraka*, of two simple dervishes in Afghanistan. And in 1342, when Sultan Shams al-Din Ilyas Shah launched the longest-lived dynasty in Muslim Bengal, he did so with the blessings of a renowned scion of the prestigious Chishti line. Struck by the awesome spiritual powers people attributed to charismatic Shaikhs, or believing that their own lease on power was somehow extended by such forceful men, new Muslim kings sought their favour, built lodges or mausolea for them, or made public pilgrimages to their tombs. Conversely, some Sufis sought royal patronage out of their own reformist impulses to bring "the world" (*dunya*) into proper alignment with their understanding of the dictates of normative "religion" (*din*).

5

Mughalistan: An Undivided Islamic Nation in Indian Subcontinent

PAKISTAN-BANGLADESH PLAN A MUGHALISTAN TO SPLIT INDIA

Mughalistan (or Mughalstan) is the name of an independent homeland proposed for the Muslims of India. This Mughal-Muslim state in the Indian subcontinent will include all of North India and Eastern India, and will be formed by merging Pakistan and Bangladesh through a large corridor of land running across the Indo-Gangetic plain, the heartland of India. This Mughalistan corridor will comprise Muslim-majority areas of Northern India and eastern India that will be partitioned for the second time in history.

The comprehensive plan for a second partition of India was first developed by the Mughalstan Research Institute (MRI) of Jahangir Nagar University (Bangladesh) under the patronage of the two intelligence agencies, Pakistan's Inter Services Intelligence (ISI) and Bangladesh's Director General of Forces Intelligence, DGFI. The "Mughalistan Reaserch Institute of Bangladesh" has released a map where a Muslim corridor named "Mughalistan" connects Pakistan and Bangladesh via India.

The Pakistani Punjabi-dominated ISI's influence on MRI is evident even in the Punjabi-centric pronunciation of the word 'Mughalstan' (without the "i"), instead of the typical Urdu pronunciation (Mughalistan). Islamic Jihadis in India have been well-armed and well-funded by the neighbouring Islamic regimes, as part of Operation Topac – the late Pakistani President Zia-ul-Haq's grandiose plot to balkanize India.

Not surprisingly, Osama Bin Laden has thrown his support behind the concept and creation of this Greater Pakistan to "liberate" the Muslims of India from the Hindus. The Mumbai underworld (led by Karachi-based don Dawood Ibrahim who executed the gruesome 1993 Mumbai bombings), Jamaat-e-Islami, Lashkar-e-Tayyaba, Jaish-e-Mohammad and Hizbul Mujahideen have declared their unified support for creating this undivided Islamic nation in the Indian subcontinent. The Students Islamic Movement of India (SIMI) and Indian Mujahideen are working in tandem with the aforementioned organizations to waged Jihad against the Hindus of India.

It is important to note that in its "holy war" against India, the Lashkar-e-Tayyaba has openly declared Hindus to be the "enemies of Islam" who should all be converted or killed. The Lashkar-e-Tayyaba group has repeatedly claimed through its journals and websites that its main aim is to destroy the Indian republic and to annihilate Hinduism. Jaish-e-Mohammed has vowed to "liberate" not just Kashmir, but also to hoist the Islamic flag atop the historic Red Fort after capturing New Delhi and the rest of India.

SIMI has championed the "liberation of India through Islam" and aim to restore the supremacy of Islam through the resurrection of the Khilafat (Islamic Caliphate), emphasis on the Muslim Ummah (Islamic) and the waging of Jihad on the Indian state, secularism, democracy and nationalism – the basic keystones of the Indian Constitution – as these concepts are antithetical to Islam. The Indian Mujahideen have sent several emails claiming responsibility for several bombings in Lucknow, Varanasi and Faizabad (in Uttar Pradesh), Bangalore, Jaipur, Ahmedabad and New Delhi in 2007 and 2008. The emails refer to notorious Islamic conquerors of India (Mohammed bin Qasim, Mohammad Ghauri and Mahmud Ghaznawi) as their role-models, refer to Hindu blood as "blood to be the cheapest of all mankind" and taunt Hindus that their "[Hindu] history is full of subjugation, humiliation, and insult [at the hands of Islamic conquerors]". The Indian Mujahideen's emails warn the Hindus to "Accept Islam and save yourselves" and or else face a horrible fate: – "Hindus! O disbelieving faithless Indians! Haven't you still realized that the falsehood of your 33 crore dirty mud idols and the blasphemy of your deaf, dumb, mute and naked idols of ram, krishna and hanuman are not at all going to save your necks, Insha-Allah, from being slaughtered by our [Muslim] hands?"

BACKGROUND

Pakistan's emergence in 1947 was as a "mutilated, truncated, moth-eaten Pakistan, in M.A. Jinnah's own words, because the Muslim League's original plan did not envisage the partition of Punjab and Bengal. Today, Mughalistan is Jinnah's dream come true.

The Partition of India provided temporary respite to the Indians and merely postponed the inevitable outcome. By 1971, all across Sindh, Western Punjab, Gandhara (Kandahar) and Eastern Bengal, the native populations of the Indian Religionists (Hindus, Sikhs, Buddhists, Jains) have been wiped out almost entirely by conversion, massacre and mass exodus. Extrapolating this scenario, we find ominous results. This Islamic beach-head, which squeezes India from both sides (Pakistan and Bangladesh), gradually links up with a Fifth Column within India and gains fresh territorial and demographic victories within the last two decades (Kashmir valley, several districts of West Bengal and Assam, Malappuram district in Kerala and the Hyderabad-Deccan region). The Islamic Anschluss creeps steadily and bloodily, until the Western beach-head (Pakistan) is linked up demographically with the Eastern beach-head (Bangladesh) through the formation of a Islam-dominated belt called "Mughalstan", that will then run through Jammu, Mewat, Uttar Pradesh, Bihar, West Bengal and Assam.

JAMMU & KASHMIR

It is an open secret that wherever the Muslims are in a majority, the rights and freedom of the non-Muslims are severely curtailed. Take for example Kashmir. It's the only state in India which is a

Muslim majority and let us see what happened there. Hundreds of temples were razed, Hindus were forced to flee, their women were raped, children were killed and houses forcibly occupied. The entire Kashmiri Hindu population (known as Kashmiri Pandits) having been driven away, killed or converted between 1990 and 2000 in a silent, mass genocide. The Muslims in Kashmir have been enjoying a special status under Constitution's Article 370, hardly any central law is enforced there, the number of income-tax payers is among the lowest and unlike other poor states, J&K gets 90 per cent central financial assistance as grants and only 10 per cent as loans. Still there are complaints that a 'Hindu central government discriminates'. The other minority, Buddhists mostly located in Ladakh, too, are harshly treated and discriminated against by the mainly Sunni Muslim governance in Srinagar. The Buddhist Association, Leh, has been submitting memorandums to the central government about how Buddhist youths are denied jobs and a fair chance to join the Kashmir Administrative service and professional colleges in spite of clearing the entrance exams. The number of Buddhist minorities is fast decreasing causing concern amongst their leaders. Even their dead are not allowed to be buried in Muslim-majority Kargil area and monasteries have been denied to be built. Leh district continues to see rampant conversions of Buddhist women to Islam.

The Kashmir Valley today has a 98 per cent Muslim population. Poonch district, which is contiguous with Pakistan, has a Muslim majority. Jammu district has seen regular attacks on Hindu civilians and temples. The Hindu-population of the adjacent district of Doda is being squeezed out by Islamic violence. As a result, Doda is now a Muslim-majority district, where the population ratio between the Muslims and the Hindus in Doda district is now 55:45. Doda town has a 90 per cent Muslim population. Out of the seven subdivisions, Banihal, Kishtwar and Balesa are Muslim dominated areas. Bhaderwah, Thathri and Ramban have a Hindu majority. In Ladakh, Kargil district has a Muslim majority.

NORTHERN INDIA

In the backward Mewat region of Haryana (and Rajasthan), Muslims form 66% of the local population. In 2005, the Congress

(I) state government in Haryana quietly created a Muslim-majority district called Mewat, by vivisecting Gurgaon district. This move strengthened the clout of Islamic groups in the region. After all, it was in Haryana's Mewat region in 1992, that Muslim mobs in Nuh town had hacked Hindus, destroyed Hindu temples and brazenly slaughtered cows openly on streets after seizing them from Gau Shalas (cow shelters). Today, the mass conversion of Hindu villagers to Islam, purchasing tens of thousands of Hindu girls for use as sex-slaves, cow-slaughter and social boycott of Hindus is common in Muslim families in Mewat. The average Muslim birth rates of 12-15 children per household in Mewat is increasing even more by cases like the Mohammed Ishaq family where the patriarch has sired 23 kids from his wife, Bismillah.

The 2008 bomb blasts targeting Hindu temples and civilians in Jaipur underscore the rising tension in Rajasthan.

Muslim-majority cities like Old Delhi and Malerkotla (in Indian Punjab) provide not only shelter to Jihadi terrorists, but also geographic continuity to Muslim-dominated districts of western Uttar Pradesh (UP), especially Agra, Aligarh, Azamgarh, Meerut, Bijnor as well as Muzaffarnagar, Kanpur, Varanasi, Bareilly, Saharanpur and Moradabad. Muslim attacks on Hindu religious processions, religious riots and bomb blasts are common place in UP as was seen in Mau, Ayodhya, Lucknow and Kanpur. The UP state population of Muslims has risen to 18% today.

Next door, Bihar has a 17% Muslim population and religious tensions are simmering. Along the Indo-Nepal border of Uttar Pradesh and Bihar, around 1900 Islamic seminaries have come up on both sides of the Indo-Nepal border in recent times. "There has been an exponential increase of Madrassas on both sides of Indo-Nepal border in the recent past of which around 1100 are in India while the rest are in Nepal," revealed Director General of Sashastra Seema Bal (SSB) Tilak Kak. These large number of Madrassas, which serve as have come up in a disproportionate way and are not proportional to the Muslim population in the area.

India's Task Force on Border Management, in its report of October 2000, wrote about the ominous developments along the India-Nepal border: "On the Indo-Nepal border, Madrassas and mosques have sprung up on both sides in the Terai region, accompanied by four-fold increase in the population of the minority community in the region. There are 343 mosques, 300 Madrassas and 17 mosques-cum- Madrassas within 10 kilometres of the border on the Indian side. On the Nepal side, there are 282 mosques, 181 Madrassas and eight mosques-cum- Madrassas. These mosques and Madrassas receive huge funds from Muslim countries like Saudi Arabia, Iran, Kuwait, Pakistan and Bangladesh. Managers of various Madrassas and Ulema maintain close links with the embassy officials of those countries located at Kathmandu. Financial assistance is also channelized through the Islamic Development Bank (Jeddah), Habib Bank of Pakistan and also through some Indian Muslims living in Gulf countries. Pakistan's Habib Bank, after becoming a partner in Nepal's Himalayan Bank, has expanded its network in the border areas including Biratnagar and Krishna Nagar.

It is suspected that foreign currency is converted into Indian currency in Nepal and then brought to India clandestinely. Madrasas and mosques on the Indo-Nepal border are frequently visited by prominent Muslim leaders, Tablighi Jamaats (proselytizing groups) and pro-Pak Nepali leaders. Officials of Pak Embassy have come to notice visiting Terai area of Nepal to strengthen Islamic institutions and to disburse funds to them. Pro-Pak elements in Nepal also help in demographic subversion of the Terai belt."

West Bengal and Assam: The Weakest Links in the ChainAccording to the 2001 census, the Muslim population is 28% of the total West Bengal population. In Assam, the Muslim population comprises atleast 31% of the total state population.

Arun Shourie wrote this in the Indian Express in 2004: "Muslims in India accounted for 9.9 per cent (of India's population) in 1951, 10.8 per cent in 1971 and 11.3 per cent in 1981, and presumably about 12.1 per cent in 1991. The present population ratio of Muslims is calculated to be 28 per cent in Assam and 25 per cent in West Bengal. In 1991 the Muslim population in the border districts of West Bengal accounted for 56 per cent in South and North Parganas, 48 per cent in Nadia, 52 per cent in

Murshidabad, 54 per cent in Malda and about 60 per cent in Islampur sub-division of West Dinajpur. A study of the border belt of West Bengal yields some telling statistics: 20-40 per cent villages in the border districts are said to be predominantly Muslim.

There are indications that the concentration of the minority community, including the Bangladesh immigrants, in the villages has resulted in the majority community moving to urban centres. Several towns in the border districts are now predominantly inhabited by the majority community but surrounded by villages mostly dominated by the minority community. Lin Piao's theory of occupying the villages before overwhelming the cities comes to mind, though the context is different. However, the basic factor of security threat in both the cases is the same.

Figures have been given showing the concentration of Muslim population in the districts of West Bengal bordering Bangladesh starting from 24 Parganas and going up to Islampur of West Dinajpur district and their population being well over 50 per cent of the population.

The Kishanganj district (of Bihar) which was part of Purnea district earlier, which is contiguous to the West Bengal area, also has a majority of Muslim population. The total population of the districts of South and North 24 Parganas, Murshidabad, Nadia, Malda and West Dinajpur adds up to 27,337,362. If we add the population of Kishanganj district of Bihar of 986,672, the total comes to 28,324,034. (All figures are based on the 1991 Census.) This mass of land with a population of nearly 2.8 crores has a Muslim majority. The total population of West Bengal in 1991 was 67.9 million and of these, 28.32 million are concentrated in the border districts, with about 16-17 million population of minority community being concentrated in this area. This crucial tract of land in West Bengal and Bihar, lying along the Ganges/Hughly and west Bangladesh with a population of over 28 million, with Muslims constituting a majority, should give cause for anxiety for any thinking Indian."

And what if, from these figures, I had advanced two warnings. First, "There is a distinct danger of another Muslim country, speaking predominantly Bengali, emerging in the eastern part of

India in the future, at a time when India might find itself weakened politically and militarily."

And second that the danger is as grave even if that third Islamic State does not get carved out in the sub-continent into a full-fledged country? What if I had put that danger as follows?

"Let us look at the map of Eastern India – starting from the North 24 Parganas district, proceeding through Nadia, Murshidabad, Malda and West Dinajpur before entering the narrow neck of land lying through Raiganj and Dalkola of Islampur sub-division before passing through the Kishanganj district of East Bihar to enter Siliguri. Proceed further and take a look at the north Bengal districts of Darjeeling, Jalpaiguri and Cooch Behar before entering Assam, and its districts of Dhubri, Goalpara, Bongaigaon, Kokrajhar and Barpeta. A more sensitive region in Asia is difficult to locate..."

To quote Sandhya Jain's article "India's Cancer Wards" in "The Pioneer": 'Mr. R.K. Ohri, ex-IGP, Arunachal Pradesh, cautioned that an Islamic Caliphate is rising on India's flanks, from Bangladesh to West Asia, and that the shadow of the Mughalistan corridor is now visibly manifesting in various districts along the Indo-Nepal and Indo-Bangladesh border. The demand for a 'Muslim Banghboomi' has already been raised, warns ex-MP B.L. Sharma (Prem). Traveling in West Bengal to check out certain atrocities against Hindus some years ago, his convoy was attacked by Bangladeshis. When demographer J.K. Bajaj and his colleagues prepared a mathematical model of the demographic challenge facing India, they found it exactly matched the map prepared by Bangladesh's Mughalstan Research Institute. Experts feel the latter has been prepared by the ISI because the 'Mughalstan' spelling indicates a Punjabi mind!

Bangladesh's reputed human rights activist Salam Azad laments that Bangladesh is the best place in the world for the return of the Taliban. Madrasas, he said, are teaching that "Muslims are the best in the world; non-Muslims will be converted, beaten, killed, married, raped, because non-Muslim women are regarded as maal-i-ganimat (free war booty)... Minorities will be oppressed, indigenous people will be attacked, in my country there is oppression everywhere and this is being done by the so-called educated people of the madrasas."

West Bengal BJP leader Tathagatha Roy said the extent of atrocities against Hindus in Bangladesh can be seen from the fact that in several districts there was not a single woman between the ages of seven to seventy years who had not been raped in that country. He apologized for the indifference of the BJP Government which did not grant refugee status to Hindus fleeing oppression in Bangladesh. North Eastern Students Organisation chairman Samujjal Bhattacharya said all 49 tribal belts and blocks in Assam have been occupied by Bangladeshis. The shadows have spread to Arunachal, Nagaland, Manipur and Meghalaya

Today, Hindus residing within a 50-km radius of the border are feeling the heat. They are being harassed on Indian soil and forced to move as the infiltrators establish themselves along this corridor, thus de facto extending the Bangladesh border into India.'

The West Bengal administration, which had taken a serious view of the problem in the initial stages of the Buddhadeb Bhattacharjee government, now seems to have accepted it as a fait accompli. The chief minister had adopted some steps to contain the menace when the BJP strongman L.K.Advani was the union home minister from 1998-2004. But his initiative has slackened after the installation of the UPA government at the Centre since 2004.

In case the ramifications of the unfolding scenario are not yet clear to Indians, the bomb-blasts and religious riots are a roaring continuation of the 1400-year Jihad against India – an ongoing war that will culminate in the Islamisation of what's left of Hindustan. Already the demographic battle is underway and the Mughalistan scenario looks feasible. The book "Religious Demography of India" published by A P Joshi, M.D. Srinivas and J K Bajaj of the Centre for Policy Studies (CPS), Chennai, reveals that in 2001, Muslims comprise over 30% of the total population in the Indian-subcontinent (comprising India, Pakistan and Bangladesh). The total Muslim population zoomed from 12.5% (1991) to 30.3% (2001), in just 10 years (from ex-IAS officer V.Sundaram's article in "News Today": Deathly Demographic warnings for India).

According to the 2001 census report, Indian population is 1,027,015,247.3. Of this, 1.5 crore people are Bangladeshi infiltrators who are living in India. The Intelligence Bureau has reportedly estimated, after an extensive survey, that the present number is about 16 million. The August 2000 report of the Task Force on Border Management placed the figure at 15 million, with 300,000 Bangladeshis entering India illegally every month. It is estimated that about 13 lakh Bangladeshis live in Delhi alone. It has been reported that one crore Bangladeshis are missing from Bangladesh [August 4, 1991, Morning Sun] and it implies that those people have infiltrated into India. These infiltrators mainly settle in the north-east India and in West Bengal. This is shown by the fact that there has been irregular increase in the Muslim population in these states and many of the districts have become Muslim majority. The proportion of Muslims in Assam had increased from 24.68 per cent in 1951 to 30.91 per cent in 2001.Whereas in the same time period the proportion of Muslims in India increased from 9.91 per cent to 13.42 per cent. In West Bengal, the Muslim population in west Dinajpur, Maldah, Birbhum and Murshidabad 36.75 per cent, 47.49 per cent, 33.06 per cent and 61.39 per cent respectively, according to 1991 census.

This has not only caused the burden on the Indian economy, but also threatens the identity of the indigenous people of the north-east of India. In Tripura, another north-eastern state of India, the local population has been turned into a minority community over a short period of time by the sheer numbers of cross-border migrants from Bangladesh. In 1947, 56 per cent of Tripura's population consisted of tribal (or indigenous) population. Today this stands at a 25% of the total. In many districts these infiltrators are the one who decides the outcome of elections. Outcomes of the 32 per cent of Vidhan Sabha seats in Assam and 18 per cent of seats in West Bengal are decided by them. This is due to the fact that political parties are helping them to get ration cards and voters ID and hence using them to win elections.

According to the report, at present there are 80 lakh Bangladeshi infiltrators in Bengal, 55 lakh in Assom, 4 lakh in Tripura and 5 lakh in Bihar (Katihar, Purnia and Kishenganj districts) and

Jharkhand(Sahebganj district). As far as West Bengal is concerned, the concentration of infiltrators is quite marked in the border districts like North and South Dinajpur, Cooch Behar, Nadia, Murshidabad, Malda and North and South 24 Parganas. The affected areas in Assom are Dhubri, Goalpara, Karimganj and Hailakandi, while a similar scenario is noticeable in Kailashar, Sabrum, Udaipur and Belonia areas in Tripura. Pakistan's ISI is believed to have a hand behind this large-scale infiltration which has been playing havoc with the economy of Bengal and Assam. Home ministry sources say Harkat-ul-Jehadi-Islami(HUJI), the dreaded militant outfit active in Bangladesh, has succeeded in sending a large number of militants along with the infiltrators to West Bengal.

The Home ministry had laid stress on an early completion of barbed-wire fencing along the borders with Bangladesh. Of the 2216 km-long border the fencing could be completed only along 1167 km till 2007. The continuous infiltration has brought about serious demographic changes to Bengal's border areas and made the border-map, drawn after the 1974 Indira-Mujib agreement, somewhat irrelevant. The Centre has consequently sought a detailed report from the state government on changes in the population pattern in 66 blocks of nine border districts.

To facilitate Mughalistan and the concomitant partition of India and Bengal, the DGFI-ISI have jointly planned to change the demography of West Bengal and Assam on a priority basis.

As many as 53 out of 294 Assembly constituencies in West Bengal have a high concentration of voters who happen to be illegal Muslim from Bangladesh. Similarly, the fate of 40 Assembly seats in Assam depends on the votes cast by illegal Bangladeshi Muslim infiltrators. All this has been revealed by a recent report of the union home ministry on infiltration from India's neighbour. The report has been prepared on the basis of facts and figures provided by the Task Force on Border Management and Assam's former governor S.K. Sinha.

As such the Bangladeshi Muslims can control the West Bengal Assembly, and dictate terms to the state government of West Bengal in all respects. The picture of plight of majority Hindu electorates worsened in the State, as Muslim electorates have a clear majority in three districts viz. Malda, Murshidabad & North Dinajpur and 63 (sixty three) blocks in West Bengal. Again, an analysis upon the projection into the 2001 Census hints at abnormal Muslim growth everywhere in West Bengal, where the Muslim population is 28% of the total state population.

There are at least 5 powerful Muslim ministers in the West Bengal state cabinet: Abdur Rezzak Mollah (Minister of Land & Land Reforms), Anisur Rahaman (Minister of Animal Resources Development), Mortaja Hossain (Minister of Agriculture, Marketing & Relief, Minster of State), Anarul Haque (Minister of State for Public Health, Engineering) and Abdus Sattar (Minister of State for Minority Development & Madrasa Education).

In West Bengal, there are 45 Muslim Members of the Legislative Assembly (MLAs) out of 294 seats. There are 5 Muslim Members of Parliament from West Bengal out of 42 seats: Mohammed Salim (Calcutta North East), Abu Ayes Mondal (Katwa), Abu Hasem Khan Choudhury (Malda), Abdul Mannan Hossain (Murshidabad) and Hannan Mollah (Uluberia), all of whom strength the control of Islam in various government institutions and the police hierarchy.

As the UPA Central Government and the CPI(M) State Government have paid no attention for the threat of Bangladeshi Muslim infiltrators in West Bengal, the Bangladeshi Muslims have captured land, money and unequalled power of voting throughout the border districts in Bengal in many places.

With the passive support of both the UPA Central Government and the CPI(M) State Government and with the active support of all the political parties in West Bengal (except for the BJP) for winning the Muslim votebank's support, the DGFI & ISI has actively put down roots in the soil of West Bengal for their purposes. Not only are they successful in the ongoing demographic change of West Bengal by means of mobilizing the election machinery of Bengal, they have also opened their fronts everywhere in smuggling, trafficking, drug peddling, illegal cow smuggling, trans-border gang robbery and of course terrorism, with the active grassroots support to the Harakat ul-Jihad-I-Islami-Bangladesh (HUJI-B), Lashkar-e-Tayyaba and Jaish-e-Mohammad.

Now in its most advantageous position, the DGFI & ISI's joint collaboration is now promoting activities of Mughalistan in Kolkata, Howrah & other districts. The Dhaka-based Mughalistan Research Institute has identified various areas marked as "Mini Pakistan" in W.Bengal & Eastern India. This Mughalistan, as we know, comprises the entity of Greater Pakistan, right from Afghanistan to Myanmar including Bangladesh, whole of W. Bengal, Assam & many other portions of India. This Pan-Islamic movement gets petro-dollars from the Arab World and fake Indian Currency from Pakistan and Bangladesh for the maximum manifestation of their plans. The Muslim infiltration from Bangladesh gives oxygen to the Pan-Islamic movement in India. Now they have direct access into the West Bengal State Assembly and into the Ministry of Bengal within Writers Building, Kolkata. But sadly, West Bengal's vote politics undermine the situation by turning a blind eye to this colossal tragedy, unabashedly providing voters' ID cards to the Muslim infiltrators and setting a dangerous peril for Bengali Hindus and India.

The North-Eastern region is connected to rest of India by a small strip called "The Siliguri Corridor" or "Chicken's Neck". The Islamists have planned to isolate the North-East of India from the rest of India, in order to facilitate the creation of Mughalistan. This Operation is named as "Operation Pin code". For this they have planned to infiltrate 3000 Jihadis into North Eastern region. According to the Task Force, there are 905 Mosques and 439 Madrasas along Indo-Bangladesh border on the Indian side.

Some excerpts from the report, "Demography survey on eastern border" by Bhavna Vij-Aurora in "The Telegraph" are startling. "There have been reports that more Madarsas and mosques are sprouting along the borders, which in itself is an indication of increased Muslim population in the area," disclosed an intelligence official. The last such study was done by the Intelligence Bureau and the home ministry in 1992, and their report kept a secret in view of the sensitive findings. It was ultimately leaked and the estimated number of illegal migrants from Bangladesh was anywhere between 1.5 crore and 2 crore. It's time for a fresh survey, according to sources. There have been renewed intelligence reports that militants are using madarsas and mosques as safe havens, and also for storing arms and ammunition. According to reports, the largest number of madarsas and mosques has come up in bordering areas with Nepal, lower Assam and Bengal. This complements another secret survey that has revealed that nearly 40 per cent villages in the border districts of Bengal are predominantly Muslim. There are reports that concentration of the minority community, including the Bangladeshi immigrants in the villages, has resulted in the majority community moving to urban areas. Along with madarsas and mosques, a large number of Muslim NGOs have sprung up in the area bordering Nepal. Most of these madarsas are used for anti-India activities by Pakistan-backed terrorists. The NGOs ostensibly work for the social and educational uplift of the Muslim community and receive substantial and completely unregulated funding from Saudi Arabia, Kuwait, Libya and other Islamic countries," an intelligence report said."

When India was partitioned in 1947 on religious grounds and Muslims got West Pakistan and East Pakistan (now Bangladesh), they had a vulture's eye on the entire north-east. Muslims were not satisfied with both the Pakistans. They wanted the whole of the north-east region (undivided Assam) integrated with East Pakistan. Manul Haq Chowdhury, Jinnah's private secretary, who remained in Assam and later became a minister in Assam assembly, wrote to Jinnah in 1947: "Quaid-e-Azam, wait for the next thirty years, I shall present Assam to Pakistan on a platter." Since then, a sinister game plan to 'grow more Muslims in the north-east' has been going on surreptitiously.

Today, out of the total 24 districts of Assam, six districts, namely, Nagaon, Goalpara, Dhubri, Karimganj, Barpeta and Hailakanndi have 60 per cent Muslim population while other six, namely, Bongaigaon, Kokrajhar, Kamrup, Nalbari, Darang and Cachar districts have above 40 per cent of them. Out of the 126 assembly seats, the election of 54 MLAs depends on the Muslim vote bank. There are 28 Muslim MLAs and four ministers, namely, (i) Rocky Bul Hussain (Nagaon), Minister of State for Home Affairs; (ii) Ismail Hussain (Dhubri), Minister for Flood; (iii) Dr Nazurul Islam (Doboka), Minister for Food and Civil Supply, and (iv)

Misabul Hussain Laskar (Borkhola, Cachar), Minister for Cooperatives.

There are two Lok Sabha MPs in Assam, namely, Anwar Hussain from Dhubri and A.F. Gulam Osmani from Barpeta and one Rajya Sabha MP, Smt. Anwara Timur (Nagaon). The Muslim community of Assam has provided one former Muslim Chief Minister—Smt. Anwara Timur (Nagaon) and one former President of India—Fakhruddin Ali Ahmed (Lakhtokia, Guwahati). Earlier, in the Assam Gana Parishad (AGP) Ministry, headed by Prafulla Kumar Mahanta, there were two Muslim ministers, namely, Maidul Islam Bora from Kamalpur, Kamrup district and Sukur Ali from Barpeta. Several high-ranking officers including deputy commissioners are from this community. Obviously, the Muslim community, including the Indian Muslims and the Bangladeshi Muslims, have become a dominant group in Assam and it is they who decide who would be the Chief Minister of Assam and what would be the major policies of Assam pertaining to detection and deportation of illegal Muslim migrants and care of Muslim welfare.

Tarun Gogoi, the Congress(I) Chief Minister of Assam, is giving all protection to these Muslims due to political compulsions. The Assamese community has been overpowered by Muslims. These Bangladeshi Muslims are sneaking into upper Assam too, creating serious problems for the Assamese. The demography of Assam has drastically changed and the very existence of the indigenous people is threatened. The manifold growth in Muslim population has overburdened Assam and the Assamese people are feeling harassed and tortured. The livelihoods of the local people are getting snatched away by these illegal Muslim migrants. The Janjati (indigenous tribal) communities in Assam are not organized. Therefore, their land and forests are very often forcefully occupied by these Muslims. The Nelli massacre in 1983 was the worst clash between the local people and Bangladeshi Muslims in which several Lalung Janjati people were reportedly killed and many Lalung villages were burnt.

These Bangladeshis have illegally sneaked into Manipur, Mizoram, Meghalaya, Arunachal Pradesh and Tripura too. They are marrying the local girls of influential people and are thus getting protection from their in-laws' families. After marriage with a Janjati girl, they convert her to Islam. They purchase land in the Janjati belts in the name of their Janjati wives by producing Janjati certificates in her name. Now, the new generation of Muslims, i.e. the Janjati Muslims, is growing. They give Muslim names to their children but the clan remains that of local wives, like Saidullah Ningrum, Azad Lingdoh (Khasi Muslims), Nizamuddin Semia, Akram Semia (Naga Muslims), Shahabuddin Chowdhury, Akbar Laskar (Assamese Muslims) and others. In Assam, Muslims are using Assamese surnames like Hazarika, Barbhuian, Bargohain, Bhuiyan, Bora, Gohain and others. There are Meitei Muslims too in Manipur.

In Nagaland, the Muslim menace is more serious. Dimapur has become the den of these Bangladeshi Muslims. They constitute the leading labour force in the agriculture sector owned by the Naga community. The majority of rickshaw-pullers, auto-drivers and other manual labourers is now of Bangladeshi Muslims. This has given rise to robbery, theft, illegal trafficking of narcotic drugs and liquor, smuggling of pornographic films and vulgar literature and an unprecedented rise in crime, flesh trade and prostitution. This influx has narrowed the jobs of lay workers too.

The Nagaland state capital, Kohima, has become the second biggest haven for the illegal migrant Muslims who occupy most of the shops in the main market, P.R. Hills and other localities. They marry Angami girls and become sons-in-law of the Naga people.

Similarly, all the district areas such as Mokokchung, Wokha, Zunheboto, Phek, Mon and Tuensang are infested with them. They are sneaking into the interiors of Nagaland. In places like Jalukie in Zeliang area, Naginimora, Tizit and other central places of Nagaland, the pain of the presence of migrant Muslims is felt by the local Naga populace. Some ten years before, the students' bodies had agitated against these foreigner Muslims. But the agitation was silently withdrawn reportedly due to threats from Bangladesh that the Government of Bangladesh would demolish all the camps of Naga undergrounds established in the territory of that country if the Bangladeshi Muslims were harassed in

Nagaland. On seeing this unprecedented growth of Muslim population in Nagaland, S.C. Jamir, the then Chief Minister, once stated, "Muslims are breeding like mosquitoes in Nagaland."

As a result of such illegal migration of Bangladeshi Muslims and their nuptial ties with the local Naga girls, a new community called Semiya or Sumias has already emerged in the state. Their number is estimated to be several thousand. The concentration of the Semiyas is the highest in Dimapur and Kohima districts respectively. There are fears among many that the voters' list might have been doctored to accommodate the Semiyas as well other immigrants. The result of such immigration is gradually being felt in the state.

According to a Dimapur-based newspaper, on any Muslim religious day at least half of the shops in Kohima and some 75 per cent in Dimapur remain closed. It is also a fact that control over business establishments is fast receding from the hands of the locals. A recent survey conducted by the state directorate of Agriculture showed that 71.73 per cent of the total business establishments are being controlled and run by non-locals. Out of the 23,777 numbers of shops in the state, the local people own only 6,722 shops. Since the illegal migrants provide cheap labour, they are aggravating the unemployment problem. Besides, they pose a threat to the internal security as well. Reliable sources indicate that they are also involved in various unwanted activities like drug peddling and flesh trade.

THE BIG PICTURE

The following map shows the concentration of Muslims and Hindus in the Indian subcontinent today. The highlighted areas show riot-prone regions of India where aggressive Muslim populations range from atleast 20% to 100% of the population.

Lest one mistakenly thinks that Mughalistan is the culmination of the Islamisation of India and that somehow the rest of India will be spared its fate, it must be stressed that this second partition of India is only the beginning. In Hyderabad of Andhra Pradesh, northern districts of Karnataka and certain areas of Maharashtra, the growth of Muslims is very high. Likewise, in Kerala, the

Muslims now constitute 25% of the state's population. Malappuram district was carved out to create a Muslim majority district by the Communist government headed by E.M.S Namboothiripad. Today, the entire Malappuram district enforces the weekly holiday on Friday (not Sunday) for schools and businesses, while Hindus in neighbouring Kozhikode (Calicut) and Kannur are intimidated through high-profile massacres like in Marad. The planning and execution is well underway to ensure a continuing Anschluss where several Muslim majority pockets such as Moplahstan (in Kerala) and Osmanistan (in the Deccan) will gradually spread in size and link up with Mughalistan to form a Greater Mughalistan.

This Greater Mughalistan is of strategic significance as it will provide a contiguous, strategic corridor linking the Ummah into a pan-Islamic Caliphate. The ISI-DGFI-Indian Jihadi triumvirate has fondly nicknamed this pan-Islamic Caliphate as Islamistan (meaning "Land of Islam"), a synonym for `Islamic World' or `Dar-ul-Islam'. This geographical Islamic crescent will link the Islamic Middle-East to Islamic South-East Asia, with the new Islamic World stretching all the way from Morocco and Bosnia in the West to Malaysia and Indonesia in the East.

There are Muslims in India today who dream of "Mughalistan" and are working relentlessly towards a further partition of India by creating "Mughalistan" in the UP-Bihar-Bengal-Assam corridor. It remains the focus of mainstream groups like the Tablighi Jamaat (who have methodically radicalised the ordinary Muslims) as well as underground terror groups like the Students Islamic Movement of India (SIMI) and the Indian Mujahideen, who have blown up several Indian cities killing thousands of people.

Until Mughalstan is achieved, Indians will continue to see serial bomb-blasts, attacks on Hindu festivals and temples, killings of Hindu activists, conversions of Hindu women and socio-economically backward sections, and brazen cow-slaughter that will continue endlessly until the Hindu mind becomes too numb and shell-shocked to look at the bigger picture, or comprehend the future – that Mughalistan is inevitable ("Mughalstan Paindabad").

6

Islamic Fundamentalism in Pakistan

Pakistan is situated in a region where fundamentalism has been posed, of late, as one of the most threatening questions. The process initiated by the Islamic revolution in Iran has even been internationalised by the Taliban's victory in Afghanistan. At the same time, the rise of Hindu radicalism in India has further complicated the situation in Pakistan. Recently Islamic fundamentalism has risen as an alternative political phenomenon not only in Pakistan but also in the entire Muslim world. Islamic fundamentalism in Pakistan is partly a link of this international phenomenon and partly caused by specific local reasons. When analysing Islamic fundamentalism, one must understand that the religion of Islam and Islamic fundamentalism are not one and the same thing. Islamic fundamentalism is a reactionary, non-scientific movement aimed at returning society to a centuries-old social set-up, defying all material and historical factors. It is an attempt to roll back the wheel of history.

Fundamentalism finds its roots in the backwardness of society, social deprivation, a low level of consciousness, poverty and ignorance. Like fascism and national chauvinism, Islamic fundamentalism finds its base in the petty bourgeoisie. But it is not only the petty bourgeoisie that is attracted by fundamentalism; those who have fallen from among the petty bourgeoisie into the ranks of the proletariat and semi-proletariat are also impressed by the movement. Similarly, sections of the proletariat that are newly formed and not yet equipped with class-consciousness and the experience of class struggle are also likely to become supporters of this movement. They correspond to a section of petty bourgeoisie described by the *Communist Manifesto*:

> The lower middle class, the manufacturer, the shopkeeper, the artisan, the peasant, all these fight against the bourgeoisie to save from extinction their existence as fractions of the middle class. They are therefore not revolutionary, but conservative. Nay more, they are reactionary, for they try to roll back the wheel of history.

It is possible to distinguish four general causes contributing to the rise of Islamic fundamentalism.

THE CONTRADICTIONS OF IMPERIALISM

Islam has been a political religion since the beginning. When Arabs invaded other countries, the rationale was jihad (holy war) against infidels, although these wars had economic motives. In the nineteenth and twentieth centuries, when Muslim countries, one after the other, were colonised by the imperialist countries, the resistance movements used religion as well as nationalism as a launching pad for independence struggles. In countries like Indonesia and Malaysia, the national liberation movement was begun in the name of religion.

Of late, as the multinationals have stepped up their super-exploitation of the Muslim world, one of the natural reactions is hatred of the headquarters (i.e. the West) of these multinationals. During the Cold War, imperialism used Islamic fundamentalists against the left. The fundamentalist parties were the closest friends of imperialism in the Muslim world. However, in the post-Cold War era, imperialism does not need them as it did in the past. The CIA has stopped funding Islamic fundamentalists. This changed situation brought Islamic reactionaries into contradiction with imperialism. At the same time, because of the experience of centuries of colonisation and exploitation, a hatred for the West, especially for the USA, is widespread in the Muslim world, as in any Third World country. In the changed situation of the post-Cold War era, fundamentalists turned to anti-imperialist sloganeering and came to the fore as the forces challenging imperialism. Osama bin Laden became a symbol of anti-imperialism no matter what his tactics or the class to which he belongs. The terrorist methods of fundamentalism were seen by the ranks of the fundamentalists as jihad against the USA, while in general the movement was seen as a challenge to the USA.

The Inability of Capitalism to Solve the Basic Problems

Islamic fundamentalism is spreading especially rapidly in those counties where capitalism has failed to fulfil the tasks of the bourgeois democratic revolution, where it has failed to eliminate poverty and ignorance and where class contradictions are sharpening. Poverty and ignorance are concomitant. A society ridden with ignorance is fertile soil for the growth of fundamentalist ideas.

The Failure of the Left

It was in Iran that the Islamic fundamentalists had their first major victory. The Tudeh Party (Iranian Communist Party) believed in the bankrupt Stalinist two-stage theory of revolution. Despite having a mass base, the Tudeh Party, in line with its theory, forged an alliance with fundamentalists instead of offering an alternative to the masses. Not only that, but the Iranian left also failed to present itself as an alternative during the democratic movement against the shah and failed or did not attempt to link the democratic movement to the class struggle to overthrow capitalism and replace it with socialism. The alliance with the fundamentalists proved fatal. The fundamentalists on coming to power went on to the physical elimination of the communists, and did it successfully. A golden opportunity for a socialist revolution was lost and the working class had to pay a heavy price, which it is still paying. Afghanistan was the other country where fundamentalists were able to capture power. In Afghanistan, the fundamentalists came to power as a direct sequel to the socialist government. The Afghan revolutionaries who captured power surrendered to the Stalinist instructions and methods taught by Moscow.

Instead of making any genuine effort to consolidate revolution by appealing to internationalism, consolidating workers democracy and laying the material basis to prolong the revolution, they resorted to Stalinist, bureaucratic and class-collaborationist methods of running a transitional state. As a result, they failed, paving the way for the fundamentalists. Similarly in Algeria, where socialists successfully led the national liberation movement against France and remained in power for over two decades, they failed to stop the rise of Islamic fundamentalism. The fundamentalist movement in Algeria is one of the strongest movements in the Muslim world today.

Providing an Alternative Society

The fundamentalists, through their massive network of social services, have built alternative societies in the Muslim countries where they are strong. They provide hospitals, orphanages, schools and many other facilities, which weak capitalist governments have failed to provide to the masses. This adds to their influence as a social force. Their schools are the most influential tool. These seminaries not only provide religious education but also guarantee food and shelter to the children of poor parents who cannot afford education and food.

IN PAKISTAN

Pakistan is witnessing a rise of Islamic fundamentalism. Partly this is linked with international phenomena and the four factors cited above. But there are some local factors as well. Five factors are summarised here.

Pakistan is not a Nation-state

It is an unnatural and unhistorical country with its borders drawn in the name of religion. Besides Israel, it is the only country founded in the name of religion. Religion was and still is exploited to provide a basis for the country. After its creation, the ruling class, in order to keep the country intact and run the state in a multi-national country, has constantly used religion as a tool to deny the rights of small nationalities and to justify unelected regimes. This has combined state and religion. Therefore Pakistan has become a semi-theocratic state, if not a completely theocratic one.

The Ruling Class has always Exploited Religion to Justify its Regimes or to Win Popularity

The unelected governments used religion to argue that Islam and Western democracy do not match, while so-called elected governments used religion to gain popularity whenever it was threatened. Even a populist leader like Bhutto used the phrase Islamic socialism in the late 1960s, and when he was facing a movement in 1977 he decreed Friday a weekly holiday and other such cosmetic Islamic reforms. After decades of exploitation of religion by rulers, there is a developing view that if Islam is the only solution to all problems, then one might as well give the government to those who practice Islam most consistently, i.e. the fundamentalists.

Madaris Provide a Big Army of Young Fundamentalists Every Year

There are 8000 religious schools, with an estimated 2.5 million to 3.5 million students. These schools are run with money from the Saudi or Kuwaiti governments, various departments of the Pakistani government and local wealthy people, who give big donations from their corruptly obtained money to please Allah as well as to purify their corrupted money.

Poor parents are compelled by their circumstances to send their children to these schools. Their only options are to send their children to child labour or to these schools, where they will get religious education, food, shelter and a job at some mosque on completing their education. There is an additional factor: it is believed that by learning the Quran by heart at these schools, a boy will secure heaven for himself and his family.

The Rise of Islamic Fundamentalism in Pakistan Really Began in the 1980s

On the one hand, the military dictator, General Zia ul-Haq, was using religion to justify his rule and was Islamising laws and society. On the other hand, Pakistan had become a base camp for the forces opposing the Afghan revolution. Not only were thousands of Pakistani guerrillas operating from Pakistani soil but also 25,000 guerrillas from other Muslim countries reached Afghanistan through Pakistan. After the end of the Afghan war, the Pakistan Army started using these guerrilla forces to fight a proxy war in Kashmir. It is still going on. The Pakistan Army is interested in using them only in Kashmir, but the way these guerrillas are brainwashed, it is not possible to restrict them to Kashmir. They are taught to fight against all infidels; hence they reach from the Moro (Philippines) to Chechnya to help their Muslim brethren. When their foreign engagements end and they return home, they may pose a big challenge to the state. Already they are flexing their muscles. The attack on the US embassy in Islamabad in 1999 and the hijacking of an Indian plane from Nepal demanding the release of Maulana Massod, a militant leader, show their strength.

Pakistan Strategic Position also Provides a Fertile Ground for the Spread of Islamic Fundamentalism

Two Muslim countries with fundamentalist governments, Iran and Afghanistan, lie on its western border. The governments in both these countries have strong connections with the fundamentalist parties belonging to their respective sects. Pakistan borders India in the east. India is experiencing the rise and rise of Hindu fundamentalists, who have been in power now for about three years. These Hindu reactionaries use sloganeering and war mania against Pakistan to seek popularity. As a reaction to Hindu fundamentalism, Islamic fundamentalism gains popularity in Pakistan.

ISLAM IN PAKISTAN

Islam is the official religion of the Islamic Republic of Pakistan, which has a population of about 174,578,558. The overwhelming majority (95-97%) of the Pakistani people are Muslims while the remaining 3-5% are Christian, Hindu, and others. Pakistan has the second largest Muslim population in the world after Indonesia. Sunnis are the majority while the Shias make up between 10-20% of the total Muslim population of the country. Pakistan has the second largest number of Shias after Iran, which numbers between 17 million to as high as 30 million according to Vali Nasr.

Umayyad Invasion of Sindh and the Arrival of Islam

Islam arrived in the area now known as Pakistan in 711 CE, when the Umayyad dynasty sent a Muslim Arab army led by Muhammad bin Qasim against the ruler of Sindh, Raja Dahir, this was due to the fact that Raja Dahir had given refuge to numerous Zoroastrian Princes who had fled the Islamic conquest of Iran. Muhammad Bin Qasim's army was defeated in his first three attempts. The Muslim army conquered the northwestern part of Indus Valley from Kashmir to the Arabian Sea. The arrival of the Arab Muslims to the provinces of Sindh and Punjab, along with subsequent Muslim dynasties, set the stage for the religious boundaries of South Asia that would lead to the development of the modern state of Pakistan as well as forming the foundation for Islamic rule which quickly spread across much of South Asia. Following the rule of various Islamic empires, including the Ghaznavid Empire, the Ghorid kingdom, and the Delhi Sultanate, the Mughals controlled the region from 1526 until 1739. Muslim technocrats, bureaucrats, soldiers, traders, scientists, architects, teachers, theologians and Sufis flocked from the rest of the Muslim world to Islamic Sultanate and Mughal Empire in South Asia and in the land that became Pakistan.

Islam and the Pakistan Movement

The Muslim poet-philosopher Sir Allama Muhammad Iqbal first proposed the idea of a Muslim state in northwestern South Asia in his address to the Muslim League at Allahabad in 1930. His proposal referred to the four provinces of Punjab, Sindh, Balochistan, and the NorthWest Frontier — essentially what would became Pakistan. Iqbal's idea gave concrete form to two distinct nations in the South Asia based on religion (Islam and Hinduism) and with different historical backgrounds, social customs, cultures, and social mores.

Islam was thus the basis for the creation and the unification of a separate state. Allama Muhammad Iqbal in 1937, in a letter to Jinnah wrote, *After a long and careful study of Islamic Law I have come to the conclusion that if this system of Law is properly understood and applied, at last the right to subsistence is secured to every body. But the enforcement and development of the Shariat of Islam is impossible in this country without a free Muslim state or states. This has been my honest conviction for many years and I still believe this to be the only way to solve the problem of bread for Muslims as well as to secure a peaceful India.*

But just three days before the creation of Pakistan, Mohammad Ali Jinnah made a different commitment. A commitment to secularism in Pakistan. In his inaugural address he said, *You will find that in the course of time Hindus would cease to be Hindus and Muslims would cease to be Muslims, not in the religious sense, because that is the personal faith of each individual, but in the political sense as citizens of the State.* This statement of Jinnah is an object of great controversy since then and this vision of a Pakistan in which Islamic law would not be applied, contrary to Iqbal's perception, was questioned shortly after independence.

Politicized Islam

From the outset, politics and religion have been intertwined both conceptually and practically in Islam. Because Prophet Muhammad established a government in Medina, precedents of governance and taxation exist. Through the history of Islam, from the Ummayyad (661-750) and Abbasid empires (750-1258) to the Mughals (1526- 1858), Safavis (1501–1722) and the Ottomans (1300-1923), religion and statehood have been treated as one. Indeed, one of the beliefs of Islam is that the purpose of the state is to provide an environment where Muslims can properly practice their religion. If a leader fails in this, the people have a right to depose him. In March 1949, the first constituent assembly passed Objectives Resolution, which declared that the state of Pakistan will be submitted to the sovereignty of God. In 1950, thirty one Ulema passed a demand draft, called Twenty Two Points of Ulema. This drafted demanded preparation of constitution according to Objectives Resolution. It also demanded changes in the law according to Shariah. In 1977, the government of Zulfiqar Ali Bhutto outlawed alcohol and drugs and changed the weekend from Sunday to Friday, but no substantive Islamic reform program was implemented prior to General Zia-ul-Haq's Islamization program.

Starting in February 1979, new penal measures based on Islamic principles of justice went into effect. These carried considerably greater implications for women than for men. A welfare and taxation system based on Zakat and a profit-and-loss banking system were also established in accordance with Islamic prohibitions against usury but were inadequate.

Muslim Sects in Pakistan

According to the CIA World Factbook and Oxford Centre for Islamic Studies, 95-97% of the total population of Pakistan is Muslim. The majority of the Pakistani Muslims are Sunnis, while Shias are estimated 10-20%. The Muslims belong to different schools which are called Madhahib (singular: Madhhab) i.e., schools of jurisprudence (also 'Maktab-e-Fikr' (School of Thought) in Urdu). The Hanafi school of Sunnis includes the Barelvi and Deobandi schools.

The two subsects of Sunni Hanafi school, Barelvis and Deobandis, have their own Masjids. The conservative think tank The Heritage Foundation gives estimate that the vast majority of Sunni Muslims in Pakistan follows Barelvi traditions.

The Shi'a *Ithna 'ashariyah* school has its own Masjids commonly termed as Hussainias (Imambargahs). Mustaali Dawoodi Bohra and Sulaimani Bohra also have their own Masjids, while the Nizari Ismailis pray in Jama'at Khanas. Although the vast majority of Pakistani Shi'a Muslims belong to Ithna 'ashariyah school, there are significant minorities: Nizari Ismailis (Agha Khanis) and the smaller Mustaali Dawoodi Bohra and Sulaimani Bohra branches. The Salafi sect is represented by the Ahle Hadith movement in Pakistan. Many people on the Makran coast of Balochistan follow the Zikri sect of Islam. The Ahmadiyya community, a minority group is also present. Ahmadis have been declared non-Muslims by the Government of Pakistan. In 1974, the government of Pakistan amended Constitution of Pakistan to define a Muslim "as a person who believes in finality of Prophet Muhammad". For this reason, Ahmadis are persecuted on behalf of their beliefs. Ahmadis believe in Muhammad as the best and the last law bearing prophet and Mirza Ghulam Ahmad as the Christ of Muslims who was prophesied to come in the latter days and unite the Muslims. Consequently they were declared non-Muslims by a tribunal, the records of which have not been released to date. According to the last Pakistan census, Ahmadis made up 0.25% of the population. However the website adherents.com proposes that the Ahmadiyya Muslim community made up 1.42% of the population; which is likely to be a less biased source. The Economist puts the figure of Ahmadiyya adherents to 4 million. The Ahmadis claim their community is even larger. Sufism has a strong tradition in Pakistan. The Muslim Sufi missionaries played a pivotal role in converting the millions of native people to Islam. As in other areas where Sufis introduced it, Islam to some extent syncretized with pre-Islamic influences, resulting in a religion with some traditions distinct from those of the Arab world. The Naqshbandiya, Qadiriya, Chishtiya and Suhrawardiyya silsas have a large following in Pakistan. Sufis whose shrines receive much national attention are Data Ganj Baksh (Ali Hajweri) in Lahore (ca. 11th century), Baha-ud-din Zakariya in Multan and Shahbaz Qalander in Sehwan (ca. 12th century) and Shah Abdul Latif Bhitai in Bhit, Sindh and Rehman Baba in Khyber Pakhtunkhwa Province.

Laws and Customs

There is no law in Pakistan enforcing hijab and wearing of Hijab by Pakistani women is fairly uncommon. However, the practice of wearing Hijab among younger women in urban centres is slowly growing due to media influence from the Middle East and Persian Gulf countries. The episodes of sectarian violence have significantly decreased in frequency over the years due to the conflictual engagement of the Islamic militant organizations with the state's armed forces and intelligence agencies.

Media and Pilgrimages

Media and pilgrimages has influenced Pakistani Muslims to learn more about Islam as a result the local heterodox beliefs and practices are being replaced with orthodox beliefs from Quran and Sunnah. The inexpensive travel, simpler visa rules and direct air travel to Saudi Arabia has resulted in large number Pakistani Muslims going to Medina and Mecca for Haj and Umrah. This has helped to increase Pan-Islamic identity of Pakistani Muslims. The Muslim print media has always existed in Pakistan which included newspapers, books and magazines. The Muslim satellite channels are widely available and are watched by Pakistani population.

Islamic Education

The Study of Islam as a subject is compulsory for all Muslim students up to Matriculation or O'levels in all schools in Pakistan. Islamic education to the masses is also propagated mainly by Islamic schools and literature. Islamic schools (or Madrassas) mostly cater to the youth from impoverished social backgrounds and those learning to be Islamic clerics. More casual and even research oriented material is available in the form of books. While the most prominent of these schools are being monitored, the latter are being 'moderated' by both the government and some of the scholars, thereby also removing in the process the various material present in it that is used by Anti-Islam/Anti-Sunni writers. Oldest and universally accepted titles such as the Sahih Bukhari have been revised into 'summarised' editions and some of the old, complete titles, translated to Urdu, the national language, are not available for purchase now. These changes are also a herald to new outbreaks of religious controversy in the region.

IMPERIALISM AND FUNDAMENTALISM

Islamic fundamentalism provides a glaring example of imperialist hypocrisy. Now the USA and the imperialist West pose as the biggest enemy of Islamic fundamentalism and try to fool the working class in the West by presenting fundamentalism as a big challenge to world peace. But it was the same imperialism that used these fundamentalist forces against the left in various Muslim countries.

In the 1950s and 1960s there was a rise of populist, anti-imperialist and class movements. The USA worked out a plan to patronise the fundamentalists in order to weaken these populist movements, which imperialism feared could end up in socialist revolutions. The CIA, under the guidance of US Secretary of State John Foster Dulles, established a liaison between fundamentalist parties in different countries. According to the plan, a network of Akwanul Muslameen popularly known as Muslim Brotherhood (Egypt), Hamas (Syria), Sarakat ul Islam (Indonesia), Islamic Salvation Front (Algeria) and Jamaat Islami (Pakistan) was established. These parties were given full economic and political support during that period.

This process reached its peak during the 1980s, when thousands of militants or so-called Mujahideen were trained and sent to Afghanistan. The Jamaat Islami of Pakistan provided the main force, but the above-mentioned parties also sent their share.

The shameful alliance of imperialism and fundamentalism was exposed in Pakistan in 1977 during a movement against Prime Minister Zulfiqar Ali Bhutto. The fundamentalists started a movement against Bhutto in 1977 based on his rigging of elections. Some left and bourgeois parties also joined hands with the religious parties. Bhutto was a populist nationalist leader and an irritant for imperialism in the region. During this movement, the dollar was devalued in Pakistan. This was the only such instance in Pakistan, indicating the flood of dollars reaching Pakistan during those days. Similarly, a US official welcomed and waved to a rally of the Jamaat Islami when it passed before the American Center in Lahore while the demonstrators chanted slogans in favour of the USA.

In the Afghan war, thousands of guerrillas fought against the Afghan revolution at the command of the CIA and the Pentagon. Osama bin Laden was a hero then. But the post-Cold War situation, as mentioned, brought them into contradiction for at least three reasons. There was a political vacuum because the collapse of the USSR had hurt the trade union and the left movement in the Muslim world, as it had elsewhere. The imperialist political and economic support for the fundamentalist parties stopped. Imperialism now needed another potential enemy in place of the Communists.

In the new situation, it was in the interest of both fundamentalism and imperialism to become enemies. The fundamentalists started gaining politically by posing as anti-imperialists, while imperialism now had Islamic terrorists to fool its working class and justify big defence budgets. But is this imperialism-fundamentalism enmity real and long-lasting? No. As soon as a working-class movement begins threatening the class structure and imperialism, the old hypocritical alliance of imperialism and fundamentalism will be renewed. However, before that, because of the strong consciousness among the working classes in the West against fundamentalism, imperialism will not openly support any fundamentalist movement. There may be underhanded deals with fundamentalist governments in Afghanistan or Iran, or with Chechen rebels, but not an open alliance. Similarly, after the experience of the Taliban, imperialism would hardly support any fundamentalist movement coming to power. But it cannot be completely ruled out everywhere; because of the internal contradictions of imperialist countries, a section of imperialism may support particular fundamentalist movements while another section of imperialism opposes them. It is most likely that, unless a revolutionary situation arises, the present contradiction between fundamentalism and imperialism will suit both of them, and fundamentalists from time to time may make trouble for imperialism.

THE GROWING RELIGIOUS FUNDAMENTALISM IN PAKISTAN

The religious fundamentalists in Pakistan are once again on the full swing. They are very much encouraged by the outcome of the general elections in Pakistan. In overall, they have got over 16% of the total votes caste in the elections. But in the national assembly, they have emerged the second largest parliamentary group leaving behind Pakistan Peoples Party. Thanks to the support of the conservative Muslim League Nawaz MLN that their nominee for the prime minister Fazal Rehman got 86 votes while PPP trailed behind with 71 votes. The pro military Muslim League Q group was able to fetch the needed 172 votes for the Prime Minister lot.

The upsurge in the fundamentalist support was witnessed on 19th November 2002 when over 70,000 turned up for the funeral of Aimal Kansi in Quetta Baluchistan. This was the largest ever funeral in the whole history of Baluchistan. Aimal, body was brought from US where was awarded the death sentence after found guilty of killing two CIA officers in 1993. Till his last breath, he was very much proud of what he has done to the American imperialism. He has become another hero of the fundamentalists after Assama Bin Laden.

Another sign of the growth in religious fundamentalism was seen on 24th November when activists of Lashkar Tayaba, the banned religious group in Pakistan took over for six hours two temples in Jammu district of Indian held Kashmir. The incident resulted killing of the two and 10 more in the struggle to re-hold the temples by the Indian forces. There have been more incidents like this during the week in Kashmir resulting over 20 deaths mainly of Indian army men. This is no incident. The leader of Lashkar Tayaba Hafiz Saeed was released last week in Pakistan. The Pakistan authorities would not accept at Lahore High Court only a month before that he is held up with them. ? Withdraw your writ petition if you want your husband to be released? Was the message of the intelligence agencies to the wife. Later the wife of Hafiz Saeed was forced to withdraw her write petition. Hafiz Saeed as brought to his hometown after being held for over a year and was house arrested. Lahore High Court declared the move as illegal. Since his release on 18th November, he has addressed many thousands in several cities of Punjab. At Faisalabad, the third largest city of Pakistan, he spoke to over 50,000 who came to greet him after his release. Many women threw their children in the air and begged him to take them for Jihad. ? Jihad can not be stopped by any mean,? he declared at the meeting.

Lashkar Tayaba was the main religious group promoted by the military intelligence of Pakistan during the nineties to carry on jihad in the Indian held Kashmir. Many youth were provided the military training at camps set up by the group in different parts of Pakistani held Kashmir. "Suicidal missions are the only way forward to further the message of Jihad" was the main philosophy of the group training. The 11th September 2001 changed the priorities of the military intelligence. The Lashkar Tayaba was asked to wind up the camps. The leader was kidnapped. The military intelligences thought that it would be all over by these actions. That is been proved all wrong. The ghost of religious fundamentalist propped up by the military intelligence is out of control and is in a process of changing its colour. From pro military group, it is fast becoming an anti military group in Pakistan.

In the eighties, the religious fanatics were very closely linked with American imperialism. In the nineties, they left them on their own. From the beginning this century, the fanatics have taken roots among the general consciousness of the masses in Pakistan as an anti imperialist force. ?It is war between Islam and American infidels,? says Samee-ul-Haq, one of the main leaders of MMA, the religious political alliance in Pakistan. He was also the main supporter of the Talban regime.

While in the nineties, the American imperialism has left them on their own but not the major part of the establishment in Pakistan. They wanted to use them against their traditional rival Indians. They had also the illusions that a stable regime in Afghanistan would give them access to the markets of the Central Asia. So the formation and the support for Talban were the main priorities. All that changed with 11th September.

The crushing of Talban in Afghanistan by bombing of US imperialism has not curbed the spread of religious fundamentalism. It has spread in a different form in Pakistan at present. Leon Trotsky, the architecture of the Soviet revolution of 1917 in Russia, once quoted ?You can not crush the will of the masses to change the society?.

The will of the most of the masses to change the society has not emerged, as was the case in the past, through the left forces in the region. Rather through the religious sentiment. The general elections in Pakistan held on 10th October gives some glimpse how they have emerged as a serious political force in Pakistan. The fundamentalist united in one main group called Mutehida Majlas Ammal MMA (United Action Forum) won the most seats in two provinces. They took considerable votes in all other constituencies. But the most alarming fact was their support in the two major cities, Lahore and Karachi. At Lahore, they won three national assembly seats out of 13 and in Karachi, a neck-to-neck fight against the MQM, the immigrant mass force. MMA got 5 out of 20 seats in Karachi but it was very closely defeated in all the other 15 seats. MQM fetched 12 in the end. The MMA anti US rhetoric, which played a seminal role in wooing voters elsewhere in the country, played important part in their victory. But their campaign in Karachi was also centered on the issues like health and education. Mayer belonging to MMA already rules the local government in Karachi. MMA captured 29 out of 35 National and 52 out of 99 provincial assembly seats in North West Frontier Province (NWFP). In Baluchistan, it got 6 out of 13 National and 14 out of 51 provincial seat. In over all, MMA got nearly 3.2 millions votes. While the main bourgeoisie party MLQ got 7.3 millions. PPP fetched the most votes, nearly over 7.4 million votes. The total vote caste in Pakistan was over 28.9 millions. MMA got over 52 per cent of its seats in the low turnout areas. The fragmentation and disenchantment of the secular vote coupled with increased mobility and motivated election campaign by the MMA are definitely factors that cannot be ignored.

The conservative Muslim League, the main bourgeoisie party in Pakistan was split on the question of the support for military. A large part of it went to support the military rule while the rest under MLN supported the religious fundamentalist on the name of seat adjustment in many parts of Pakistan. MLN was taking revenge from the military as their leader Nawaz Sharif was ousted from power in October 1999. Later he was forced to leave Pakistan and now reside in Saudi Arabia. In the process, the MMA got more votes and seats than the MLN. MLN strategy made the fundamentalist stronger and is now no more close associates of the MLN. In fact MLN is fast becoming a tail end of the fanatics in Pakistan. MMA took more advantage of the lowering of the vote age from 21 to 18 than another political group. The Pakistan Talban from the Madrasas, the religious schools, over 70,000 of them in Pakistan, energetically worked for the successful campaign of the MMA. ? He who has the youth has the future,? Lenin said once. The majority of the youth is fed up with the system. "They are all corrupt", is the argument presented in most of the discussion among youth. ?Only Islamic revolution is the answer? you hear very often.

After the general election, the strategy of MMA was to give an impression to the masses of Pakistan that they are ready to shares the power but it has to be on their principal position. To attract and enlarge their support among the petty bourgeoisie, the MMA in words at least has become champions of the democracy and defendant of the 1973 constitutions.

The constitution, unanimously passed by parliament under Bhutto government, is a combination of capitalist democratic values and religious norms. The MMA also opposed the constitutional amendments by General Pervaiz Musharaf regime to give him more dictatorial powers as president. The Legal Framework Order (LFO) was announced on 21st August 2002, giving powers to president to sack the government anytime he likes and also powers for important postings in the establishment. This strategy has earned MMA some more respect and they are not seen as power hungry as was the impression of them in the past. The religious fanatics have supported most of the military regimes in Pakistan history. Only this time, they opted to remain in opposition in the center. They are more likely to form the provincial government in North West Frontier Province (NWFP) which is next to Afghanistan and could be part of the government in Baluchistan. They have not gone to share the government at the center because of their perspective to become a mass force at national level. ? Had Punjab been awoke like the other province, the Islamic revolution in Pakistan would have been complete in this elections? cried Qazi Hussain Ahmed, the main leader of the most organized Jamaat-i-Islami; JI is a decisive component of MMA. It is JI successful political strategy of forming political alliance of all the religious forces that has won the mass support for the MMA. ?They are never united and can never be united? was the main arguments of the some of the Left intellectuals during the past years. MMA has at least made these intellectuals think twice before they bring this argument against them.

The unity process of the religious forces started long before the 11th September realizing the political vacuum after the failure of the successive civilian regimes to solve any of the basic problems of the masses in Pakistan. The 10 years of successive failed regimes of PPP and MLN after the fall of the last military regime in 1988, has provided the opportunity to the religious forces to exploit the opportunity.

In 1993, the JI formed a Pakistan Islamic Front with some minor Islamic groups to contest the general elections. The PIF failed badly and fetched less than 3 per cent of the total votes. In 1995, Mutehida Jakjehti Council (United Solidarity Council) was formed mainly to address the question of sectarian killings. In 2000, almost 29 religious groups formed the Islamic Mutehida Inqilabi Mehaz IMAM (Islamic United Revolutionary Front. This was mainly to deal with the Western ideas spread by the NGOs in the NWFP and Baluchistan. Jamiat Ulemai Islam under Fazal Rehman played the main role in this group. In June 2001, MMA was founded at the initiative of Jamaat-i-Islami. After 11th September, over 40 different religious groups formed Pak Afghan Defense Counsel. The MMA all eyes are on Punjab, the most populated province with over 64% of the total inhabitants living in this rather prosperous area of Pakistan. Many villages in Punjab particularly in Southern Punjab have young martyrs. Those who have been killed Kashmir or Afghanistan. These ?sacrifices? are laying a strong foundation for the possible growth of the religious political influence on those areas where MMQ is yet to become a majority. MMA activists unlike the main bourgeoisie parties are not driven by careers or greed. They are from the middle and working class background committed for a change. Most of the elected members of MMA from NWFP are from poor background and are seen by many all the time on cycles. This is contrary to elected members of rich parties who are on land cruisers and Mitsubishi Pajeros. The class question is very much in the mind of many who have gone to support the MMA in the recent elections. In the absence of the any significant left force in Pakistan MMA have echoed the class sentiments mixed with religion.

Would the American imperialism tolerate the growing influence of religious fundamentalism in Pakistan? The Americans has so for relied on the military generals to do the dirty job. Musharaf has done it very happily. But the political situations are getting out of control. The formation of the MMA government in

NWFP will bring new contradictions between the new government in he center with the provincial government. The under ground Talban will feel easier in surfacing in NWFP under a religious government. Already new social tensions have emerged in the area. Women rights, human rights advocated in the province are under attack. ?NGO, s in these fields must wind up their offices? is the hidden message by the fanatics. The Sunday regular weekly off day will be once again replaced by Friday by the new provincial government. ?Beard is a must,? the new young elected leaders of MMA are advocating for every Muslim. ?Women must obey the Islamic norms and must cover themselves?. It is Talbanisation of Pakistani society in a different form. It is not yet advocating an open Jihad like the Alqaida did. But it is in the oven.

So NWFP and Pakistan could be the next target of all the propaganda of the US imperialism after Iraq. Any attempt by the center to dissolve or suspend the provincial government at NWFP will result in more civil war like situation. In 1974, the united government of the nationalist and religious fundamentalist was dissolved by Bhutto under the pressure of Shah if Iran, a guerilla war started in Baluchistan. Many were killed and many went to Afghanistan in exile. Now nationalist have diminished to large extent for the time being in this election, as they were seen as pro imperialists force. Many of these nationalists supported the American bombing in the false hope that it will crush the religious threat at home as well.

More dark period is heading Pakistan unless new initiatives is been taken by the Left and progressive forces to stop the onslaught of the fanatics. The handing over the recorded message of Asama Bin Laden in Islamabad to Algezeera tele network shows how things can develop in Pakistan. The possibility of the presence of Asama Bin Laden in Pakistan, the pro Talban provincial government in NWFP, the growing influence of religious fundamentalism in Punjab and Sind can force the newly elected pro Musharaf regime to take drastic actions against them. This in return will make the life of ordinary Pakistani more difficult. And it will make the ideas of religious fundamentalism more popular. Labour Party Pakistan had foreseen the recent growth of religious fundamentalism. It has declined to side with them on any issue. It has opposed the American bombing alongside with the condemnation of religious terrorism. It is adopting the policy to oppose the recently formed new civil pro Musharaf regime. The new civil regime is no change for the masses. It is the continuation of the Musharaf regime in civilian cloths. It will carry the IMF; World Bank dictated policies on the name of reform agenda. The religious fundamentalist will also oppose the reform agenda but only in words. Initially they are showing a very liberal face to the West. They have already said that privatization is a must. But under the pressure of the masses, they can make big noise against the economic exploitation of the people by the Multi nationals alongside with the social and political repressions. The hypocrisy of the fundamentalist can only be exposed with a united action of the trade unions, Left and progressive forces.

7

Rise of Muslims under the Sultanate

Muslim population in India grew with the expansion of Turkish rule in Hindustan. Its rise was due mainly to the immigration of Muslims from abroad and conversion of Hindus to Islam. There were Muslim losses also, in wars, famines, and through reconversions, and there was the growth of Muslim numbers through natural procreation in years and decades. We study all these processes, to begin with between C.E. 1200 and 1400.

THE SULTANATE PERIOD: MEDIEVAL MUSLIM EMPIRES

By the thirteenth century, the Abbasid empire was a sprawling, fragmented, deteriorating commonwealth of semiautonomous states, sultanates, governed by military commanders. It was an empire in name only. The fictional unity of the *umma,* symbolized by the caliph in Baghdad, stood in sharp contrast to the underlying reality of its political and religious divisions. Invaded and ruled successively by the Buyids and then the Seljuks, it was completely overrun in the thirteenth century by the Mongols. Pouring out of Central Asia, the armies of Genghis Khan had subjugated much of Central Asia, China, Russia, and the Near East. In 1258, the Mongol army under Hulagu Khan, the grandson of Genghis Khan, captured Baghdad, burned and pillaged the city, slaughtered its Muslim inhabitants, and executed the caliph and his family. Only Egypt and Syria escaped the Mongol conquest of the Muslim empire. In Egypt, the Mamluks ("the owned ones"), Turkish slave soldiers who served as a sort of praetorian guard, seized power from their Ayyubid (Fatimid) masters. The Mamluk sultanate successfully resisted the Mongols and ruled until 1517.

Although the destruction of Baghdad and the abolition of the Abbasid caliphate brought an end to the caliphal period and seemed to many an irreversible blow to Muslim power, by the fifteenth century Muslim fortunes had been reversed. The central caliphate was replaced by a chain of dynamic Muslim sultanates, each ruled by a sultan, which eventually extended from Africa to Southeast Asia, from Timbuktu to Mindanao, as Islam penetrated Africa, Central and Southeast Asia, and Eastern Europe. Among the principal missionaries of Islam were traders and Sufi *tariqas.* Muslim power peaked in the sixteenth century. Three major Muslim empires emerged in the midst of the many sultanates: the Ottoman Turkish empire, centered in Istanbul but encompassing major portions of North Africa, the Arab world, and Eastern Europe; the Persian Safavid empire, with its capital in Isfahan, which effectively established Shii Islam as the state's religion; and the Mughal empire, centered in Delhi and embracing most of the Indian subcontinent (modern-day Pakistan, India, and Bangladesh). Baghdad's successors were the imperial capitals of Istanbul, Isfahan, and Delhi. Political ascendancy was accompanied by a cultural florescence. As in Abbasid times, great sultans, such as the Ottoman, Sulayman the Magnificent (reigned 1520-1566), Shah Abbas in Persia (reigned 1587-1629), and the Mughal emperor Akbar (reigned 1556-1605) in India, were patrons of learning and the arts.

Rulers bore the title sultan (the one who possesses power or authority). Their rule was based on a blend of military strength and religious legitimacy. The sultan appropriated the caliph's charge as defender and protector of the faith Islamic law continued to enjoy pride of place as the official law of the state. Religion not only supported the state but was itself supported by state patronage. In particular, many of the *ulama* became part of a prosperous religious establishment that assisted the sultan's attempt to centralize and control the educational, legal, and social systems. They educated the military, bureaucratic, and religious élites in their schools, supervised and guided the interpretation and application of Islamic law in the Sharia courts, and oversaw the disbursement of funds from religious endowments *(waqf)* for educational and social services from the building of mosques and schools to hospitals and lodges for travelers. During this time, a number of the nonofficial *ulama* in particular developed strong international linkages. Many people came from far and wide to study at Mecca and Medina or at the renowned al-Azhar University in Cairo. After years of study and interchange, they returned to their home territories or took up residence in other parts of the Islamic world. *Hadith* scholars, in particular, often traveled throughout the Muslim world to study with great masters and collect traditions. Islamic learning and interpretation possessed truly international character due to the sacrifice and commitment of these learned men. As the *ulama* developed and prospered, so too did the Sufis. Their eclectic, syncretistic tendencies enabled Islam to adapt to new environments and absorb local religious beliefs and customs. This complemented and enhanced the general process of adaptation pursued by the sultans and attracted droves of converts as Islam spread at an astonishing rate in Africa, India, and Southeast Asia. Established Sufi orders, like the Naqshbandi, spread from the Indian subcontinent to the Mediterranean, becoming vast international networks, and orders sprang up and prospered.

Within the diversity of states and cultures, Islamic faith and civilization provided an underlying unity, epitomized by a common profession of faith and acceptance of the Sharia, Islamic law. Islam provided the basic ideological framework for political and social life, a source of identity, legitimacy, and guidance. A sense of continuity with past history and institutions was maintained. The world was divided into Islamic *(dar al-Islam,* the land of Islam) and non-Islamic *(dar al-harb,* the land of warfare). All Muslims were to strive to extend Islam wherever possible. Thus, merchants and traders as well as soldiers and mystics were the early missionaries of Islam. The sultan was the protector and defender of the faith charged with extending the Islamic domain. Citizenship, taxation, law, education, social welfare, defense, and warfare were based on Islam. The *ulama* in particular successfully asserted their role as protectors and interpreters of the tradition. Thus, both the political and the religious authorities, the "men of the sword" and the "men of the pen," appealed to Islam to legitimate their authority. For the majority of believers, there was a continuum of guidance, power, and success that transcended the contradictions and vicissitudes of Muslim life, and validated and reinforced the sense of a divinely mandated and guided community with a purpose and mission.

MUSLIM IMMIGRATION

In the armies of Turkish conquerors Muslims of many tribes like Khitai, Qara-Khitai, Qipchaqi, Garji and Ilbari came to India, and they stayed on here. Fakhre Mudabbir writes that the army of Qutbuddin Aibak was composed of Turks, Ghoris, Khurasanis and Khaljis. Thus in the early years of Turkish conquest immigrant soldiers comprised an important segment of Muslim population in India.

Also with the establishment of Muslim rule, batches of other types of Muslim began to arrive in Hindustan from Central Asia, Persia, African Muslim countries, and what is now called Afghanistan. India was rich and fertile as compared with their own lands, and with the extension of Muslim political power, many immigrants - soldiers and traders, saints and scholars, political refugees and adventurers, and even musicians,. jesters and jugglers - attracted by the abundance of wealth in cash and kind - began to flock to India. Only a few instances of such immigration may be mentioned. Minhaj Siraj says that people from Persia (and adjoining countries) came to India in various capacities. A great scholar of Iltutmishs reign was Amir Ruhani; he had come from Bukhara to Delhi during Chingizs upheaval. Qazi Hamid-ud-din Nagori had also come from abroad. Fakhr-ul-Mulk Isami, who had been Vazir at Baghdad for thirty years but then had suffered some disappointment, arrived in India and was appointed Vazir by Iltutmish. Nuruddin Muhammad Ufi, the author of *Jama-ul-Hikayat* had also come to Delhi during Iltutmishs reign. Their important positions in India as well as the influence of the Abyssinian slave Yaqut at the court of Raziyah shows the presence of all types of foreign Muslims in India.

During the reign of Iltutmish, the Khwarizmi prince Jalaluddin Mangbarani fleeing before Chingiz escaped into India with 10,000 followers (1221). Even after his return (1224), some of his followers stayed on here. Because of the Mongol upheaval, again, in the court of Iltutmish there arrived twentyfive princes with their retinues from Iraq, Khurasan and Mawaraun Nahr. During the reign of Sultan Balban fifteen more refugee princes arrived from Turkistan, Mawaraun Nahr, Khurasan, Iraq, Azarbijan, Persia, Rum and Sham. It appears that each one came with a large number of followers because Balban allotted for their residence a locality (*mohalla*) each. These followers comprised masters of pen and of sword, scholars and *mashaikh*, reciters and musicians. The fact that Balban had garrisoned the forts of Gopalgir, Kampil, Patiali, Bhojpur and Jalali with thousands of Afghan troops, and in the royal procession 500 Sistani, Ghori, Samarqandi and Arab soldiers with drawn swords used to march by his side, indicates that a large number of foreigners had come to India during his reign.

The Mongols, who had sent central and west Asian refugees fleeing into India, themselves occasionally arrived as invaders and stayed on in the country. Some also came, as in 1244, from the eastern passes of Tibet into Bengal. A large number of Mongols who had arrived with large armies and sought service under Balban entered into relationships with Muslim nobles. In 1291, the Mongol invader Alghu with 4,000 Mongols and their families, made India his home. The colony of these neo-Muslims came to be called Mughalpura. Under Alauddin Khalji also many Mongol captives embraced Islam and settled down in India. According to Ziyauddin Barani, many needy persons from Khurasan, Iraq, Mawaraun Nahr, Khwarizm, Sistan, Herat, and Demascus came to Hindustan to receive bounty from Muhammad bin Tughlaq. Ibn Battuta says that no new comer from Khurasan was allowed to enter into Indian territory unless he came with the express intent of staying permanently in Hindustan. Battuta was himself required to write a bond to that effect. Under Muhammad bin Tughlaq especially, foreigners are said to have been preferred to Indian Muslims on important posts and their immigration encouraged. Foreign slaves, male and female, too arrived from countries as far off as China and Abyssinia.

Then there is the fact of foreign traders and merchants coming to India in large numbers. They came both by land and by sea. Horse traders in particular came from the north-western side to Sind, Gujarat, Punjab and U.P.; some also came through the eastern passes into Bengal leading to the establishment of an Arab traders colony in Chittagong. It is said that the ancestors of Lodi rulers in India (1451-1526) were horsedealers. We hear a little later that the best houses in Delhi belonged to the Khurasani merchants, which shows that they had built permanent homes in India.

Such was the position in North India. In the South, the coastal towns like Calicut, Cochin, and Quilon, to mention only a few, were hub of international trade. There were Muslim colonies on the West Coast from very early times. Indigenous converts added to the numerical strength of foreign Muslims. How quickly their numbers swelled may be inferred from the fact that when, early in the fourteenth century, Malik Kafur marched into Maabar (Malabar), about 20,000 Musalmans who had settled in South India for long and were fighting on the side of the Hindus, deserted to the imperialists and were spared. During the thirteenth century Muslim territorial expansion was rather restricted.

Till the very end of the century Muslim rule could not extend beyond what it had been by 1206. In the fourteenth century, however, Muslim arms penetrated into the south also encouraging Muslim immigration. With the founding of the Bahmani kingdom, in the middle of the fourteenth century, the avenues of Muslim employment increased still further and so also their immigration.

What could be the quantum of this immigration? It is true that ever since the inception of Muslim rule in India we come across references to Abyssinians (Habshis), Arabs, Afghans, Mongols, Persians, people from Khurasan, Rum and Sham, and of course the Turks, as constantly arriving or living in Hindustan. It is also true that the whole atmosphere of the courts of the Turkish sultans was Islamic; all high officers were Muslim. Their repeated mention in the chronicles creates the impression that they were flooding the country. But repeated references to foreign Muslim elements may not have been due so much to their large numbers as to the important positions they held. It appears that the number of actual immigrants could not have been large. A somewhat detailed discussion on this point will follow later on.

Conversions

One important mission of Islam was to spread throughout the world. The Quran, the Hadis, the Hidaya and the Sirat-un-Nabi, the four all important works of Islam, direct the faithful to fulfill the above task. Therefore, there was never any doubt in the minds of the Muslims of their right to spread over the earth The *Hidayah* is quite explicit about the legality of *jihad* (holy war) against infidels even when they have not taken the offensive The Muslim Turks found the moral justification for their advance into India in the induction to propagate Islam.

As this could not, in the opinion of kings and warriors, be achieved without the subjugation of non-Muslims and occupation of their territory, the propagation of Islam became identical with war and conquest. In simple language, conquerors and rulers converted people by force. It has been seen that during the Arab invasion of Sind and the expeditions of Mahmud of Ghazni, defeated rulers, garrisons of captured forts, and civilian population were often forced to accept Islam. Turkish rule in Hindustan was established in the teeth of Rajput opposition and the process of war and conversion never ceased. Malik Kafur, the general of Alauddin Khalji, gave the Raja of Dwarsamudra a choice between Islam, death or payment of a huge idemnity. But under Muhammad bin Tughlaq there is greater insistence on the vanquished Hindu princes to embrace Islam. The most glaring example of this is that during the Warangal campaign all the eleven sons of the Raja of Kampila were made Muslims. Muhammad bin Tughlaq converted many people in this fashion. When Firoz Tughlaq invaded Jajnagar (Orissa), he captured the son of the Rai of Sikhar, converted him to Islam, and gave him the name of Shakr Khan.

Ordinarily, captivity for a Rajput was out, of the question; his sense of honour and the dire punishments with which he was visited in case of captivity, excluded any attempt on his part to save his life by surrender. He either died on the field of battle or escaped. But in war civilians and non-combatants could easily be taken. Kafur Hazardinari from Gujarat or Hasan (Khusrau Khan) from Malwa would not be the only ones who were captured.

They rose into prominence and therefore the circumstances of their enslavement and conversion are known. Large numbers became Musalmans in this way. Muslim rulers were keen to obtain captives in war and convert them. During warfare it was still more easy to enslave women and children. It was almost a matter of policy with the Turkish rulers and their commanders, from the very start of Muslim rule, to capture and convert or disperse and destory the male population, and carry into slavery women and children. Ibn-ul-Asir says that Qutbuddin Aibak made war against the provinces of Hind He killed and returned home with prisoners and booty. In Banaras, according to Ibn-ul-Asir, Shihabuddins slaughter of the Hindus was immense, none was spared except women and children, Who were destined to be made slaves. No wonder that slaves began to fill the household of every Turk from the very inception of Muslim rule in Hindustan. Fakhre Mudabbir informs us that as a result of the Turkish achievements under Muhammad Ghori and Qutbuddin Aibak, even a poor householder (or soldier) who did not possess a single slave (before) became the owner of numerous slaves

In 1231 Sultan Iltutmish attacked Gwalior, and captured a large number of slaves. Minhaj Siraj Jurjani writes that his (Balbans) taking of captives, and his capture of the dependents of the great Ranas cannot be recounted. Talking of his war in Avadh against Trailokyavarman of the Chandela dynasty (Dalaki wa Malaki of Minhaj), the chronicler says: All the infidels wives, sons and dependents and children fell into the hands of the victors. In 1253 in his campaign against Ranthambhor also Balban appears to have captured many prisoners. In 1259, in an attack on Hariyana (the Shiwalik hills), many women and children were enslaved. Twice Balban led expeditions against Kampil, Patiali, and Bhojpur, and in the process captured a large number of women and children. In Katehar he ordered a general massacre of the male population above eight years of age and carried away women and children.

The process of enslavement during war went on under the Khaljis and the Tughlaqs. Alauddin had 50,000 slaves some of whom were mere boys, and surely many captured during war. Firoz Tughlaq had issued an order that whichever places were sacked, in them the captives should be sorted out and the best ones (fit for service with the Sultan) should be forwarded to the court. Soon he was enabled to collect 180,000 slaves. Ziyauddin Baranis description of the Slave Market in Delhi (such markets were there in other places also) during the reign of Alauddin Khalji, shows that fresh batches of slaves were constantly replenishing them.

Muhammad bin Tughlaq became notorious for enslaving women, and his reputation in this regard spread far and wide, so that Shihabuddin Ahmad Abbas writes about him thus: The Sultan never ceases to show the greatest zeal in making war upon the infidels Everyday thousands of slaves are sold at a very low price, so great is the number of prisoners. Ibn Battutas eyewitness account of the Sultans arranging the enslaved girls marriages with Muslims on a large scale on the occasion of the two Ids, confirms the statement of Abbas.

Such was their influx that Ibn Battuta writes: At (one) time there arrived in Delhi some female infidel captives, ten of whom the Vazir sent to me. I gave one of them to the man who had brought them to me, but he was not satisfied. My companion took three young girls, and I do not know what happened to the rest. Thousands of non-Muslim women were captured in the minor yearly campaigns of Firoz Tughlaq, and under him the Id celebrations were held on lines similar to those of his predecessor. In short the inflow of such captives never ceased, and it need hardly be stated that in the hands of their Muslim masters the slaves, whether captured or purchased, became Musalman sooner or later.

The numbers thus captured and converted during the thirteenth and fourteenth centuries cannot be ascertained. But from the details given by the chroniclers, it appears that enslavement during war brought the largest number of converts and, as years passed by, they and their progency seem to have formed the bulk of the Muslim population.

Only two instances may suffice to show how this agency contributed to the rapid rise of Muslim numbers. Bashir Sultani was originally a Hindu slave. He converted to Islam and became an important nobleman (Imadul Mulk) under Firoz Tughlaq. He purchased 4,000 slaves. Later on they were all manumitted and married, and could have produced other thousands of Muslims in a single generation. Khan-i-Jahan Maqbul too was originally a Hindu. He converted, became Prime Minister, and collected 2,000 women in his harem. How many slaves he had is not known, but for such a high dignitarys household of two thousand, at least a few thousand slaves would have been required. The point to note is that all these women and slaves, if not originally Muslim, would have embraced Islam in course of time.

EARLY MUSLIMS

No integrated contemporary account exists to say how Islam spread in India. Medieval chroniclers very graphically describe the achievements of Muslim invaders, conquerors, monarchs, governors, rulers of independent Muslims kingdoms, and even officials, in effecting conversions. Muslim hagiological works, some reliable others not so reliable, too report on addition to Muslim population through conversions. But the actual numbers who embraced Islam year after year and decade after decade are not known. Some Muslims no doubt came from abroad as conquerors and soldiers. Some scholars and religious men also arrived either in the train of conquerors or at the invitation of Indian sultans or as refugees. Arabs, Abyssinians, Egyptians, Persians and Transoxionians, all find mention as having come to India to seek refuge or fortune. But the majority of Muslims are converts from Hinduism. One has, therefore, to collect facts and figures contained in stray references of medieval writers, especially Persian chroniclers, to make a conversion-cum-immigration survey to be able to estimate the growth of Muslim population.

On a study in depth on the growth of Muslim population, one is struck by the fact that as against the zig-zag pattern of rise and fall of the overall population in the medieval period, Muslim population shows only a constant rise. Another is that in spite of centuries of exertion in the field of proselytization, India has been converted only but partially. This proves that in contrast to the quick conversion of some West Asian countries,

Islam received a definite check in India. In other words, while countries like Arabia, Persia, Mesopotamia and Syria succumbed to the onslaught of Islam and converted *en masse,* the sword of Islam was blunted in India. This check provided provocation and enthusiasm to some Muslim conquerors and rulers to take to the task of proselytization with great zeal and earnestness. Their exertions and achievements find repeated mention in official and non-official chronicles and similar other works. Sometimes, besides broad facts, actual data and figures in this regard are also available. All this information is very helpful in estimating Muslim numbers as they grew from almost a cipher.

By the year 1000 of the Christian Era the extreme north-western parts of India, in the trans-Indus region, had become introduced to Islam. As early as C.E. 664, consequent upon an invasion of Kabul and its environs (which then formed part of India), by Abdur Rahman, a few thousand inhabitants are reported to have been converted to Islam. Subuktagin also fought against the Hindus and converted some of them. But all these events took place in the trans-Indus region, and we may, therefore, agree with Lanepoole in saying that in C.E. 1000 there were no Muslims in northern India east of the Indus.

However, there were some small settlements of Muslims in Sind, Gujarat and the Malabar Coast. Parts of Sind were conquered by Muhammad bin Qasim Sakifi in C.E. 712. Whichever towns he took, like Alor, Nirun, Debul and Multan, in them he established mosques, appointed Muslim governors, and propagated the Muhammadan religion. In Debul, for instance, he enslaved and converted some women and children, and left a contingent of 4,000 Muhammadans to garrison the place. In Multan about 6,000 persons were made to accept Islam. Al Biladuris narrative indicates that the people of Sawandari, Basmad, Kiraj, and Alor were converted in large numbers. The reports of Muhammad bin Qasim Sakifi to Hajjaj also point to large number of conversions. Caliph Umar wrote to some Indian rulers in C.E. 717 inviting them and their people in Sind and Hind to become Musalmans. It is said that in response to his appeal some people turned Musalmans and took Arab names.

Muhammad bin Qasim remained in Sind for a little more than three years. After his recall not only the Arab power in Sind declined rapidly, but also most of the neo-converts returned to their former faith. Al Biladuri informs that in the days of Tamim, the Musalmans (had) retired from several parts of India nor have they up to the present time (he wrote in the middle of the ninth century) advanced so far as in days gone by. When Hakim succeeded Tamim, the people of India had returned to idolatry excepting those of Kassa, and the Musalmans had no place of security in which they could take refuge. Sir Dension Ross also says that after the recall of Muhammad bin Qasim, the Muslim retained some foothold on the west bank of the river Indus, but they were in such small numbers that they gradually merged into Hindu population. In Mansura (the Muslim capital of Sind) they actually adopted Hinduism.

In brief, because of the efforts of Muhammad bin Qasim and Caliph Umar II (C.E. 717-24) some Hindus in Sind had been converted to Islam, but by the time of Caliph Hashim (724-43), when Tamim was the governor of Sind, many of these Sindhi converts had returned to Hinduism. Those who continued to retain the new faith remained confined mostly to cities, particularly Multan. After Mahmud of Ghaznis attack on Multan their number seems to have gone up for, writing in the twelfth century, Al Idrisi says: The greater part of the population (of Multan) is Musalman, so also the Judicial authority and civil administration. However, up to C.E. 1000 there were very few Muslims in Sind.

Similar was the situation in Gujarat. A military expedition was sent out in C.E. 636 from Oman to pillage the coasts of India. It proceeded as far as Thana (near Bombay). About the same time expeditions were sent to Broach and Debul, but because of Caliph Umars opposition to hazardous voyages, the policy of armed interference by sea remained in abeyance. Meanwhile commerce by sea continued. In the eighth century, Arab fleets attacked Broach and port towns on the Kathiawar coast. Thus because of armed attacks, but more so through the channel of trade, foreign Muslims and indigenous converts began to be seen in the coastal towns of Gujarat. Ibn Hauqal (C.E. 968) observes that from Kambaya to

Saimur is the land of Balhara It is a land of infidels, but there are Muslims in its cities. Masudi, who visited India in 916, found Muslims of Siraf, Oman, Baghdad and Basra at Saimur (modern Chaul) besides others who were children of Arabs born there. There were Jama Masjids at Famhal, Sindan, Saimur and Kambaya. All these facts indicate the presence of some Muslims in Gujarat. But their number was small. This finds confirmation in the fact that in an anti-Muslim riot in Cambay, in the middle of the eleventh century, only eighty persons had been killed. Besides, the population of traders is by nature and profession migratory, and the number of Muslims in Gujarat does not seem to have been large.

Arab Muslims first settled on the Malabar coast about the end of the seventh century. These Arab traders who settled down on Indias coast between the seventh and the ninth centuries were treated with tolerance by the Hindus, and so they grew in numbers. In the early part of the eighth century, Hajjaj bin Yusuf (who sent Muhammad bin Qasim to Sind), drove out some persons of the house of Hasham, and they left their homeland to settle in Konkan and the Cape Camorin area.

Refugees or traders, Muslims were welcome in India, and apparently, facilities were given to them to settle and acquire lands and openly practice their religion In course of time mosques were erected at eleven places on the Malabar coast. But till the end of the tenth century their settlements were only too small. The Muslim Arab historiog-raphers, while describing the achievements of Muslims on the Malabar Coast, exaggerate their numbers and influence. They also miss to mention the Hindu reabsorbtion of neo-converts, for Sulaiman, who visited India in the ninth century, states that he did not find any Muslims or Arabic speaking people on the western coast.

In short, while there can be no doubt about the presence of some Muslims in Sind, Gujarat and on the western coast of India, their number till the end of the tenth century was almost microscopic. In Hindustan proper, east of the river Indus, there were hardly any Musalmans in C.E. 1000.

In the year C.E. 1000 the first attack of Mahmud of Ghazni was delivered. The region of Mahmuds activity extended from Peshawar to Kanauj in the east and from Peshawar to Anhilwara in the South. In this, wherever he went, he converted people to Islam. In his attack on Waihind (near Peshawar) in 1001-3, Mahmud is reported to have captured Jayapal and fifteen of his principal chiefs and relations some of whom, like Sukhpal, were made Musalmans. At Bhera all the inhabitants, except those who embraced Islam, were put to the sword. Since the whole town is reported to have been converted the number of converts may have been quite large. At Multan too conversions took place in large numbers for, writing about the campaign against Nawasa Shah (converted Sukhpal), Utbi says that this and the previous victory (at Multan) were witnesses to his exalted state of proselytism. In his campaign in the Kashmir Valley (1015) Mahmud converted many infidels to Muhammadanism, and having spread Islam in that country, returned to Ghazni.

In the latter campaigns, in Mathura, Baran and Kanauj, again, many conversions took place. While describing the conquest of Kanauj, Utbi sums up the situation thus: The Sultan levelled to the ground every fort, and the inhabitants of them either accepted Islam, or took up arms against him. In short, those who submitted were also converted to Islam. In Baran (Bulandshahr) alone 10,000 persons were converted including the Raja.

During his fourteenth invasion in C.E. 1023, Kirat, Nur, Lohkot and Lahore were attacked. The chief of Kirat accepted Islam, and many people followed his example. According to Nizamuddin Ahmad, Islam spread in this part of the country by the consent of the people and the influence of force. Conversion of Hindus to Islam was one of the objects of Mahmud. Al Qazwini writes that when Mahmud went to wage religious war against India, he made great efforts to capture and destroy Somnat, in the hope that the Hindus would then become Muhammadans. Sultan Mahmud was well-versed in the Quran and was considered its eminent interpreter. He ardently desired to play the role of a true Muslim monarch and convert non-Muslims to his faith. *Tarikh-i-Yamini*, *Rausat-us-Safa* and *Tarikh-i-Ferishtah*, besides many other works, speak of construction of mosques and schools and appointment of preachers and teachers by Mahmud and his successor Masud. Wherever Mahmud went, he insisted on the people to convert to Islam. Such was the insistence on the conversion of the vanquished Hindu princes that many rulers just fled before Mahmud even without giving a battle. The object of Bhimpal in recommending the flight of Chand Rai was, that the Rai should not fall into the net of the Sultan, and thus be made a Musalman, as had happened to Bhimpals uncles and relations, when they demanded quarter in their distress.

There is thus little doubt that during the first thirty years of the eleventh century, consequent upon the invasions of Mahmud of Ghazni, some thousands of people were converted to Islam. During and after his raids, a few Muslim colonies were also established, some in as far off places as Kanauj, Banaras, and Bahraich. This is partially corroborated by the sixteenth century Lama historian Taranatha who refers to the settlements of the Turks in the Antarvedi or the Ganga-Jamuna Doab. He further adds that during the time of Lavasena and his successors, prior to the invasion of Odantapuri and Vikramsila (1203), the Turks had increased in number in Magadh. The traditional history of Maner and an inscription found there also corroborate the presence of Turks in Bihar in the twelfth century.

In Mahmud Ghaznis time some conversions had taken place in Gujarat and Kashmir also. Besides king Kalasa of Kashmir (C.E. 1063-89) employed some Turkish architects to erect a golden parasol over the temple of Kalasesvara. Another king of the same state, Harsha, employed Turks in his army.

In spite of his great success the sway of the descendants of Mahmud in Punjab was precarious, and their proselytizing efforts could not have been quite rewarding of success. Therefore, the number of Muslims in the Punjab, like in Sind, Gujarat and Malabar could have been only small.

Islam being a proselytizing religion, its followers have not only taken pride in winning converts but also often exaggerating the numbers of real or imaginary conversions. For instance it is claimed that in Gujarat some members of the depressed classes like Kunbis, Kharwars and Koris were converted to Islam by Nuruddin Nur Satgur. But Nur Satgurs figure is one which is more legendary than real, at least in determinable historical tenns. The story of the conversion of Cheraman Perumal of Malabar too is only legendary. There is no doubt that the invasions of Mahmud of Ghazni brought good crop of converts, and a few more Muslims were added through the influence of Muslim Mashaikh and traders in Gujarat and Malabar.

But if the example of Sind provides any precedent, it is possible that many Hindus forcibly converted to Islam during Mahmuds raids returned to their former faith. Very few Muslims were left in Sind after the decline of Arab rule. A local Karmatian Muhammadan dynasty was, however, ruling at Mansura and Multan. Mahmud of Ghazni destroyed it root and branch (1010) and Multan was deserted. There was another wave of Shia immigrants. In 1175 Shihabuddin Ghori attacked, defeated, and massacred them; and the majority of survivors began to live in the guise of Hindus.

Thus while the story of the conversions to Islam has been very enthusiastically narrated by Muslim chroniclers, the attitude of the Hindus to conversion and the endeavours of the hurriedly converted Hindus to revert to their former faith, has not been even referred to by them. Alberuni mentions a number of restrictions imposed upon reconversion to Hinduism, but he has probably noted only the extremely orthodox Brahman opinion. On the other hand *Devalasmriti* and many other similar works, lay down liberal rules for the reconversion of men and women who might have stayed with the *mlechchhas* for even as long a period as twenty years.

All this points to a keenness on the part of the converted to return to Hinduism. We know that Nawasa Shah reverted to Hinduism at the earliest opportunity. There is also the case of Rai Sal. Between Mahmud of Ghaznis death (1030) and Muhammad Ghoris invasion (1191-92) such opportunities of reconversion were many, even on a large scale. Consequently, during this Period of more than a century and a half, Muslim numbers do not seem to have shown any great rise.

About the end of the twelfth century, Muhammad Ghori established Muslim rule in India on a durable basis. When he captured Bhatinda in 1190-91, he placed in its command Qazi Ziyauddin with a contingent of 1200 horse. In 1192 he invaded Hindustan with an army of 120,000. A good number of his soldiers would have been killed in the sanguinary battle with Prithviraj. A major portion of the remainder would have stayed on in India under Qutbuddin Aibak, who must not have been left empty handed in an alien and hostile country.

Aibak entered upon a series of conquests. He despatched Ikhtiyaruddin Bakhtiyar Khalji to the East and himself captured Kol (modern Aligarh) in 1194. There those of the garrison who were wise and acute were converted to Islam, but those who stood by their ancient faith were slain with the sword. In 1195 when Raja Bhim of Gujarat was attacked, 20,000 prisoners were captured, and in 1202 at Kalinjar 50,000, and we may be sure that (as in the case of Arab conquest of Sind) all those who were made slaves were compelled to embrace the religion of the masters to whom they were allotted. Ferishtah specifically mentions that on the capture of Kalinjar fifty thousand *Kaniz va ghulam*, having suffered slavery, were rewarded with the honour of Islam. According to Ferishtah three to four hundred thousand Khokhars and Tirahias were also converted to Islam by Muhammad Ghori.

Ikhtiyaruddin Bakhtiyar Khaljis military exploits in the east also resulted in conversions to Islam. About the end of the twelfth or the beginning of the thirteenth century, he marched into Bihar and attacked the University centres of Nalanda, Vikramshila and Uddandapur, erecting a fortress at the site of Uddandapur or Odantapuri.

The Buddhist monks in these places were massacred and the common people, deprived of their priests and teachers, turned some to Brahmanism and some to Islam. Buddhism did not die out immediately or completely in Bihar. But Bakhtiyars raid on Bihar did deliver a shattering blow to Buddhism and its lost followers were gained mainly by Islam. Muslim sway extended from Varanasi through the strip of Shahabad, Patna, Monghyr and Bhagalpur district, and the presence of Muslims in this tract from early times indicates that conversions by the Khaljis warriors were common in this region. Bakhtiyar converted some tribes in the Himalayan foothills also, and one chieftain, known after his conversion as Ali the Mech, had exchanged his native beliefs for the religion of Islam.

During the time of Qutbuddin Aibak a large number of places were attacked and prisoners captured for which actual figures or written evidence are available. Figures of any conversions during campaigns to Kanauj, Varanasi (where the Muslims occupied a thousand temples). Ajmer (attacked thrice), Gujarat, Bayana and Gwalior, and the campaigns carried out right up to Bengal are not available. However, since the notices of medieval chroniclers are usually full of exaggeration where figures of the defeated or captured non-Muslims are concerned, it would be reasonable to take into consideration only those which are specifically mentioned, any exaggeration being rounded off by those which are not.

I have calculated elsewhere that the numbers converted between 1193, when the rule of the Turkish Sultanate was established at Delhi, and 1210, when Qutbuddin Aibak died, and the immigrant Muslims were about two and a half lakhs. To this may be added the Muslims converted, migrated and procreated since the days of Mahmud of Ghazni in the Punjab, U.P., Gujarat and the South.

Thus by the beginning of the thirteenth century, there surely was emergence of a Muslim community in India. Structurally, the term community connotes a geographical area with definite legal boundaries occupied by residents engaged in interrelated economic activities and constituting a politically self-governing unit. Thus in a community is discerned a process of social interaction, interdependence, cooperation, collaboration and unification and a conscious sense of belonging. In modern times means of communication have broken community boundaries. In medieval times human associations like family, relatives, marriages, class (or caste), status, and neighbourhood played a very important role in the communitys life. Even now, despite modern times, it is to be noted that in rural areas, villages and smaller cities the community process is still more closely related to family, neighbourhood, religious beliefs and institutional factors. With this conceptual framework let us examine the structure and organization of Muslim community in Hindustan in the eleventh and twelfth centuries. Punjab saw the emergence of Muslims as a local community consequent to the invasions of Mahmud of Ghazni. But for a few immigrants in the shape of Ghaznavid officers and soldiers, the bulk of Muslims were converts from the indigenous Hindu population. Similar was the case in pockets of Sind, Gujarat, Bihar and Malabar. The process of their conversion was hurried. All of a sudden the invader appeared in a city or a region, and in the midst of loot and murder, a dazed, shocked and enslaved people were given the choice between Islam and death. Those who were converted were deprived of their scalp-lock or *choti* and, if they happened to be caste people, also their sacred thread. Some were also circumcised.

Their names were changed, although some might have retained their old names with new affixes. They were taught to recite the *kalima* and learnt to say the prescribed prayers. But beyond this, to them their conversion would have meant little. These neo-converted Muslims lived, as before, among the vast majority of the Hindus. Their interest lay, as before, in co-operating with their erstwhile friends and relations rather than with their foreign co-religionists whose main occupation was to fleece the Punjab and exploit the people. They continued in their old professions and vocations; perhaps they were given some preferential treatment in the redistribution of the conquered land, but there was hardly any change in the economic set-up with its inter-dependence, cooperation and collaboration, and they remained as intimately associated with their old social and economic order as in days before they were made Musalmans. Situated as they were, some of them might have even tried and succeeded in reverting to Hinduism.

But no community, however newly born, however weakly constituted it may be, exists without a moral power which animates and directs it. After the passing of a few generations, Indian Muslims would have forgotten the circumstances of their conversion, and developed a sense of oneness amongst themselves.

With time, they would have begun to be considered a distinct and separate entity in the caste-oriented Hindu society.

The Hindus were so well organized in their social and religious life, that a few conversions had not even made a dent in their social organization, and gradually they would have tended to become indifferent towards those who had become Musalmans, thereby creating in the latter a sense of oneness and cohesion amongst themselves. As the influence of the parent society on them declined and the influence of Muslim regime and religion increased, the Indian Muslims began to look more and more to foreign Muslim ruling and privileged classes for guidance, help and protection, and in return gave them their unflinching cooperation. Much more important than the recession of Hindu moorings and the ascension of Muslim beliefs and culture in their life and thought, was the fact that these Muslims were governed by a new set of laws - the Shariat. They prayed in a different fashion now, in congregation and many times a day. They began to marry amongst themselves. The magic word of Islam would have given them a unity of thought, interest and action. Lahore and Delhi were their political and cultural centres.

PROSELYTIZING ACTIVITY OF THE GOVERNMENT

It was not during expeditions and wars alone that conversions were effected. For increasing the number of their co-religionists, Muslim rulers made free use of the governmental machinery in peace time. This was done not only by the sultans of Delhi, but by all Muslim rulers - of Bengal, Kashmir, the Deccan - wherever Muslim rule was established. Another step was the building and maintenance of mosques, Khanqahs and Sarais from government funds. The buildings were often constructed on the sites of Hindu shrines and from materials obtained by demolishing them. These mosques, besides being houses of worship and centres of Islamic learning, often provided asylum to the needy and the indigent, who could be potential converts. Sometimes conquests were undertaken with a missionary motive. Some rulers like Sikandar Butshikan of Kashmir (1394-1417) just compelled their subjects to embrace Islam.

An important and effective means of obtaining converts was economic temptation or pressure. Ibn Battuta writes that Sultan Qutbuddin Mubarak Shah Khalji (1316-1320) used to encourage Hindus to accept Islam by presenting a convert with a robe of honour and a gold ornament. In Bengal the landlords and Rajas who could not deposit land revenue by a certain date had to convert to Muhammadanism. Under Frioz Tughlaq (1351-88) the state openly became an agency of conversion. Shams Siraj Afif says that he ordered his Amils to convert Hindus to Islam. Firoz Tughlaq himself writes that he rescinded the Jiziyah to lure people to become Muhammadans, and this measure brought him groups of converts day by day from every quarter. And so were Indian Muslims made.

Contemporary sources do not supply any figures of the converted in this way. But the number of converts was perhaps not small. Ibn Battutas assertion that Qutbuddin Mubarak Shahs system of proselytization provided a convenient handle to his enemies to murder him by introducing into the palace a large number of Hindus declaring them to be possible converts, shows that Qutbuddin was accustomed to converting large numbers.

Voluntary Conversions

Side by side the efforts of the Muslim ruling classes was the proselytizing activity of the Sufi Mashaikh. It is, however, not known to what extent the Sufis were interested in the work of conversion, and this problem will be taken up in some detail at a later stage. Here it would suffice to point out that not many reliable references to their proselytizing activity are available in genuine hagiological works. They may have helped those who showed any inclination to become Muslims. Occasionally they resorted to force also to convert people.

Closely related to the work of missionaries is the question of voluntary conversions. There are some references in the chronicles about individual Hindus accepting Islam because of dissatisfaction with their own faith. Al Biladuri mentions such a case. The son of (a) king fell sick, and he desired the ministers of the temples to pray to the idol for the recovery of his son But the youth died.

Then the king attacked the temple, destroyed the idol, and slew the ministers. He afterwards invited a party of Muhammadan traders who made known to him the unity of God and (he) became a Musalman. *Tarikh-i-Tahiri* mentions the case of the younger brother of Dalu Rai, the ruler of Sind, who, of his own accord, became a Musalman and got married at Mecca. Similarly one hoping through conversion to obtain his object of love, succession to property., etc, would have voluntarily embraced Islam. Some, whose relatives had converted but who were not prepared to cut themselves off from them, too would have followed suit. These are solid assumptions, often backed by references in Persian chronicles.

The groups which converted to get relief from the Jiziyah, referred to by Firoz Tughlaq, obviously belonged to the poor, economically vulnerable sections. The few caste groups which converted to Islam did so because of professional and vocational compulsions.

Such conversions took place mostly in urban areas, especially among artisans, mechanics, handicraftsmen. The Zamorin ordered some fishermen of Malabar to convert to Islam in order to man his warships. Some urban tailors also converted. The inter-dependence of cotton-carders, weavers (*dhunia, julaha*) and tailors would have encouraged the former to embrace Islam. Beggars accepting cooked food from Muslims would have become Musalmans automatically. Butchers would have become Musalmans because their vocation found a ready and sympathetic clientele among Muhammedans.

MUSLIM LOSSES

Side by side the rise in Muslim numbers through immigration and conversion, there was decimation of Muslim population also. Muslim rulers had to struggle hard to preserve and expand their territory not only against Hindu Rajas but also against rebel Muslim governors and adventurers. There were wars against Hindu rulers for extension of Muslim political power and there were wars of succession and military campaigns against defiant Muslim governors. Withal foreign invaders had to be kept in check All these processes entailed loss of Muslim lives.

A glance at a few historical events can give an idea of this loss. During the first year of their conquest the Muslims had captured Ajmer, Hansi, Kuhram, Sarsuti, Baran, Meerut, Kol and Ranthambhor. But in 1193 the Chauhan prince Hariraja, collected a Rajput force and besieged Ranthambhor where, earlier in the year, Aibak had placed a garrison under Qivam-ul-Mulk.

The Chauhans also occupied Ajmer. In 1194 Aibak is stated to have crossed the Jumna a second time to capture Kol, but the next year again he had to proceed to the relief of its garrison. On his return to Delhi in 1195 news arrived of fresh trouble in Ajmer, which was again besieged by the Rajputs in 1195 and Aibak had to fight hard for its relief; and it could be saved only by the timely arrival of reinforcements from Ghazni. But a little later, in Ghazni itself Yaldoz was creating trouble for the Delhi Sultan. Such troubles recurred constantly; as a consequence of which there was loss of Muslim numbers. The best instances of such losses are found in the east where Bakhtiyar Khaljis ambition to conquer Tibet and China destroyed his whole army, or in the west where a Hindu king, after defeating a Muslim army shorly after the initial Turkish conquest, openly regarded himself as restoring to India its original name of *Aryavarta* by killing off the *mlechchhas*.

Sultan Iltutmishs accession (1210) was resisted by Delhi *Jandars*, and in the battle he put most of their horsemen to the sword. His wars with Yaldoz and Qubacha again must have meant depletion of Muslim numbers (fighting on both sides) continually. In his attack on Malwa - Vidisha, Ujjain etc., again some Muslim soldiers would have perished. During his attack on Nagda, the capital of the Guhilots, he was driven away by its ruler Kshetra Singh, with heavy losses.

But the most interesting fact is that Kalinjar, Gwalior, Ranthambhor and even Badaon and Kanauj, which had been captured earlier, had to be reconquered by him. Obviously the Muslim garrisons in these places had been destroyed by the Rajputs. Minhaj Siraj makes mention of a Hindu Raja of Avadh, Bartu (?) by name, under whose hands and sword (in 1226) more than 120,000 Musalmans had received martyrdom. The figure may be inflated, but the fact is important. Raziyahs rule was full of bloodshed. Armies of Delhi, Lahore, Bhatinda and Sirhind were involved in war. Karmatians had created trouble in Iltutmishs reign: in Raziyahs reign a thousand of them openly attacked the Muslims in the Jama Masjid, killed many of them and then were themselves killed. Ranthambhor had once again to be evacuated during her reign.

Since perhaps during the period of the early sultans there was not muh Indianisantion of the army, the losses in war may have been mainly of the Muslims. Alauddin Masud Shah had acquired the habit of seizing and killing his nobles (and certainly other Muslims too). In Nasiruddins reign two attempts on Ranthambhor (1248, 1259) seem to have been made without success but surely entailing loss of Muslim soldiers. In wars in Avadh, Narwar, Gwalior, Chanderi, Malwa etc., again, many Muslims would have lost their lives.

Add to these losses the Mongol killings in India. In 1241 the Mongols under Tair Bahadur captured Lahore, slaughtered the Muhammadans and made their dependents captive. Hasan Qarlugh wrested Multan in 1245 and the whole of Sindh was lost to the Mongols. It was recovered by Ulugh Khan (Balban) but the next year the Mongols again arrived under Sali Bahadur. By 1254, the territory up to and including Lahore had been taken by them. During Balbans reign the Mongol pressure increased all the more. His son, the Prince Martyr, lost his life fighting them. So great was the loss on this occasion, that according to Amir Khusrau, in Multan, in every house there was some dead to be wept for. Vigorous Mongol attacks. continued right up to the first decade of the fourteenth century; and this alone can give an idea of the losses suffered by Muslim (and Hindu) population.

Meanwhile fighting at home never ceased. Balban did not mount any major attacks on neighbouring rulers, but even so his campaigns against the rebellious Bengal and Mewat would have only added to the depletion of Muslim numbers. Barani says that the Mewatis had killed a hundred thousand of his personal troops. Jalaluddin Khaljis accession was attended by loss of Muslim lives. What Ranthambhor meant to him (and had surely meant to his predecessors too), is candidly confessed by him.

He had marched to it in 1291, but recoiled from attacking it because he feared that its capture would entail great loss of Muslim lives. With murdering Mongols he purchased peace. Although Alauddin Khalji rarely suffered defeat, yet there is no doubt that Muslim soldiers lost their lives in good numbers in the Bengal campaign, at Ranthambhor and Chittor and against the recurring terrific Mongol invasions.

The rebellions of Ikat Khan, Haji Maula and Umar and Mangu Khan too would have killed many Muslims. The massacres of neo-Muslims under Balban and Alauddin (30,000 under Alauddin only) would have added to the depreciation of Muslim numbers, and so also in Ghayasuddin Tughlaqs expeditions to Warangal, Jajnagar, Tirhut, and Bengal.

Muslim blood was shed most recklessly under Muhammad bin Tughlaq. Many of his schemes were costly in terms of human life. In the Qarachal venture 100,000 soldiers are said to have perished. Many of these, if not all, would have been Muslims. A modern historian recounts twenty-two rebellions during his reign, twenty of which were of Muslim nobles or governors, and the details point to loss of Muslim lives on both sides, rebel as well as royalist.

During the transfer of the capital, according to the same scholar, it were mainly Muslims who were asked to go from Delhi to Devagiri, and it is they who suffered and died in the exodus. Ibn Battuta and Ferishtah credit this Sultan with a love for shedding blood. Not a little of this blood was Muslim.

Under Muhammad Tughlaqs successor Firoz Tughlaq, Shams Siraj Afif notices a demographic recovery. When he wrote about it, he was naturally thinking in terms of his co-religionists also. But after Firozs death civil wars and other disorders began to decimate Muslim numbers. Most of the 180,000 slaves were done away with by his son Nasiruddin Muhammad Shah.

Muhammad Bihamad Khani gives vivid details of how with the weakening of the Sultanate, Muslim forces were repeatedly defeated and destroyed by even local rulers like Adharan and Sumer, and how Muslims were ousted from Chandwar, Bhongaon,

Bercha, Kalpi and many other places, of course with great losses in men. As the fourteenth century closed, Timur arrived to kill indiscriminately, not only Hindus but also Muslims. Muslim numbers would also have contributed their share to famines, pestilences etc. commonly recurring in India.

NATURAL GROWTH OF MUSLIM POPULATION

These contradictory scenes in Muslim demography apart, about one thing one can be sure. While the overall demographic trend of India showed a decline, the Muslim population showed only an upward tendency. It is true that many a time statistical victories through conversions were scored off by losses in wars, yet an overall rise in Muslim population - sometimes slow, at others accelerated - is clearly discernible.

The rise seems to be slow between 1200 and 1300, and rapid between 1300 to 1400. Historical facts vouch for this behaviour. Up to the end of the thirteenth century, government effort towards proselytization is hesitant.

For example, when some Ulema approached Iltutmish and suggested to him to confront the Hindus with a choice between Islam and death, Nizam-ul-Mulk Junaidi, the Wazir, replied: But at the moment in India the Muslims are so few that they are like salt (in a large dish).

If the above orders are to be applied the Hindus might combine and the Muslims would be too few in number to suppress (them). However, after a few years when in the Capital and in the regions and the small towns, the Muslims are well established and the troops are larger, it will be possible to give Hindus, the choice of death or Islam.

Iltutmish, Balban and Alauddin Khalji were practical administrators, and but for the captives and converts obtained by them during wars, they did not act as royal missionaries. Besides, with the Hindus politically strongly entrenched right up to the end of the thirteenth century, Muslim proselytizing activity had to be cautious. Alauddin subdued the major Hindu powers. With their submission and extension of Muslim political power to most parts of the country Hindu vulnerability to proselytization increased. Therefore, between 1300 to 1400, under Qutbuddin Mubarak, Muhammad and Firoz Tughlaq, conversions were effected at an accelerated pace, and immigrants also arrived in larger numbers.

In brief till about the end of the thirteenth century, Muslims in India were only like salt in a large dish. The main reason for this phenomenon was that during the whole century there was little Muslim territorial expansion. To what had been acquired by 1206, nothing substantial was added till about 1300, and all the energies of the Sultanate were concentrated on preserving their acquisitions rather than expanding territorially.

Such a situation was discouraging both to proselytization and even immigration. Even in the capital city of Delhi and its environs the Muslims were few, a fact which probably made Barani suffer from an incurable Hindu-phobia.

From the time of Alauddin Khalji, however, Muslim population in India began to grow a little faster due to the spreading of the Muslim rule to almost the whole of India after 1300, and it is rightly claimed that the establishment of the Vijayanagar Empire in the South was effected with a view to preserve Hinduism from the onslaughts of Islam.

But contemporaneously the Bahmani kingdom of the South was also founded and it took to proselytising work usual with a Muslim regime.

By the close of the fourteenth century, the situation was like this. Kashmirs introduction to Islam had started since the days of Mahmud of Ghazni. Sind and Punjab were being effectively Islamised by rulers and Mongol invaders.

In Gujarat, Deccan and Malwa also, because of the campaigns of local Muslim rulers against Hindu chiefs, the number of Muslims had risen. By the last years of the century, in the heartland of Muslim power, Muslim population of Delhi and its adjoining regions rose greatly, a fact which prompted Afif to write from the qasba of Indrapat (present Indraprastha Estate) to the Kaushik-i-Shikar (present Delhi University area), five kos apart all the land was occupied There were eight public mosques, and one private mosque The public mosques were each large enough to accommodate 10,000 suppliants. This clearly indicates a fairly large Muslim population in the capital city.

There is yet another, though indirect and not unimpeachable, evidence for this rise. Alauddin Khalji had abolished the jagir system, lest local officials should turn contumacious. But by the time of Firoz Tughlaq the number of dependable Muslims (or Muslims of a few generations) had increased, and he could safely entrust jagirs to them, and during the forty years of his reign he devoted himself to generosity and the benefit of Musalmans, by distributing villages and lands among his followers in lieu of salary.

8

The 'Problem' of Muslim Minorities

It is not difficult to see why Muslims who live as a minority in non-Muslim countries like India or Israel are seen by them as a problem. The reasons are relatively simple. Wherever Muslims live as minorities they increasingly face problems of discrimination. These are partly due to historical and political factors, partly due to the media, which have confirmed for many that Muslims are violent, unreliable and prone to anarchy.

There is another reason. Most non-Muslim countries in which Muslims live have an image of themselves as plural, tolerant, secular and modern societies. Muslims somehow challenge this image. They provoke the worst aspects of the state. In the main, instead of solving the problems of the Muslims in a manner that would be mutually beneficial, the state tends to ignore or minimize them.

In the former state of Yugoslavia the Serbs went one step further with their Muslim minority. They systematically killed them and drove them from their homes in Bosnia. The world called it 'ethnic cleansing' and did nothing. Bosnia was added to the list of recent Muslim losses. What offends Muslims living in a country as the minority community? What is the Muslim 'problem'? There are two or three things that Muslims are most sensitive about. The most important is religion. Muslims would like to be able to visit their mosques and say their prayers peacefully without interruption, without being beaten up, without being picked up for interrogation. They would also like privacy in their homes where they can lead their lives as Muslims.

They would like dignity and honour for their families - in particular, for the elderly, the women and the children. They don't like police or paramilitary forces to burst into their homes and humiliate their families. They would like some control over their lives, some perpetuation of their own customs and values, the construction and maintenance of mosques which are the focus of social and cultural life, the capacity to read the Qur'an and the chance to live as Muslims and by Muslim traditions. These include family laws, inheritance, religious holidays and religious festivals. When these are threatened, Muslims are threatened; confusion and anger ensue.

It is not difficult for non-Muslim rulers to concede these facilities to Muslims; when they have been conceded, Muslims have lived harmoniously. History confirms this. It is the modern state that creates the problem. Because the modern state is so centralized and because it often lacks imagination in dealing with its minorities, Muslims are constantly under pressure. Merely wishing for the minimum, Muslims are seen as people who demand separation and indeed secession.

There is a cultural problem also for Muslims living as a minority. Non-Muslim tourists visiting Muslim holy places cause offence by eating there and loitering, playing loud music on their radios. Islamic culture, adab, is directly challenged. In some cases there is a direct physical threat to these holy places, such as the demolition of Babar's mosque in Ayodhya, India. The inevitable religious clashes cost lives. There is also the more sinister danger of actual history being changed and Muslim culture being depicted in official textbooks as barbaric and worthless (as has happened in Spain). A discussion of Muslims as a minority is important for several reasons. First, the populations we are discussing are large. Indeed, Muslims who live as a minority constitute about a quarter of the total number of Muslims. The problem is serious because it is ongoing and does not involve only one or two countries - it is global. A list of countries in which Muslims live as a minority includes the USA, India, Russia, the UK, France, Germany, Israel and Singapore. In India alone there are said to be anywhere around 110 million Muslims. No religion in the world has so many people trapped in an alien environment as the Muslims. Neither Christians nor Jews, nor Hindus, none of the major world religions have such large numbers in so many countries dominated by people of other religions.

The second reason is that the sharpest and most brutal political confrontation is taking place in these societies. We learn of the most compelling stories of injustice and brutality as Muslims struggle for self-dignity and identity. The images that are shown on television and the reports in the press confirm for us the plight of the Muslims.

Thirdly, because of the notion of the ummah, because of the manner of the suppression of these groups, Muslims in neighbouring countries are deeply concerned. The struggle of the Kashmiris in South Asia and the Palestinians in the Middle East draws in large Muslim populations outside the national borders. The geo-political situation remains tense; indeed it can escalate to war at any time. It is well to recall that the major powers in both areas have gone to war three or four times because of these Muslim minorities. Finally, some Islamic ideas place Muslims and the non-Muslim majority on a confrontation course. The Islamic ideas are notions of the ummah, which transcends national borders, and the idea of jihad, struggle, the need to fight for a just and correct order. On the other hand, these non-Muslim nations need to respond to security requirements and geopolitical strategy. The Muslim minority is often caught in the crossfire.

There are agonizing dilemmas facing Muslims living as a minority in certain areas. In a different time, in a previous age, Muslims persecuted by the majority could do one of two things: they could pack up and leave, that is, exercise the right to adopt hijra, or they could fight for their rights, that is jihad. Today, because of the power, the highly centralized security and administrative structures and the strongly manned borders of state, neither option is really feasible. Besides, it would be difficult to exercise the option of hijra. As recent history shows us, migrant communities do not settle down easily and merge; they take a long time to do so. Any influx of large numbers of refugees causes all kinds of social and political problems to the host community, however welcoming they may have been at first.

This leaves the option of jihad. That too is difficult in our age. A small deprived minority cannot easily take on the power of the state, but it can try. The attempt to assert independence, to fight for one's dignity and culture, explains what is going on in Kashmir and Palestine. Communication between the government and these groups appears to have broken down. For Muslims the state is represented by the brute force of soldier and policeman. The women in the area live in dread of their honour and dignity being violated; young males are in the constant fear of being picked up for interrogation and torture at any time on any flimsy pretext. For the elders there appears to be no real alternative but to give free rein to the youth in their attempt to break loose and create their own response to the world, whatever the costs. It is a dreadful choice, full of pain and disruption. But when dialogue breaks down it appears to be the only one open for the time being.

An important aspect of these movements is their direct involvement with the geo-politics of the region. The Kashmir movement is seen in India as entirely a creation of Pakistan. This perception is simplistic and disregards numerous factors: the notion of the ummah which generates sympathy for Muslims wherever they are in trouble (although the Kashmiri cause has great sympathy in Pakistan, so does the Palestinian one); the strong feelings of injustice in Pakistan regarding the legality of the state of Kashmir and the manner it was incorporated into India; the many Kashmiris who have settled in Pakistan; the failure of the central government over the last decades to integrate these areas into the larger body of the nation. All these factors militate against integration. There are also certain Muslims who out of enthusiasm or ignorance or even mischief would make demands which not only clash with the state but suggest its disintegration. These create problems for everyone concerned. For instance Dr Kalim Siddiqui's call for a Muslim parliament created all kinds of doubts in Britain in the early 1990s. Did Muslims want to create their own country in Britain? Did they want independence? Were their threats of forcing an Islamic order on to Britain to be taken seriously? Such questions obviously cause resentment and anger in the majority. This reaction, when fed into the existing stereotypes about the minority, creates a sense of contempt and revulsion against it. Muslims appear to be largely unaware of this aspect of their relationship with the majority.

THE TREATMENT OF RELIGIOUS MINORITIES IN MUSLIM LANDS

Just as Muslims are 'in context' in some countries, they are 'out of context' in others-usually when they are in the minority. The 'communication' of the clothing message does suffer from distortion in these contexts. Often the 'message sent' by the wearer is not understood by the 'receiver'-or is understood to have a very different meaning from that intended (or sent) by the wearer.

This emphasises issues of identity for minorities:

- For example, a Syrian Muslim woman living in an urban area in Syria would probably emphasise neither her nationality nor her religion. For the same woman to live in Britain, however, her 'Muslim-ness', her nationality, her class and probably her gender would be matters of concern, and she would identify herself in these terms. In Muslims' encounter with non-Muslims, Islam therefore tends to become the identity marker no matter what relation the person has to Islamic rules and regulations. As long as one is part of the mainstream culture or belongs to the majority in society there is no need for an urgent quest for identity, but in minority situations these matters tend to be contrasted with mainstream opinions or characteristics and are rendered problematic.

More personally for the individual:

- Identity can be divided into smaller components. It has as much to do with how one views oneself, *i.e.*, one's self-definition, as it has to do with how one is perceived by others. In certain situations, selfdefinition might concur with others' perceptions. In minority/majority conflicts, however, others' perceptions tend to be expressed in stereotypical

> terms. Self-definitions also tend to change according to circumstances. For an Arabic-speaking Muslim woman living in a Western European country, her self-awareness of being a Muslim would be pronounced in an environment of non-Muslims.... A Muslim immigrant woman would often stress her Muslim identity in her meeting with Western researchers. Sociologically speaking she is defined as a Muslim, and according to sharia' (Islamic law) she would be defined as a Muslim.

Translated into the context of clothing, the extreme visibility of Muslim women observing Islamic clothing requirements in a Western society becomes a very big identity issue-especially if the social reactions to her dress are hostile or negative:

- As interaction between Muslims and the majority population in most of the West European countries seems to be limited, the apparent, *i.e.*, the outstanding, characteristics of the other cultural group become those which are highlighted in comparison with one's own ideological stance. Apart from judging one's own group according to an ideal standard and judging outsider groups according to their actual practice or behaviour, individuals belonging both to the majority and the minority group tend to 'stereotype themselves as well as others in terms of their common attributes as group members'.

Moreover, Roald observed that there is a tendency on both sides to perceive the other group in terms of what is most 'extreme' in relation to one's own stance or practice. Roald goes further, using the work of Kenneth Ritzen to show that the members of the majority society who have contact with immigrants and 'transmit their impressions to the rest of society' are likely to be those, such as social workers, who work with people who have problems, and this, combined with the vested interests of the media (there not being much news value in harmony or homogeneity), can lead to a harsh misrepresentation of the minority group. This is especially true if symbols (such as the Islamic head-covering), which have a very specific meaning in Islam, are divested of their accepted contextual meanings and invested with other or foreign meanings usually by those who do not cover their heads. This brings us to the 'oppositional' paradigm.

'The veil' has various connotations in a Western context:

- A Christian nun wearing a veil might be seen as an image of sincere religiosity, purity and peace, whereas a Muslim woman wearing a veil is likely to be seen as a symbol of the oppression of women and as making a political-religious statement.... The visibility of her religious commitment may be seen to signal a 'holier than thou' attitude and thus evokes resentment in the non-Muslim. In... many... Western countries, religion is regarded as a private matter. Thus a common statement is that 'religiosity should not be visible but should be a matter of the heart and one's inner-most feelings'. The acceptance of the nun's veil seems unaffected by such complaints against the Muslim woman's veil, even though both share the same visibility. Why? Because the nun represents commitment to the prevailing religious tradition. She is an 'insider'. The Muslim woman, on the other hand, symbolises the intrusion of alien beliefs contrary to the prevailing religious tradition. This response is further reinforced by negative media reports about Muslim immigrants or Muslims in other countries.

El Guindi also makes this point:

- In 1931 Crawley wrote: 'A Muslim woman takes the veil, just as does a nun'. This is an example of a very commonly presumed analogy that results from examining the veil as an object with universal (Christian) meaning. So the veil of the nun and the veil of the Muslim woman are presumed identical. Nothing can be more different than these two veils. The difference is in the meaning, the symbolism, the ideology, the constructed womanhood, and the notion of sexuality.

This 'deconstruction' of symbols leads to misrepre-sentations on both sides. 'The instrumentalist interpretation of the phenomenon of Islamic veiling has its base in the nature of in-group/out-group communication.... [W]hen Islamist women meet non-Islamist or even non-Muslim women, their discussions are governed by what they perceive are the "premises of the other". For example, in discussion with a researcher, Islamist women might try to convince her of the benefits of veiling on rational, apologetic grounds. Thus socio-political arguments might be used'. Religion is not used as a unit of analysis in the consideration of Islamic veiling. 'The analysis of Islamic veiling by social researchers must be understood in the context of recent social research which abandons religion as an instrument of analysis'.

This clearly limits the explanation. 'Secularist-bound scholars either deny the existence or ideologically dismiss any scholarly discussion of such formulations as apology'. With regard to the veil as protest, a commonly quoted instance is the act in 1923 of the Egyptian feminist Huda Shaarawi who, upon returning from a conference in Rome, '... pulled off her veil. There was a gasp of disbelief. Then by the hundreds others started removing theirs. The "de-veiling" of the Arab women had begun....'". In Shaarawi's own memoirs, however, the incident looks somewhat different: she '... drew back the veil from her face'.

This was, in fact, an act against cultural norms and separations between economic classes: 'Early Egyptian feminism not only challenged the patriarchal order but was an ideology that superseded class and was all the more threatening to the old order because it was grounded in Islam'. The 'veil' Shaarawi removed was the face veil; she did not remove her head-scarf, nor did she reject Islam. Consider this example: 'In the face of modern women who exhibit their femininity by the care they give to their bodies and clothes, Muslim women conceal their femininity behind veiling and thus present the "sacred body" against the "aesthetic" one... Veiled women, like their predecessors, enter into public life with the slogan "Personality But Not Femininity"'. The total lack of understanding of the observed phenomena here is astounding.

Furthermore:

- The overarching assumptions of feminist theory have generally been Eurocentric and ethnocentric. These limitations are especially apparent in the generally reductive and ahistorical scholarship on Middle Eastern women, which commonly centres on the harem, the veil, gender segregation, arranged marriages, clitoridectomies, and other presumed pathologies of Islamic culture.

Fundamentally, 'it is important not to overlook the fact that the hijab is worn by women out of sincere religious conviction and is primarily meant to convey piety and respect for religious values rather than political radicalism and anti-Westernism, but the potential for it to symbolise a political stand is very powerful'.

This is an interesting quote from Azzam, because she acknowledges the religious motivation. Azzam uses both the religious and the political in her debate but, by including the religious, she offers a seldom considered perspective. Clearly, Islamic teachings on modesty and normative social clothing practice in Western societies clash; but the Western paradigm sees women 'who cover' as opposing them, when in fact the 'social interaction' component of Muslim women's clothing choices is often considered a distant second to 'vertical concerns'. This point is expanded below in the discussion of sharia'. In Islam the head-covering is not a sign of celibacy, but the opposite. 'The moral standards of Islam are designed to accommodate enjoyment of worldly life, including a sexual environment. [The head-covering] posed no tension between religion and sexuality'. 'Within Islam, a woman's sexuality does not diminish her respectability. Islam in fact supports this combined image of womanhood'. This point is most easily illustrated by the fact that young Muslim women are required to observe suitable dress (including head covering) from the age of puberty.

RELIGIOUS CONFLICT

Muslim-Hindu conflict

Before 1947

The conflict between Hindus and Muslims in the Indian subcontinent has a complex history which can be said to have begun with the Jihad of the Umayyad Caliphate in Sindh in 711. The persecution of Hindus during the Islamic expansion in India during the medieval period was characterised by destruction of temples, often illustrated by historians by the repeated destruction of the Hindu Temple at Somnath and the anti-Hindu practices of the Mughal emperor Aurangzeb.

From 1947 to 1991

The aftermath of the Partition of India in 1947 saw large scale sectarian strife and bloodshed throughout the nation. Since, then, India has witnessed sporadic large-scale violence sparked by underlying tensions between sections of the Hindu and Muslim communities. These conflicts stem in part from the ideologies of Hindu Nationalism and Islamic Extremism. Since, independence, India has always maintained a constitutional commitment to secularism.

Since, 1992

The sense of communal harmony between Hindus and Muslims in the post-partition period was compromised greatly by the rasing of the Babri Mosque in Ayodhya. The demolition took place in 1992 and was perpetrated by the Hindu Nationalist Bharatiya Janata Party and organisations like Rashtriya Swayamsevak Sangh, Bajrang Dal, Vishwa Hindu Parishad and Shiv Sena. This was followed by tit for tat violence by Muslim and Hindu fundamentalists throughout the country, giving rise to the Bombay Riots and the 1993 Bombay Bombings.

Gujarat (2002)

One of the most violent events in recent times took place during the Gujarat riots in 2002, where it is estimated one thousand people were killed, most allegedly Muslim. Some sources claim there were approximately 2,000 Muslim deaths. There were also allegations made of state involvement. The riots were in retaliation to the Godhra Train Burning in which 50 Hindus pilgrims returning from the disputed site of the Babri Mosque, were burnt alive in a train fire at the Godhra railway station. Gujarat police claimed that the incident was a planned act carried out by extremist Muslims in the region against the Hindu pilgrims. The Bannerjee commission appointed to investigate this finding declared that the fire was an accident.

In 2006 the High Court decided the constitution of such a committee was illegal as another enquiry headed by Justice Nanavati Shah was still investigating the matter.There was widespread communal violence in which Muslim communities suffered. In these riots, the role played by chief minister of Gujarat, Narendra Modi, and some of his ministers, police officers, and other right wing Hindu organisation has been criticised. Narendra Modi was even accused of genocide. In 2004, several Indian school textbooks were scrapped by the National Council of Educational Research and Training after they were found to be loaded with anti-Muslim prejudice.

The NCERT argued that the books were "written by scholars hand-picked by the previous Hindu nationalist administration". According to *The Guardian*, the textbooks depicted India's past Muslim rulers "as barbarous invaders and the medieval period as a dark age of Islamic colonial rule which snuffed out the glories of the Hindu empire that preceded it". It was purported that the Taj Mahal, the Qutb Minar and the Red Fort — all examples of Islamic architecture — "were designed and commissioned by Hindus".

In 2010 Deganga riots began on 6 September when an Islamist mob resorted to arson and violence on the Hindu localities of Deganga, Kartikpur and Beliaghata under the Deganga police station area. The violence began late in the evening and continued throughout the night into the next morning. The district police, Rapid Action Force, Central Reserve Police Force and Border Security Force all failed to stop the mob violence, army was finally deployed. The army staged a flag march on the Taki Road, while Islamist violence continued unabated in the interior villages off the Taki Road, till Wednesday in spite of army presence and promulgation of prohibitory orders under section 144 of the CrPC.

Muslim-Sikh Conflict

Sikhism emerged in the Punjab during the Mughal period. Conflict between early Sikhs and the Muslim power center at Delhi reached an early high point in 1606 when Guru Arjan Dev, the fifth guru of the Sikhs, was tortured and killed by Jahangir, the Mughal Emperor. After the death of the fifth beloved Guru his son had taken his spot Guru Har Gobind who basically made the Sikhs a warrior religion. Guru ji was the first to defeat the Mughal empire in a battle which had taken place in present Sri Hargobindpur in Gurdaspur After this point the Sikhs were forced to organise themselves militarily for their protection.

Later in the 16th century, Tegh Bahadur became guru in 1665 and led the Sikhs until 1675.

Teg Bahadur was executed by the Mughal Emperor Aurangzeb for helping to protect Hindus, after a delegation of Kashmiri Pandits came to him for help when the Emperor condemned them to death for failing to convert to Islam. At this point Aurangzeb had instituted forceful conversions for which they would charge citisens with various accusations granting them to have charges and execution waved off if they converted this led to a high increase of violence between the Sikhs and Hindus as well as rebellions of Aurangzeb's empire.

This is an early example which illustrates how the Hindu-Muslim conflict and the Muslim-Sikh conflicts are connected. After which Guru Gobind Singh and the Sikhs helped the next successor of the throne of India to rise who was Bahadur Shah Zafar for certain period of time good relations were maintained some what like they were in Akbar's time until disputes arose again. The Mughal period saw various invaders coming into India through punjab with which they would loot and severely plunder. Better relations have been seen by Dulla Bhatti, Mian Mir, Pir Budhu Shah, Pir Bhikham Shah, Bulleh Shah. In 1699, the Khalsa was founded by Guru Gobind Singh, the last guru. A former ascetic was charged by Gobind Singh with the duty of punishing those who had persecuted the Sikhs. After the guru's death, Baba Banda Singh Bahadur became the leader of the Sikh army and was responsible for several attacks on the Mughal empire.

He was executed by the emperor Jahandar Shah after refusing the offer of a pardon if he converted to Islam. The decline of Mughal power during the 17th and 18th centuries, along with the growing strength of the Sikh Confederacy and later, the Sikh Empire, resulted in a balance of power which protected the Sikhs from more violence. The Sikh Empire was absorbed into the British Indian empire after the Second Anglo-Sikh War of 1849.

Massive population exchanges took place during the Partition of India in 1947, and the British Indian province of Punjab was divided into two parts, and the western parts were given to the Dominion of Pakistan, while the eastern parts were given to the Union of India. 5.3 million Muslims moved from India to West Punjab in Pakistan, 3.4 million Hindus and Sikhs moved from Pakistan to East Punjab in India. The newly formed governments were completely unequipped to deal with migrations of such staggering magnitude, and massive violence and slaughter occurred on both sides of the border. Estimates of the number of deaths range around roughly 500,000, with low estimates at 200,000 and high estimates at 1,000,000.

Muslim-Christian Conflict

In spite of the fact that there have been relatively fewer conflicts between Muslims and Christians in India in comparison to those between Muslims and Hindus, or Muslims and Sikhs, the relationship between Muslims and Christians have also been occasionally turbulent. With the advent of European colonialism in India throughout the 16th, 17th and 18th centuries, Christians were systematically persecuted in a few Muslim ruled kingdoms in India.

Anti-Christian Persecution by Tippu Sultan in the 17th Century

Perhaps the most infamous acts of anti-Christian persecution by Muslims was committed by Tippu Sultan, the ruler of the Kingdom of Mysore against the Mangalorean Catholic community from Mangalore and the erstwhile South Canara district on the southwestern coast of India. Tippu was widely reputed to be anti-Christian. The captivity of Mangalorean Catholics at Seringapatam, which began on 24 February 1784 and ended on 4 May 1799, remains the most disconsolate memory in their history. The Bakur Manuscript reports him as having said: *"All Musalmans should unite together, and considering the annihilation of infidels as a sacred duty, labour to the utmost of their power, to accomplish that subject."*

Soon after the Treaty of Mangalore in 1784, Tippu gained control of Canara.

He issued orders to seize the Christians in Canara, confiscate their estates, and deport them to Seringapatam, the capital of his empire, through the Jamalabad fort route. However, there were no priests among the captives.

Together with Fr Miranda, all the 21 arrested priests were issued orders of expulsion to Goa, fined ₹2 lakhs, and threatened death by hanging if they ever returned. According to Thomas Munro, a Scottish soldier and the first collector of Canara, around 60,000 of them, nearly 92 per cent of the entire Mangalorean Catholic community, were captured, only 7,000 escaped. Francis Buchanan gives the numbers as 70,000 captured, from a population of 80,000, with 10,000 escaping. They were forced to climb nearly 4,000 feet (1,200 m) through the jungles of the Western Ghat mountain ranges. It was 210 miles (340 km) from Mangalore to Seringapatam, and the journey took six weeks.

According to British Government records, 20,000 of them died on the march to Seringapatam. According to James Scurry, a British officer, who was held captive along with Mangalorean Catholics, 30,000 of them were forcibly converted to Islam. The young women and girls were forcibly made wives of the Muslims living there. The young men who offered resistance were disfigured by cutting their noses, upper lips, and ears. According to Mr. Silva of Gangolim, a survivor of the captivity, if a person who had escaped from Seringapatam was found, the punishment under the orders of Tippu was the cutting off of the ears, nose, the feet and one hand.

The Archbishop of Goa wrote in 1800, *"It is notoriously known in all Asia and all other parts of the globe of the oppression and sufferings experienced by the Christians in the Dominion of the King of Kanara, during the usurpation of that country by Tipu Sultan from an implacable hatred he had against them who professed Christianity."* Tippu Sultan's invasion of the Malabar had an adverse impact on the Syrian Malabar Nasrani community of the Malabar coast. Many churches in the Malabar and Cochin were damaged.

The old Syrian Nasrani seminary at Angamaly which had been the center of Catholic religious education for several centuries was razed to the ground by Tippu's soldiers. A lot of centuries old religious manuscripts were lost forever. The church was later relocated to Kottayam where it still exists to this date. The Mor Sabor church at Akaparambu and the Martha Mariam Church attached to the seminary were destroyed as well.

Tippu's army set fire to the church at Palayoor and attacked the Ollur Church in 1790. Furthernmore, the Arthat church and the Ambazhakkad seminary was also destroyed. Over the course of this invasion, many Syrian Malabar Nasrani were killed or forcibly converted to Islam. Most of the coconut, arecanut, pepper and cashew plantations held by the Syrian Malabar farmers were also indiscriminately destroyed by the invading army. As a result, when Tippu's army invaded Guruvayur and adjacent areas, the Syrian Christian community fled Calicut and small towns like Arthat to new centres like Kunnamkulam, Chalakudi, Ennakadu, Cheppadu, Kannankode, Mavelikkara, etc., where there were already Christians. They were given refuge by Sakthan Tamburan, the ruler of Cochin and Karthika Thirunal, the ruler of Travancore, who gave them lands, plantations and encouraged their businesses. Colonel Macqulay, the British resident of Travancore also helped them.

His persecution of Christians also extended to captured British soldiers. For instance, there were a significant amount of forced conversions of British captives between 1780 and 1784. Following their disastrous defeat at the battle of Pollilur, 7,000 British men along with an unknown number of women were held captive by Tipu in the fortress of Seringapatnam. Of these, over 300 were circumcised and given Muslim names and clothes and several British regimental drummer boys were made to wear *ghagra cholis* and entertain the court as *nautch* girls or dancing girls.

After the 10 year long captivity ended, James Scurry, one of those prisoners, recounted that he had forgotten how to sit in a chair and use a knife and fork. His English was broken and stilted, having lost all his vernacular idiom. His skin had darkened to the swarthy complexion of negroes, and moreover, he had developed an aversion to wearing European clothes. During the surrender of the Mangalore fort which was delivered in an armistice by the British and their subsequent withdrawal, all the Mestizos and remaining non-British foreigners were killed, together with 5,600 Mangalorean Catholics. Those condemned by Tipu Sultan for treachery were hanged instantly, the gibbets being weighed down by the number of bodies they carried. The Netravati River was so putrid with the stench of dying bodies, that the local residents were forced to leave their riverside homes.

Muslim-Buddhist Conflict

In 1989 there was a social boycott by the Buddhists of the Muslims of Leh district. The boycott remained in force till 1992. Relations between the Buddhists and Muslims in Leh improved after the lifting of the boycott, although suspicions remained.

MODERN TRADITIONS FOR WOMEN

If you live in the West, or in a westernised country, it's often difficult to wear traditional Muslim clothing. You may feel as if everyone is staring at you, which defeats the purpose of women's Muslim clothing: to allow women to be modest and discreet. However, there are ways to maintain tradition and still be modern and ordinary enough to satisfy modesty.

The hijab is vital to the Muslim woman. It covers her hair for modesty's sake, and it gives her a constant reminder to be pure in the name of God. The hijab is the only unusual requirement of a woman's dress. The Quran specifies that a woman should be modest and cover everything but her face and hands; it does not specify that you should wear abaya and veil, which is guaranteed to make you stand out in Western society. That leaves a lot of leeway.

When you wear hijab in public, be cheerful and matter-of-fact about it; don't allow anyone to embarrass you. If you aren't comfortable wearing hijab in public, try wearing a chiffon scarf or something similarly modern-looking to cover your hair. Wearing hijab and ensuring nothing shows but your hands and your face are enough to satisfy Muslim restrictions in clothing if you are a woman; but some women, even in the West, choose to veil their faces with the bashiya and the niqab. And though it's not necessary according to the Quran, many women also choose to wear black because it's so traditional a colour for outer women's clothing in Muslim countries.

Physical Modesty

The concept of modesty is addressed in Islamic teachings from many angles. In physical terms, modesty is connected with the awra', an Arabic term meaning 'inviolate vulnerability' or 'what must be covered' and consisting of the private body parts of a human being.

For men, the awra' is from the navel to the knee. For women, the awra' is more extensive and a more complicated matter entirely. A woman's awra', with respect to men outside her mahrem and non-Muslim women, consists of her entire body, with the exception of her face and hands.

There are twelve categories of mahrem and these people may see a woman's 'hair, ears, neck, upper part of the chest, arms and legs. Other parts of her body, such as the back, abdomen, thighs and two private parts, are not to be exposed before anyone, man or woman, excepting her husband'.

Some scholars have also ruled that a woman's awra', with respect to other Muslim women, is 'the area between her navel and knee'. We may consider the areas of awra' as 'navel to knee' for men, and 'women's whole bodies excepting her face and hands'. In practical terms, this means that these areas of the body are not to be shown to anyone except the spouse (or, if necessary, a doctor) and, in the case of women, it refers to what she must cover when in public-not when she is at home or with her family members in a private area.

As a result of the awra' concept, Muslims are very physically modest, and many ahadith relate to situations where modesty should be observed:

- The Messenger of Allah saw a man washing in a public place without a lower garment. So he mounted the pulpit, praised and extolled Allah and said: Allah is characterised by modesty and concealment. So when any of you washes, he should conceal himself.

Marriage as an act of Modesty

Marriage is encouraged in Islam, and marriage is seen as the 'completion' of every human being as well as an act that protects modesty. 'In general Muslims regard marriage as an essential of life.... The family, whether the extended or the nuclear family, is considered to be the main institution of society'. 'Marriage is worship by which man completes half of his deen'.

Two ahadith relating to this are:

1. Whoever Allah blesses with a righteous woman then He has assisted him with half of his deen, then let him fear Allah with regard to the other half.
2. O young people! Whoever among you can marry, should marry, because it helps him lower his gaze and guard his modesty, and whoever is not able to marry, should fast, as fasting diminishes his sexual power.

In Islamic teaching, the only permissible (halal) intimate physical contact between a man and a woman occurs within marriage. Any other intimate contact is forbidden (haram). Obviously, legal marriage comes with responsibilities and rights for both parties, and these are also clearly addressed in the teaching.

Haya' as a Form of Faith

Modesty is also considered an important part of faith.

As it says in these ahadith:

- Faith consists of more than 60 branches. And haya is a part of faith.
- Avoid being naked, for with you are those who never leave you...; so observe modesty before them and honour them.

The reference to 'those who never leave you' may seem odd but, as the religious writer Karen Armstrong notes, Muslims have a very pervasive 'God-consciousness', which makes them ever aware of the 'unseen' and the omnipresence of Allah. This focus on Allah and, as a consequence, the afterlife, makes for a very different way of looking at the world from that most common in Western societies.

Speech, Thought and Action

Humility and a lack of verbosity are other forms of modesty and are highly valued as these four ahadith illustrate:

- Modesty and inability to speak are two branches of faith but obscenity and eloquence are two branches of hypocrisy.
- Modesty is part of faith and faith is in Paradise, but obscenity is a part of hardness of heart and hardness of heart is in Hell.
- Indecency disfigures everything and modesty (haya) enhances the charm of everything.
- Coarse talk does not come into anything without disgracing it and modesty does not come into anything without adorning it.

For these reasons, such acts as swearing, lewd speech or connotation, showing off, watching intimate acts on television or in movies or performing them in public and the like are contrary to Islamic teaching.

Obviously protecting one's modesty requires knowing what that means in Islam and then taking self-disciplinary steps to do so:

- An Islamic principle is that if something is prohibited, anything which leads to it is likewise prohibited. By this it means Islam intends to block all avenues to what is haram (prohibited). For example, as Islam has prohibited sex outside marriage, it has also prohibited anything which leads to it or makes it attractive, such as seductive clothing, private meetings and casual mixing between men and women, the depiction of nudity, pornographic literature, obscene songs and so on.

9

Muslim Women

Like women from other communities, Muslim women are differentiated across gender, class, caste and community and are subjected to the interface between gender and community within the Indian social, political and economic context. After five decades of independence majority of Muslim women are one of the most disadvantaged, least literate, economically impoverished and politically marginalized sections of Indian society. Islamic Scholars argue that Islam treats both men and women as equals and cite verses from Quran to prove their argument. They say that in the Holy Quran the doctrine of human equality including sex equality is comprehensively stated and give following verse as an example :

"O people be mindful (of your duty) to your Lord. Who created you from a single being and created its mate of the same (kind) and spread from these two, many men women".

Besides the above mentioned verse, there are a number of other verses which enshrines equality of status and rights for both men and women. However, it is interesting to note that Quran at the same time places husband above the wife. This is reflected in the following verse. "Wives shall with justice have rights similar to those as against them, although husbands are a degree above them".

However a few Muslim Scholars project two tier model of society where men have superiority over women in certain spheres of life particularly in political and economic activities. Despite the claim that Quran bestows equal status and rights on both men and women, the reality is different if one examines the existential conditions of Muslim women both in the middle east, and in other Eastern Countries including India with substantial Muslim population.

In these countries the Muslim women have lower status than their men and do not enjoy equal rights both in the family and outside. In India, as elsewhere the inferior status of women is probably due to the restrictions placed on their role and confined to the role of mother and wife and further based on conventional pattern of sexual division of labour. Moreover, the rules and restrictions placed on women are guided by existing notions of Islam and becomes difficult for the women to break away from the shackles of both religion and tradition.

Abida Samiuddin and R.Khanam (2002) states that it is a matter of great sorrow that Islam came to India in its bigoted farm specially with purdah which became the prominent hallmark of feudalism with high status and respectability. Its enforcement became so pervasive that women found without a veil was ruled as shameless and outside of decent society. If one examines the status of Muslim women in India during the period of Muslim rule they were treated as lower in status and even not considered full persons. After the disintegration of Muslim rule, particularly the Mughal empire, even the upper class Muslim women got degraded.

During the British period the system of modern education was introduced, though there was some initial hesitation among the Muslims to go for modern education, ultimately the community accepted the necessity of modern education but only for men. Even today this trend of denying modern scientific education to Muslim women by their own community prevents the creation of critical consciousness among the Muslim women to fight for their own status and rights. No doubt women's education in India has made considerable progress and even Muslim parents are showing some interest to educate their daughters along with their sons. Still their progress is painfully slow because of their seclusion and life of submission.

Another important factor is the use of purdah by the women and majority of them accept this as custom and tradition. Once this custom was prevalent among the upper class Muslims and but today it has caught up with lower class and poor Muslims. It is treated as a mark of prestige. The social and psychological restrictions associated with purdah continue to operate hindering their socio and educational progress and hitting at their economic independence. But there are indications that the inroads of education and modernisation are influencing the Muslim women also. In metropolitan areas rigorous use of purdah has been relaxed to a certain extent. Young school and college going girls and women working in white collar jobs leave the houses with purdah but after reaching the destination remove it.

The Institutions of marriage and family among the Muslims discriminate against women. Unlike among Hindus and Christians, marriage among Muslims is not a sacrament but a contract which is called "Nikah". The main objective of 'nikah' is procreation and legalisation of children. The only substantial factor in favour of Muslim women at the time of their marriage is the payment of 'Mehr' by the bridegroom to the bride which would become the personal property of the bride. However, Muslim law discriminates women in marriage. For example, a man can have as many as four wives while women cannot have more than one husband and a Muslim man can marry a non Muslim women but vice-versa is not permitted. It is reported that largest number of bigamous marriages are found among Indian Muslims and also a man abandoning his first wife without divorce and secure another wife is also common among Indian Muslims. This method is followed to avoid payment of maintenance allowance (dower) to the abandoned wife. The Muslim law gives unlimited right of divorce to the husband. It is an arbitrary power of divorce. Husband's can divorce their wives at any time without giving any reason by uttering 'Talaq' three times. Now a days it has became a fashion for the Muslim men to divorce their wives through telephone and e-mails. If a Muslim wife wants a divorce from her husband, she can only have it on the grounds of impotency and cruelty of her husband.

The structure of Muslim family, it is observed is not conducive to women's freedom. The stumbling blocks are purdah and the joint families where women are sequestered behind the doors preventing them to mix freely with other non-Muslim women. No doubt as per the Islamic scripture one of the objectives of marriage is procreation but their reproduction is controlled by their husbands and other family members indicating she has very little freedom either to space her reproduction or to put an end to it. Of course, this observation applies to non-Muslim women also in the country. Socio-political reasons on the question of identity creates many problems and restrictions in the sphere of reproduction among the married Muslim women. Even in the sphere of production the Muslim women are treated as non producers despite the fact they shoulder the whole responsibility of domestic work in their families. Not only this, Muslim women are also traditionally engaged in a few household industries which does not require their going out for work, still they lack economic independence and access to education, this is an important cause for their lower status and lack of initiative to fight for their rights.

Maintenance of Muslim divorced women has become a controversial issue in India as reflected in the case of Shah Bano in 1985. Shah Bano a Muslim divorced women, approached the apex court for maintenance for her life from her former husband. The supreme court in its judgement applying Criminal Procedure code Section 125 accepted her appeal and delivered the judgement in her favour. The Muslim leadership in India objected to the judgement as it goes against the Muslim law, according to which a divorcee can get maintenance only for the 'Iddat' period (i.e., a period of waiting for 3 months after divorce is pronounced). The Muslim leaders felt that the Supreme Court has no right to go against the Muslim law. The Government of India conceding to the opinion of the Muslim leaders enacted a bill in the Parliament in 1986 and according to this Act, the Muslim law on the maintenance of divorced woman was restored back. Tahir Mahamood (2006) writing on Muslim personal law vis-a-vis the status of Muslim women says that Muslim women are being treated as secondary members in the Muslim community because of distorted and misinterpretation of Muslim law by its own scholars and elites. According to Tahir Mahamood "Muslim womens unfettered freedom of choosing a life-partner by their free will, negotiating the terms of a proposed alliance, maintaining their independent identity and rights during marriage, walking out of an irretrievably broken marriage without any hassles, and enjoying unrestricted ownership of all property that comes to their hands by inheritance or other wise, are some of the salient features of Muslim law.

Three distinct opinions are being expressed on the status of Muslim women in India. One opinion says that Islam and Islamic law has nothing to do with present disadvantaged status of Muslim women. This view stresses that the status of Muslim women is similar to that of in other caste women in the country, the most important reason being poverty and illiteracy. The second view is that Islam imposes many restrictions on its women and gives higher status to the men and concentrates power in the hands of men. The third view is that Islamic law treats both men and women as equals but unfortunately the Islamic scholars and religious leaders are misinterpreting the Islamic law giving the men power over the women.

However it may be mentioned that all is not lost in the case of Muslim women. Many educated Muslim women have come forward in the country to fight against the gender discrimination in the community. Human rights groups in general and those among the Muslims in particular started examining the status of Muslim women and fighting for to put an end to gender discrimination. There are a number of Muslim and non-Muslim associations in the Country trying to increase the literacy standards of the Muslim women believing that education would equip them to fight for themselves. Gradually secular education as against Madarasa education is being preferred both for the boys and girls. Educated Muslim women entering into white collar jobs both in public and private sectors has become quite common. But progress achieved so far in the upliftment of Muslim women is meagre and requires concerted efforts from all the groups like Governments, Muslim elites, Muslim women activists etc.

Various Departments/Ministries of Government both Central particularly Ministry of Women and Child Development and State are implementing various development programmes such as awareness programmes, health and nutrition, vocational training cum production centres, micro credit to self help groups for starting income generating activities, girls hostels for students, working women hostels etc., for the welfare of women.

STATUS AND ROLE

The concept status and role have been widely used by social scientists to understand the position of an individual or a group in the society. According to Linton (1936) status means a position in a social system occupied by designated individuals and the role means the behavioural patterned expectations attributed to their status. Both status and role are derived from culturally defined expectations of behaviour patterned and inherent relationships which Merton (1957) calls as the social structure. The term status also signifies the culturally ascribed roles to the individuals and even to the groups which have to be played according to the cultural norms. The concept of status and role also connotes the notions of rights and obligations of superordination and subordination in relation to power, authority and grading. When making attempt to study the status of women in any society or community three dimensions are usually examined. They are: 1) the traditional method of assessing the roles of women in relation to the men, 2) the extent of actual control enjoyed by the women over their own lives and 3) their role in decision making process within their families and outside.

The status of women is a complex question and has to be studied as an integral part of the socio-economic structures in which the women live and it cannot be dissociated from it. Changes that have taken place in her position is part of the socio-economic structures in which the women is a part. The changes that take place in her position is a part of the process of transformation of traditional societies. In the past, womens position was based on custom which carried the sanction of generations of practice and tradition behind it. Though it is mentioned by scholars on Indian society that during the Vedic period Indian women enjoyed equal status and equal rights along with the men, the fact remains that if we look into the history of Indian Society women never enjoyed equal status along with men and also many traditions and customs go against them curtailing some of their rights. In the contemporary Indian society despite legislation, women empowerment programmes and growth of women and feminist movements, still the Indian women do not enjoy equal status on par with the men and their rights are curtailed. They are still treated as chattals, exploited and abused.

Many social scientists have observed that progress and development of a country depends on the status of its women, meaning if the status of women is low the country's progress and development will be retarded and on the otherhand if the status of women is high and equal to that of men there will be rapid progress and development. The examples cited are the Eastern Countries for lower status of women and retarded progress and the Western Countries for higher status of women and rapid progress and development. Because the progress and development of a country or a society is related to and depend on the status of its women the question of women's status today has acquired great importance throughout the World. Further the human rights movements have gained momentum questioning lower status accorded to women and to other disadvantaged groups.

Apart from religion, patriarchy seems to have played a major role in treating the women as having lower status or ranking them secondary to men. Religious texts are quite often quoted as a basis for legitimising lower status of women. A women is relegated to the roles of wife, mother, as well as care taker of the house, etc., These roles of women are idealised in every society and the socialisation process internalises these ideals in the minds of the people. It is unfortunate that over the ages, women themselves believed in their lower status comparing themselves to their men. The lower status of women denies them access to resources, education, and even to health facilities. They are being exploited both by the men and the society. Even looked from the angle of human rights, traditionally men have rights and women have duties. Majority of the women in Third World Countries including India are not aware of their rights and even if a few are aware they are not empowered to exercise these rights.

The Present Study

This report is based on the field work carried out among the Muslim women of three districts in Andhra Pradesh. The study focuses its attention on the status of Muslim women of three categories i.e., 1) illiterate and non-beneficiaries, 2) Muslim women beneficiaries (Government as well as NGO programmes for economic progress) and 3) educated and white collar employed Muslim women. It is a comparative study of the status of the above mentioned three groups of women as perceived by the women themselves. The perception of the above mentioned category of women on their status was examined in relation to their marriage and family, divorce, purdah, adoption of small family norm, decision making in the families, voting behaviour and political participation etc. In addition, the opinion of Muslim men from some of the families of respondents is also incorporated in this report.

Three types of sample groups as mentioned above were selected on the assumption that the illiterate group because of lack of education will be less conscious about their status and they will have conforming attitudes towards some of the Muslim traditions determining the status of women in the community. In the case of beneficiary sample it was assumed that they will better exposed to the outside society because of their income generating activities, as a result of accessing micro credit. Added to this beneficiary women at least some of them are members of SHGs and have undergone training programmes as well as participating in the meetings of the SHGs. Hence it was assumed that this group is likely to have more consciousness about their status and also non conformative attitude to a certain extent towards aspects which determine to the status of women in the community. The third group was selected again assuming that because they are educated employed, they will be critically conscious about their status in particular and that of Muslim women in general. This group is likely to have modern attitude and non conformist behaviour when compared to other 2 sample groups. The present study is a cross section study among the Muslim women of Andhra Pradesh and makes an effort not only to examine the present status of Muslim women but also to understand the impact of education and employment as well as income generating activities on the direction of the change among Muslim women in Andhra Pradesh.

Methodology

Andhra Pradesh state is divided into 3 cultural regions namely Coastal Andhra, Telangana and Rayalaseema. One district with highest concentration of Muslim population from each of the above regions was selected for the study i.e. Guntur district from Coastal Andhra, Nizamabad district from Telangana and Kurnool district from Rayalaseema. Secondly from each selected districts 3 Mandals were purposefully selected for the study. Finally the plan was to select randomly 100 Muslim women from each of the three categories for each of the three selected districts i.e., (i) Illiterate and non-beneficiary Muslim women; (ii) Muslim women beneficiary under Government and Non-Government Organisations (mostly from SHGs) and (iii) Educated and salary employed Muslim women were randomly selected for the study. But unfortunately despite best efforts of the research investigators only 225 women sample representing educated employed could be selected from the 3 districts together (Nizamabad, Kurnool and Guntur) because very few educated employed Muslim women are found in the selected mandals of these 3 districts.

Data Collection

Both primary and secondary sources were used in the collection of data for the study. Three different interview schedules were constructed to collect the information from the three selected categories of the sample respondents. Each schedule consists of questions on socio-economic and demographic characteristics of the selected sample respondents and their families as well as on various aspects related to perception of the status based on their experiences and existential conditions. Besides the above schedules, a small schedule was used to collect information from the Muslim men from the selected sample families.

In addition to the primary data, secondary data were also collected from various offices and libraries such as Commissioner and Directorate of Women and Child Development, Hyderabad, Andhra Pradesh State Minorities Finance Development Corporation, Hyderabad, Libraries of National Institute of Rural Development, Hyderabad, Tribal Cultural Research and Training Institute, Hyderabad, Institute of Objective Studies, New Delhi etc., and published articles from different journals, books etc., for the study.

Analysis of Data

The collected data was analysed for each of the sample groups by using various indicators such as age, education, income, occupation, type and size of family (economic, educational, marriage and family and political) etc., of the respondents and their families. As far as possible data were incorporated in the statistical tables to facilitate comparison of the 3 sample groups. Statistical technique i.e., simple 'percentages' were used in the analysis of the data.

Organization of Andhra Pradesh

Andhra Pradesh lies between 12°41¢ and 22°N latitude and 77° and 84°40¢ longitude. It is spread over an area of 275,068 Sq.km. The state receives rainfall from south-west monsoon as well as north-east monsoon. It is the fifth largest state in India and forms as a major link between the north and the south of India. It is the biggest and most populous state among the southern states. It is bounded by Madhya Pradesh, Chhattisgarh and Orissa in the north, Bay of Bengal in the east, Tamil Nadu and Karnataka in the south and Maharashtra in the west.

The state has red, black alluvial, laterite and coastal sandy soils. Shale and limestone landscapes are also present. The state is dotted with hill ranges from north to south, running erratically down the middle dividing it into western and eastern or coastal Andhra.

The hills form integral geographical entities of Andhra life and history. The state has two great perennial rivers, Godavari and

Krishna which spring from the Western Ghats in Maharashtra and flow eastward and joins Bay of Bengal.

The state is divided into 3 regions - Rayalaseema, Coastal Andhra and Telangana. There are 23 districts with 1200 mandals in Andhra Pradesh. The total population of Andhra Pradesh as per 2001 census is 76,210,007. Out of them 38,527,413 are males and the rest 37,682,594 are females. Total Muslim population in Andhra Pradesh is 69,86,856. The sex ratio is 978 females per 1000 males. Out of the total population of the State Scheduled Castes and Scheduled Tribe are 12,339,496 and 50,24,104 respectively. Literacy rate in the state is 61.11%. Of them, 70.3% are males, 50.4% are females. Literacy rate among the Scheduled Castes and Scheduled Tribes is 53.51% and 37.03% respectively.

Agriculture is the lifeline of the state economy, contributing over a third of its domestic product and providing livelihood for over 70% of its population. Nearly 80% of the total workers in the state are still engaged in agriculture (cultivators and agricultural labourers). Paddy, tobacco, cotton, mirchi, and sugarcane are the important crops. The State also started making important strides in the fields of information technology and biotechnology.

Kurnool

Kurnool district lies between the Northern latitudes of 14°54' and 16°18' and the Eastern longitudes of 76°58' and 79°34'. The district is bounded on the north by Tungabhadra, Krishna rivers and the district of Mahabubnagar, on the east by Prakasam district, on the west by Bellary district of Karnataka and on the south by Anantapur and Cuddapah districts. Total area of the district is 17658 Sq.km. According to Census of 2001, population of the district is 35,29,494. Out of them, 17,96,214 are males and 17,33,280 are females. Muslim population of the district is 5,72,404. Of them 2,91,577 are males and 2,80,827 are females. The district has 54 mandals, 12 towns and 915 villages. Scheduled Castes and Scheduled Tribes population of the district as per 2001 Census is 6,28,637 persons and 69,635 persons respectively. 2,712,030 persons live in rural areas and 8,17,464 are in urban areas. Literacy rate in the district is 54.43%. 2,63,390 persons are literates among the

Muslims in the district. Of them 1,62,542 are males and 1,00,848 are females. 2,35,480 persons are total workers among the Muslims in the district. Out of the total workers 1,59,943 are males and 75,537 are females. Cultivators among the Muslims are 24,047, of them 16,728 are males and 7,319 are females. Agricultural labourers among the Muslims in the district are 82,785, of them 36,944 are males and 45,841 are females.

Main languages spoken in the district are Telugu, Urdu and Kannada. Important rivers of the districts are the Tungabhadra, its tributary the Handri, the Krishna, the Kunderu and the Gundlakamma. Agriculture is the main stay of the district. Main crops produced are paddy, jowar, cotton and pulses. Kurnool has a fairly large number of agrobased units.

Guntur District

Guntur District is located in the geographical coordinates of 15-18 and 16-50 of Northern Latitude and 70-10 and 80-55 of Eastern longitude. The district is bounded on the North by Krishna river, on the South by Krishna district and Bay of Bengal. The district has a coast line of 42 Kms. comprising parts of Repalle, Nizampatnam, Nagaram and Bapatla mandals. The total geographical area of the district is 11,33,000 Ha of which 1,62,000 Ha is covered by forests. The barren and uncultivable waste land amounts for 34,000 ha. and the land put to non-agricultural use is 1,56,000 ha. The cultivable waste land is 36,000 ha. constituting 3.17% of the total geographical area. The net area sown is 6,17,000 ha.

Total population of the district as per 2001 census is 44,05,521. Of them 22,20,305 (50.40%) are males and 21,85,216 (49.60%) are females. Muslim population in the district is (2001 census) 4,87,839. Of them 2,45,622 are males and 2,42,217 are females. Out of the total population of the district 12,31,233 (27.95%) are found in urban areas and the rest (72.05%) in rural area. Of the total population, Scheduled Castes are 8,18,005 and Scheduled Tribes are 2,08,157. The density of population in the district is 389 per Sq.km. The literacy rate of the district is 62.80% as against the State literacy of 61.11%. Literacy rate in the district is 62.80%. 2,52,214 persons are literates among the Muslims in the district. Of them 1,49,451 are males and 1,02,763 are females. 2,09,590 persons are total workers among the Muslims in the district. Out of the total workers 1,45,019 are males and 64,571 are females. Cultivators among the Muslims are 14,850, of them 10,272 are males and 4,578 are females. Agricultural labourers among the Muslims in the district are 81,940, of them 36,818 are males and 45,122 are females. Main languages spoken in the district are Telugu and Urdu.

Predominant crops grown in the district are paddy, cotton, chillies, tobacco, blackgram, sesamum, greengram and redgram. An area of 58,887 ha. is under cultivation of food-crops and 2,54,600 ha. is under non-food crops.

The important river in the district is river Krishna, which traverses about 250 Kms. through the northern boundary of the district irrigating an area of 4,79,409 ha. through its two major irrigation projects namely Nagarjuna Sagar Projet and Krishna canal. Important rivulets are Naguleru, Chandravanka and Gundlakamma.

Nizamabad District

Nizamabad district, is bounded on the North by Adilabad district and on the east by Karimnagar district, on the South by Medak district and on the West by Nanded district of Maharastra State and Bidar of Karnataka State. For the administrative purpose it is divided into 33 Mandals and 3 Municipalities. The population of the district is 20.38 lakhs, of which Muslims constitute 3,38,824. Of them 1,71,621 are males and 1,67,203 are females. Population of Scheduled Castes and Scheduled Tribes in the districts are 3,48,158 and 1,65,735 respectively. Literacy rate in the district is 53.26%. 1,81,030 persons are literates among the Muslims in the district. Of them 1,03,262 are males and 77,768 are females. 1,13,831 persons are total workers among the Muslims in the district. Out of the total workers 80,016 are males and 33,815 are females. Cultivators among the Muslims are 7,631, of them 6,009 are males and 1,622 are females. Agricultural labourers among the Muslims in the district are 22,997, of them 14,366 are males and 9,631 are females. Main languages spoken in the district are Telugu, Urdu and Marathi. Nizamabad District is also predominantly agriculture and most of the population depend on cultivation and allied activities. The major crops grown in the district are paddy, sugarcane, maize, Jowar and pulses. In non command areas, green gram, blackgram and redgram are grown.

QUR'ANIC REFERENCES TO WOMEN'S CLOTHING

The word hijab is used several times in the Qur'an, but only once does it refer to women's clothing.

The two items of clothing mentioned for women are khimar (the head-veil) and jilbab (a long gown), which had not been newly introduced by Islam but were most likely already part of the wardrobe of the time.

Surat Al Nur (Qur'an 24:1) opens with the verse:

- [This is] a chapter which We have revealed and made obligatory and in which We have revealed clear communications that you may be mindful.

This ayat is understood to be referring to the content of the whole surah, which deals with the conduct of Muslims, especially that between men and women, that is obligatory (fard).

Within Surat Al Nur is an often quoted Qur'anic verse, which specifically refers to the Islamic dress code for Muslims:

- Say to the believing men that they cast down their looks and guard their private parts; that is purer for them; surely Allah is Aware of what they do. (Qur'an 24:30)
- And say to the believing women that they cast down their looks and guard their private parts and do not display their ornaments except what appears thereof, and let them wear their head-coverings over their bosoms, and not display their ornaments except to their husbands or their fathers, or the fathers of their husbands, or their sons, or the sons of their husbands, or their brothers, or their brothers' sons, or their sisters' sons, or their women... and let them not strike their feet so that what they hide of their ornaments may be known; and turn to Allah all of you, O believers! so that you may be successful. (Qur'an 24:31)

Another direct mention of suitable dress occurs in Surat Al Ahzab:

- O Prophet! say to your wives and your daughters and the women of the believers that they let down upon them their over-garments; this will be more proper, that they may be known, and thus they will not be given trouble; and Allah is Forgiving, Merciful. (Qur'an 33:59)

The Qur'an is a difficult book to understand-especially when it is in translation-but also, in its original Arabic, for modern-day native speakers. The Islamic tradition does not allow for individual interpretation of the Qur'an, and so any reference to it by someone who is not a fully trained and qualified Islamic scholar should be accompanied by a tafsir (explanation):

The Prophet said: If anyone interprets the Book of Allah in the light of his opinion even if he is right, he has erred. (Abu-Dawood, 3644)

Keeping this in mind, a well-regarded tafsir by the renowned Egyptian scholar Mohammed Ash-Sharawy shall be provided here for the verses above. The word surat, which is translated as 'chapter' in terms of Surat Al Nur (meaning the chapter of light), also means 'boundary' or 'perimeter'. So, '[t]his is a surat/chapter which We have revealed and made obligatory' (Qur'an 24:1) actually means that the whole surat or chapter is obligatory, and the contents of the chapter are bounded-from beginning to end what is contained within the chapter is obligatory. This is the only surat in the Qur'an that begins this way, and it is universally agreed by the scholars that what is contained within the parameters of this surat is obligatory. Verses 30 and 31 of this surat deal with modesty: verse 30 is directed at men and 31 at women. Here the believing women are told to 'cast down their looks' or lower their gaze-which is just what men are told to do in Verse 30. Interestingly, in Arabic idiomatic usage the image means to avoid something in your field of vision-a part of the whole of what you can see- rather than to stare at the ground as if ashamed or chastened.

The head covering should be fastened and opaque and should cover the whole chest area. The verse addresses all believing women; the explanation is that khimar-translated here as head covering-means any cover that meets the requirements of 'fastened, loose, large and covering the head, neck and chest'. The surat recognises that beauty is inherent in women and that the selective exposure of it is desirable. Similarly, what is worn under the covering should not be 'exposed' by way of sound or any other mode. Concerning Surat Al Ahzab (Qur'an 33:59), the command is oriented first to the wives, then the daughters of the Prophet (PBUH), and then to the other female believers.

This means that he does not command his nation in anything that excludes himself. The inclusion of the word 'say' proves that the command is from Allah and not from the Prophet (PBUH), because it is an unnecessary word if the Prophet just needs to convey this information to his family himself.

This reinforces that the Prophet (PBUH) is no more than the messenger; he is not the issuer of the command, just the transmitter of commands from Allah. The family of the Prophet consists of all Muslims, so the command extends to all Muslims. The word used for women here is nisa', which is a plural form; and there is no singular form from its root.

The root of nisa' is annasi', which means 'delayed', and refers to the creation of Hawa (Eve) coming after that of Adam. 'Let down upon them their over-garments' is an example of the jussive mood (which is a feature of the Arabic language), and is a command for the second person (*i.e.*, the wives, daughters and believing women).

So, the first person command was 'say' (direct to the Messenger) and the command for the second group was 'let down...'. The second part of this is a response to the first (Qur'an 22:27). The wives, daughters and other Muslim women have been commanded to cover; if they do not, a condition of iman (faith) within them becomes imperfect or deficient.

The root of the words 'let down upon them their over-garments' is dannia', which means 'low and near'. So, this section means that women's clothing should be near the ground. And aleihin (upon them (female)) means that it includes the whole body, and that it is wrapped around (the body), dropping to the ground. The 'over-garment' (jilbab) must be long and covering, and should fulfil the clothing requirements (non-transparent, loose etc.). The last part of the verse explains the wisdom behind the command: Muslim women will be known by their clothing and their modesty.

MAJORITY MUSLIM LANDS

Muslims wearing Islamic clothing are 'in context' in majority Muslim lands-there is no distortion in terms of the basic communicated meaning; the 'meaning' sent by the clothing is understood by both the 'sender' (wearer) and the 'receiver'. In a series of interviews I conducted recently in Morocco as part of my fieldwork, the basic question 'why do you cover your head?' was included in a schedule of questions for women who do so. The first and most common response was that it is fard.

This is an Arabic term which best translates as 'obligatory' (required by Allah). A similar sentiment expressed in response to this question, usually along with the response fard, was that of takwa. The term takwa is often translated into English as 'fear of Allah'. However, an 'angry God' is not how takwa is understood in a Muslim context.

First, Allah does not have human characteristics and so does not get angry or feel anger as a human does. Secondly, takwa has a double meaning, because takwa has two roots-one can be translated as 'safeguard' (it-tiqa') and one as 'power' (quwwa). So, the summary of the din from Adam until the last Prophet is 'do this and do not do that'. Take positive actions and don't take negative actions; so, as there is a negative and a positive, we take from the positive what is beneficial (power) and we push away the harmful negative (safeguard). It means that you fear what Allah has forbidden, and you need to push away the harm, and also to attract the good. This is consistent with the Islamic understanding that Allah, who is without human characteristics and is genderless, does not favour one gender over another, and gives the guidance he does as practices to be followed which are 'better for you and for them'. Therefore, wearing Islamic clothing-defined as clothing which meets the standards set out in the texts and rulings-*i.e.*, loose, covering, non-transparent, subdued, clean, neat and tidy-is an act of worship and submission to Allah.

Misunderstandings Based on Translations

It is often difficult to obtain quality translations. Translations depend on the culture, knowledge and background of the person doing the translation. For instance, hijab is not the Arabic word for 'veil'. 'It is not a recent term; but neither is it that old. It is a complex notion that has gradually developed a set of related meanings... the term had a well-defined meaning by the ninth century AD... [and] it had become part of the Arabian Arabic vocabulary in early Islam'. Amongst Muslims it is the word commonly used for the headcovering Muslim women wear, although in some countries it is used to refer to a complete ensemble that conforms to Islamic clothing rules. Both Muslim men and women are encouraged to use coverings, both as a form of protection and modesty, and also as a clear sign that they are followers of Islam:

"Hijab is derived from the root h-j-b; its verbal form hajaba translates as 'to veil, to seclude, to screen, to conceal, to form a separation, to mask'. Hijab translates as 'cover, wrap, curtain, veil, screen, partition'. The same word refers to amulets carried on one's person (particularly as a child) to protect against harm. Another derivative, hajib, means 'eyebrow' (protector of the eye) and was also the word used during the caliphal periods for the official who screened applicants who wished for audience with the caliph. The European term 'veil' (with its correlate 'seclusion'), therefore, fails to capture these nuances, and oversimplifies a complex phenomenon.

However, '[t]he Western word "veil" is "sexy" and marketable in the West. It thus tends to be overused, invariably out of or without context, in titles of books, articles, conferences, press, films and popular literature in a way disproportionate to the relative significance of the veil in Middle Eastern (Muslim) affairs, and irrespective of the quality of knowledge about the veil... the veil has come to replace the earlier obsession with "harems" and hammams (public baths).

"Harems" and hammams then, and the "veil" now, evoke a public sexual energy that early Christianity, puritanist Western culture, and contemporary elements of fundamentalist Christianity have not been able to come to terms with, comprehend, or tolerate. In the West harem/veil/polygamy evoke Islam and are synonymous with female weakness and oppression'. El Guindi has 'harems' in quotation marks, because this is another very good example of mistranslation and misrepresentation. 'Harem' is a term which evolved from the Arabic harim, referring to the women's wing of the house, a private place 'off limits' to non-mahrem men.

AN ISLAMIC PERSPECTIVE ON WOMEN'S DRESS

No subject seems to receive more attention as an issue unique to Muslims than that of women's dress. Muslims and non-Muslims alike dwell on this issue, using women's appearances to categorize others in an effort to understand them.

In some instances, the dress of the Muslim woman ends up meaning more to others than it does to the woman herself with often far-reaching political and social implications. Examining the reasons for such obsession is beyond the scope of this position paper, but deserves consideration nevertheless, as we ask ourselves why so many people are so preoccupied with the appearance of Muslim women.

Our purpose here is to at least develop a basic understanding of this issue from the point of view of the Islamic texts, that is, the Qur'an and then hadith. We are not interested in coming to conclusions that result in a set of rules on how to dress. This has been done in numerous books and articles written over the centuries, including many authored very recently. Rather, we seek to understand the spirit and focus of the original texts to get an overall sense of the message being conveyed. In general, the overriding principle that comes through is one of modesty for both men and women.

Qur'anic Text

From Yusuf Ali or Muhammad Asad translations: Say to the believing men that they should lower their gaze and guard their modesty: that will make for greater purity for them: and God is well acquainted with all that they do.

And say to the believing women that they should lower their gaze and guard their modesty; that they should not display their zeenah (charms, or beauty and ornaments) except what (must ordinarily) appear thereof; that they should draw their khimar (veils) over their bosoms and not display their zeenah except to their husbands, their fathers .... and that they should not strike their feet so as to draw attention to their hidden zeenah (ornaments). (24:31-32)

O Prophet! Tell your wives and daughters and the believing women that they should draw over themselves their jilbab (outer garments) (when in public); this will be more conducive to their being recognized (as decent women) and not harassed. But God is indeed oft-forgiving, most merciful. (33:59) And know that women advanced in years, who no longer feel any sexual desire incur no sin if they discard their thiyab (outer garments), provided they do not aim at a showy display of their zeenah (charms or beauty). But it is better for them to abstain (from this); and God is all-hearing, all-knowing. (24:60)

These are the only verses which address the issue of clothing so specifically. Clearly, the basic principle is that of modesty. The first verse emphasizes the importance of one guarding her or his modesty, lowering one's gaze in order to remain pure.

This means that, in order for women and men to have respectful relationships (such as at work or school, etc.) they must focus on modesty in their behavior. This is enhanced by dressing in a way that reinforces one's image as a modest person. It must be emphasized that behavior and appearance are both important in setting the tone of respectful interaction between men and women.

In addition, the second verse shows that the purpose of covering oneself is to "be recognized (as decent women) and not harassed." Many women who cover their hair and dress modestly do notice that men are more respectful and people are more inquisitive about their faith, so they are "recognized" not just as decent women but also as Muslims. Occasionally, women who cover their hair may also experience harassment and discrimination because of stereotyping and misunderstandings about Islam and women.

Interestingly, the Qur'an is really not that explicit about the exact definition of modest dress. By reading the Qur'anic verses above, women are advised to cover their breasts and put on their outer garments in a way that enables them to avoid harassment. In addition, women are advised not to draw attention to their "beauty" (zeenah). This term has been translated as both beauty and ornaments (as women used to strike their feet to draw attention to hidden ornaments such as ankle bracelets). Of note is that the Qur'an uses the term zeenah elsewhere, perhaps showing that in different contexts the word has slightly different meanings:

O Children of Adam! Wear your beautiful apparel (zeenah) at every time and place of prayer...(7:31)

The exact rules defining women's dress have been determined based on interpretation of these verses and incorporation of concepts established in hadith. The inclusion of a head covering is derived from interpretation of the word khimar in 24:31 above. Most translators and commentators agree that this was a loose scarf worn at the time of the Prophet (pbuh) which covered a woman's head, neck and possibly shoulders, leaving the rest exposed. Women were thus ordered to use the khimar to cover their breasts. Naturally, a woman would continue to cover her neck, head and shoulders and would then also cover her breast. This understanding of the khimar as a head-covering explains why Muslims believe that the Qur'an tells us to cover our hair. The injunction, however, regarding covering the hair in addition to everything else is implied, not specified in the Qur'an.

In addition, the verse says not to display one's zeenah except to husbands, fathers, sons, etc. except "what naturally appears thereof". Most scholars writing on the subject consider a woman's chest, hips, legs, neck (basically her whole body) as zeenah, which should thus be covered. Yet, as mentioned above, the Qur'an itself reveals that, in different settings, the word may have different implications; also, the (perhaps intentional) lack of specificity in defining zeenah may actually allow for differing interpretations based on a variety of circumstances.

Similarly, traditional interpretation considers the phrase "what naturally appears thereof" (illa ma zahara minha) to be limited to the hands, feet and face (although some feel that the face is also part of a woman's beauty and should be covered). Again, when referring to Qur'an alone, the exact determination as to what naturally or ordinarily appears is left unclear.

In the second verse (33:59), the word jilbab refers to outer garments, used to cover in a way that lends oneself to be recognized and not harassed. The jilbab was commonly understood to mean loose fitting clothing and, more specifically, a long loose dress or overcoat worn by many Muslim women today. But again, the focus of the verse is on the result, avoiding harassment and preserving one's dignity, and not on the details of the actual article of clothing.

The basic message and instruction expressed in the Qur'an is for Muslims to act modestly, dress modestly, and avoid drawing attention to oneself, especially those features that are physically attractive and perhaps enticing to the opposite sex. This applies for both men and women.

The Term "Hijab"

Literally, the word hijab means "curtain". In the Qur'an the term hijab is not used as a reference to women's clothing; rather, it was the screen behind which the Muslims were told to address the Prophet's wives. (The term is also used to describe the "screen" separating God from Moses, as he received divine revelation.) When the Prophet's wives went out, the screen consisted of a veil over their face. It does not appear that covering the face was adopted by the other Muslim women at the time since it was a special injunction for the Prophet's wives as is clear in the verses below:

And (as for the Prophet's wives) when you ask for anything you want (or need), ask them from behind a hijab (screen), that makes for greater purity of your hearts. (33:53)

O wives of the Prophet! You are not like any of the (other) women: If you do fear (God) be not too complaisant of speech, lest one in whose heart is a disease should be moved with desire: but speak with a speech (that is) just. (33:32)

Among Muslims today, hijab refers to the head scarf worn by many women. It is a term used to distinguish between women who cover their hair (muhajabat) and those who do not, even if the rest of their clothes are equally modest.

Finally, the Qur'an also talks about our clothing as something both to cover our nakedness and serve as an adornment, reflecting the beauty of God's creation. But, as in the verses above, it is behavior and attitude that are most important. Regardless of how we dress, we must have faith and taqwa, God consciousness or righteousness:

O you Children of Adam! We have bestowed libasan (clothing or raiment) on you to cover your nakedness and as a thing of beauty. But the raiment of righteousness (taqwa), that is the best. Such are the signs of God, that they may receive admonition. (7:26)

O Children of Adam! Wear your beautiful apparel (zeenah) at every time and place of prayer: eat and drink: but waste not by excess, for God loves not the wasters. (7:31)

Those are all of the verses in the Qur'an which speak to the issue of dress.

Hadith Text

The hadith also address women's (and men's) dress. The most oft-quoted hadith attributed to the Prophet (pbuh) is as follows:

Aisha said, "Asma, daughter of Abu Bakr (that is, Aisha's sister), entered upon the Apostle of God (pbuh) wearing thin clothes. The Apostle of God turned his attention from her and said, "O Asma, when a woman reaches the age of menstruation, it does not suit her except that she displays parts of her body except this and this," and he pointed to her face and hands. (Sunan Abi Dawud)

This hadith is found only in the hadith collection of Abu Dawud (no. 4095). According to Abu Dawud, it is considered weak because the narrator who transmitted it from Aisha is not known (mursal). Other hadith found elsewhere talk about not wearing see-through clothes or clothing intended for wear by the opposite sex. Also, Aisha reported that when the verse above was revealed about covering the breast (24:31), the women tore their thick outer garments to make veils. Based on the interpretation and understanding of the above verses and hadith, the scholars (namely, from the major Sunni and Shi'a schools of thought) have determined that hijab (covering from head to toe) is a religious obligation (fard). The notion of ijma'a , or consensus of scholars and or schools of thought, is a well-established component of Islamic jurisprudence from which numerous laws have been derived. Needless to say, determining exactly which scholars and which opinions qualify as "consensus" is not without controversy, a topic that needs expanded discourse among learned Muslims today.

Discussion

Without a doubt, God in His wisdom advises the believers to dress and behave in a way that elevates their status both in this life and the hereafter. Most Muslims do not view modest dress as an imposition meant to oppress either women or men. Indeed, many women who voluntarily wear hijab actually feel liberated; free from society's rules about women's looks, free from being slaves to fashion, free to reserve their beauty for their husbands and so on.

A more important question in this discussion is whether individuals, Muslim or non-Muslim, should be forced to dress in a certain way. Every society is entitled to establish minimum standards of dress (in the US, we do have limits as well, defining "indecent exposure" according to this society's norms). How those standards are enforced and to what extent individuals are punished for violations is of extreme importance in those countries which strongly regulate the dress code.

When reviewing both Qur'an and hadith, there is no precedence for how to deal with such violations; the Prophet (pbuh) or his wives and companions simply reminded others to follow the guidelines. Not a single example of violence, imprisonment, humiliation or coercion can be found during the lifetime of the Prophet (pbuh)that would imply that such practices today are consistent with his example.

The Qur'an does not spell out any punishment (hudud) for violations of a dress code. Also, in the verses outlined above, the Qur'an clearly addresses "the believing women" meaning Muslims, so that it is difficult to find an argument to justify the imposition of an "Islamic" dress code on non-Muslim women. Thus, by inference the decision to dress a certain way is left to the individual who will face the consequences for all actions in this life, to her benefit or detriment, as God sees fit.

The Qur'an also says "There is no compulsion in religion" (2:256). Those who choose to behave a certain way as a reflection of their belief in God and His message and thus accept the challenges therein are not the same as those who behave to satisfy other people or laws set in place. The freedom and ability to choose to do good make the reward that much greater.

Among many Muslims today, hijab is often equated with piety, both by those who cover their hair and those who do not. Unfortunately, too many assume that a woman who covers must naturally be more religious or conservative that one who does not. This generates expectations and pressure on Muslim women in hijab , whose behavior is held to different standards, perhaps undesired on the part of the woman. On the other hand, according to popular opinion, the Muslim woman who does not cover her hair (even if she is otherwise dressed modestly) has not quite arrived at the perceived goal of all righteous believing women. The scarf, an article of clothing, has sadly become a litmus test for a Muslim woman's faith and devotion to God. Indeed, the importance which some Muslims have attached to hijab has made some sarcastically refer to it as the "Sixth Pillar" of Islam, on par with prayer, fasting, alms-giving, pilgrimage and bearing witness to the oneness of God.

While our faith is manifested in our deeds, only God can judge our piety and righteousness. The Prophet himself (pbuh) would not venture to say who, for certain, would reach Paradise. Such knowledge is with God alone such that the judgement of one person regarding another's religiosity is totally irrelevant.

How Muslims dress is only one aspect of our identities. For many women, dressing conservatively and covering one's hair are felt to be acts of faith. Therefore, discriminating against a woman for dressing a particular way violates her freedom to practice her religion, a fundamental right cherished here in the United States. The non-Muslim community, particularly the media, needs to get beyond its own narrow one-dimensional view of the conservative dress of the Muslim woman as a sign of oppression. It is a choice that American Muslim women make, perhaps not the same as that of other women, but equally valid. Ultimately, what really matters is the attitude, behavior and demeanor of the person in question.

A Source of Division?

Among Muslims, the division and intolerance expressed regarding women's dress is one factor that impedes our growth and development as a meaningful presence in the world today. All Muslims struggle with matters of faith, identity, and community. With the pressing issues facing the Ummah today such as poverty, illiteracy, violence, warfare and other ills, we must ask ourselves if we want to be consumed and paralyzed by the issue of women's dress. Placing the burden primarily on women without calling for the accountability of men to control themselves and their sexual appetites is in violation of the spirit of the Qur'an which is about self-control and self-restraint. In addition, the extremely negative attitudes which consider women who do not cover as somehow unchaste are most egregious and unjustifiable. Wrongful accusations against a woman's honor are met unequivocally with severe consequences as mentioned in the Qur'an (24:4-20).

Only together, through cooperation, tolerance and forbearance, as exemplified by the Prophet (pbuh) can Muslims overcome the obstacles to success in this life and the hereafter that often are expressed in our attitudes towards women.

MUSLIM WOMEN'S SCENE IN INDIA AND PAKISTAN

Both in India and Pakistan, there has emerged a vast corpus of literature on gender location and construction. Particularly, in Pakistan, much of the debate on gender has revolved around what has been termed as Islamic resurgence or fundamentalism. The concrete reasons for this explanation lie in the basic ideology on the basis of which Pakistan came into being in 1947 and the issue of gender in an independent Pakistan cannot be understood apart from struggles over the state.

Immediately after independence, Pakistan had to deal with establishment of a state machinery, constitution, foreign exchange shortage, weak infrastructure and lastly resettlement of refugees, who had migrated to Pakistan at a tremendous material and personal cost. The first two and last two factors had farreaching implications for women in Pakistan. The question most pertinent facing the ruling elite was as to how Pakistan's Muslimness or its identity as distinct from a common Indian culture was to be expressed and concretized.

Further compounding the problem was the fact that, some Ulama (Muslim religious scholars and teachers concerned primarily with Islamic laws) who had been staunch opponents of the idea of Pakistan including Maulana Maudoodi, later migrated to Pakistan and were demanding the construction of Pakistan as an Islamic state. During Jinnah's lifetime this took the form of a nod to Pakistan's Muslim heritage, through the official inclusion of the term in referring to the state.

Immediately after his death, Liaqat Ali formulated the Objective Resolutions of 1949, which sought simultaneously to appease the population by promising that Pakistan would be a democratic state, in which minority rights would be guaranteed and one in which, "all Muslims would be able to build their life in accordance with the teachings and injunctions of Islam". Ulama were employed as advisors to the legislatures. Islam was made the state religion and gradually the role of the Council of Islamic ideology was strengthened.

Rather than go directly to the people for support, those in power decided to use religious ideology as a political crutch, whereby, they could garner support. The roots were thus, laid for theocracy rather than democracy. Once again, Pakistan's religious leadership was by no means united. Individuals like Ghulam Ahmad Parwiz and Maulana Shabbir Ahmad supported and provided theological justifications for Pakistan's credentials. Others including Maulana Maudoodi initially opposed it, All agreed, however, that Pakistan should have an Islamic 'Character', which meant giving primacy to particular (albeit divergent) interpretations of religious laws at the levels of the state. Indeed it was the Jamiat-ul Ulama-i-Islam that led the call for a formation of a Board of Talimat-i-Islamia (Islamic teachings), a demand granted by the Constituent Assembly's Basic Principles Committee.

This board, recommended: "The Head of the State should be a Muslim with ultimate powers... government should be run by an elite of pious Muslims chosen for their piety by the Muslim electorate... the community of Ulama should decide what legislation was repugnant to the injunctions of Holy Quran and the Sunna and was therefore, invalid... a Legislative Assembly, which they identified with the Islamic... in fact, Arabian Shura or Tribal Consultative Assembly should be empowered to demand the resignation of the Head of State in certain circumstances".

These recommendations, although turned down are significant in terms of the politics of the time and of the struggle over state ideology and its institutional framework. Critical as well is the distinction between religious elements lately co-opted by the state and those who continued to oppose it.

A schism arose within those adhering to a scripturalist position an Islam with Maudoodi and the Jamaat-i-Islami taking the most extreme positions. The fact remains that historically the struggle for women's rights in Pakistan has been one of consistent opposition from the religious orthodoxy. Beginning in 1949, just after the country's creation, with the protest over the presence of two women parliamentarians in the Constituent Assembly of Pakistan, any movement for even, minimal rights for women has encountered opposition from these forces.

"The decade of the 1980s, has truly been a decade of women of Pakistan", wrote Hamza Ahtvi. His reference was to the women's resistance to Zia-ul-Haq's military regime and its proclaimed Islamic measure that in effect downgraded women. The eighties were significant for the crystallization of Anti-Women's Rights Movement in urban Pakistan, which strongly challenged on both religious and political grounds the government's so-called

Islamization process. However, the same period also saw the entry of heavily veiled women on the public scene, who projected themselves as defenders of Islam and denounced those women questioning state initiated measures—a point.

Gender and class politics frame the current debate on women's role and position in Pakistani society. Essentially located in urban centers it has been a debate between obscurantist men from the lower middle class and the newly rich middle class with aspirations for political power and women's rights activists belonging to the professional middle and upper middle class.

Initiated by men, the debate reflects, their perception of middle and upper class women as threats to the existing order. It has led to the politicization of gender, whereby, those advocating women's emancipation are viewed as modern and as such opposed to Islam. The debate manifested through opposition of women on the basis of religion remained marginal until 1977.

Led by a small group of Ulama and Maulvis, dispersed over a number of religiously defined political parties, it failed to make much impact on the evolutionary process of women's emancipation. But it intensified after 1977, with the military government's use of religion to legitimize its rule. With the government's patronage with them, the position of male antagonists of women's rights was bolstered as were their efforts for cultural hegemony. The implementation of Hudood ordinances provided an additional avenue for expressing social and familial conflicts.

The fact, that over 50 per cent of the cases appealed to the Federal Shariat Court (FSC), were overturned, warrants the conclusion that many cases filed are brought to the courts for the purpose of exerting social control alone. Added to the normal social control mechanisms available to them, parents, husbands and guardians have been empowered by the introduction of the Hudood ordinances with the real or implicit threat of bringing criminal charges against their children and wives. Finally the implementation of the Hudood ordinance has been disproportionately skewed towards Pakistan's lower socio-economic strata. Very few middle or upper class Pakistanis have been charged with the commission of Hudood crimes. Neither of the outcomes is the fault of the courts nor of the laws, but rather is reflective of the in egalitarian structure of Pakistani society. Charles H. Kennedy in his study, "Islamization and Legal Reform in Pakistan, 1977-1987", has argued that Islamic reforms (Nizam-Mustafa) promulgated by General Zia-ul-Haq have had only a minor impact upon the legal, social and economic institutions of the state.

This observation, definitely marks a departure from the conventional interpretation, because the politicization of the process of Islamization has played a very significant role in the political environment of Pakistan during the 1980s. Zias government perceived the reforms as leading Pakistan in the direction of becoming 'truly Islamic'. Opponents of the reforms argued that the reforms were reactionary, anti-democratic and discriminatory to women. Charles Kennedy in his study, further contends that it was just rhetoric and political noise with little significance, as they were very seldom implemented. The continued vitality and relevance of the Nizam-i-Mustafa despite its 'non-implementation' can be gauged from the fact, that none of the governments, since Zia's death have made any sincere effort to repeal these laws.

The PPP election manifesto in the 1988, election pledged to eliminate inequitable practices by promising to become a signatory to the United Nations Convention on the Elimination of all Forms of Discrimination Against Women (a promise not kept); improve working conditions and prospects for women including the establishment of maternity leave (nothing was accomplished in this regard), repeal of all discriminatory laws against women (another broken promise), reform personal law to bring it in line with the demands of contemporary socio-economic realities (again a broken promise) and to take special measures to promote the literacy of women.

Again, in this regard, except for foreign donor efforts not only could the PPP government achieve any success towards promoting literacy, it had not even, made any significant effort in this direction. In 1988-89, groups such as the Women's Action Forum (WAF), Pakistan Women lawyers Association (PWLA) and a transformed

All Pakistan Women's Association (APWA), lobbied the state to introduce new laws, which would empower women. Within few months of the PPP coming to power, however, they became disillusioned as they realized they were still fighting an uphold battle.

While Benazir's government had been able to prevent the implementation of the Ninth Amendment and the Shariat Bill during its tenure, it was less successful in its attempts to repeal some of the earlier legislation passed during Marital Law, owing to the Eighth Amendment restrictions introduced in 1985, by Gen. Zia. Importantly, while the platform on which the PPP had won favoured women's empowerment, most members of the provincial and national assemblies remained entrenched in patriarchal views on women's place in society. However, Benazir government took some steps for empowering women by releasing Report of the Pakistan Commission on the 'status of women', fulfilling her promise that Pakistan would become a signatory to the United Nation's Convention on the Elimination of all Forms of Discrimination Against Women and ensuring the continued reservation seats for women in Parliament, which had expired in 1988, though none of these were finally taken.

The existence of sharp gender disparities in access to resources is usually attributed to cultural and social constraints on women's mobility. A patriarchal system continues to prevail in Pakistan, giving males power over females through control of property and household income. Rigid cultural precepts separate the sphere of activity of men and women. The typical division allocated roles within the household to women and those outside the home to men. The cultural restraints imposed on women vary considerably by ethnicity and class. In terms of ethnic group, for example, Pathans, who live mostly in the North-West frontier province and Baluchis tend to observe a more rigid division of labour between the sexes than any other groups and to impose greater social restrictions on Women. In general, however, women in the upper echelons of society do have considerable access to education and to modern sector jobs. In some way, such women have more in common with their counterparts in the developed countries than with women from the rural areas of Pakistan. An example of this distinction can be provided with an illustration of national elections held in October 1993.

The federal government had mandated separate polling stations for women, throughout the country. In cities like Lahore, Rawalpindi and Faisalabad, this was apparently enforced and women exercised the right to vote. But, elsewhere, local officials took it upon themselves to assume that women would not come to vote and the separate booths were not set up. Anita Weiss, an expert on gender studies witnessed this phenomenon, while observing the election in District Pishin in the province of Baluchistan.

This district is, inhabited largely by Pushtun tribesmen who conform to rigid codes of conduct particularly concerning gender relations. Women observe strict Purdah. The psychological state of women themselves was more pathetic alongwith the lack of polling stations. The blank looks on their faces underscored the lack of involvement with, domains outside their homes. In every instance when she spoke with a woman, waiting to vote, she invariably related that she had been brought to the polling station by a man in her family (usually a brother or father, occasionally a husband), because he wanted additional votes cast for a particular candidate.

In District Pishin women's identity card, necessary to show before being allowed to cast one's ballot, had no picture nor the woman's own name on them, in deference to local concerns regarding female seclusion. Many of the women, she observed trying to cast their votes, even did not know the names of their fathers or husbands as they used honorific terms to address them at homes. Those who could not state the name of their father or husband as listed on the identity cards were not allowed to vote. Thus, these women were not exercising their own electoral franchise, but rather being provided another ballot to be cast for the choice of their family's men. Women's conventionally limited access to anything or anyone outside their kin group, underscored by their lack of access to education and related process that enable them to gain an understanding of the ways in which external events have an effect in their lives as the status of women virtually deny them their suffrage in a democratic election. This, of course, is a larger issue that is related both to literacy and economic transformation. This example is indicative of the degree to which many women in Pakistan live very differently and certainly in an inferior legal, social and economic status from men. This also illustrates credible evidence about sex discrimination and deep rooted social prejudices against women. There is a wide gulf between what is prescribed by religion for the protection of woman and what she gets in practice.

There are about four-fifth of the rural women who participate in farm activities, such as binding of wheat sheaves, thrashing or cleaning of grains and they are usually reported as non-working members of the household. In the usual census and labour force survey data, about 5 to 10 per cent of the women are reported to be members of the civilian labour force. One reason for such underestimation by respondents, particularly males is that the Pakistani culture defines the role of the man as the prime bread-winner and provider of food and shelter. One other factor, that seems to have a strong negative association with work participation is the practice of Purdah (the seclusion of women). There is a major conflict between norms prescribed by the Islamic Religion and cultural deviations from these norms. Cultural deviations are not uniform across the whole country. They vary by such factors as the socio-economic status of the family in which a woman is born and lives, the rural urban setting, caste group, etc. Regional group studies aimed at redefining the roles and status of women need to take these conflicts and the patterns of deviation into account.

Despite some progress in the past decades Pakistan's performance in the area of female education, as reflected in literacy and enrolment rate remains extremely poor. Over two decades the primary school enrolment rate for boys rose, gradually from 59 per cent in 1985 to 61 per cent in 1995, while the rate for girls increased from 20 to 32 per cent. At the secondary school level the gender gap is considerably wider as reflected in the 1985, ratio of 34 females per 100 males. The female drop-out rate at the primary level is as high as 50-60 per cent. Gender disparities in school attendance vary widely by province and area of residence. They tend moreover to be greatest in rural parts of the country where female enrolment rates are particularly low. According to data from the 1981 Census, the relative difference between males and females in rural areas was lowest in Punjab, but much larger in other provinces, particularly the NWFP. Even in Punjab only three per cent of rural girls in the relevant age groups were enrolled in secondary school, while elsewhere, the comparable enrolment rates were about one per cent. The 1991 Census indictates that 72 per cent of the population of Pakistan resided in rural areas a fact that should be taken into account while considering the implications of these extremely low female enrolment rates. The large gender gap in schooling in rural areas has been attributed to lack of appropriate facilities for girls and in particular, to the non-availability of female teachers. Given the cultural restrictions that hold in various degrees across all regions, segregated schools with female teachers are an important prerequisite to make female education more acceptable. Where financial resources are limited, there is usually greater economic pressure to educate sons, since schooling would lead to better -employment prospects for them. Daughters are expected to stay at home rather than to seek jobs. The outcome is that in Pakistan, only a small elite ordinarily from urban areas provide their daughters with the opportunity to acquire higher education. Women belonging to professional classes of the dominant elite have over the years managed to expand themselves and present a dilemma to men.

These women have also ventured the spheres, of activity considered to be solely male dominated—they are in politics, engineering town planning, banking and computer programming and are as competent as men in their work. This explains why the, discourse in Pakistan over women's rights and their position in society has been between 'fundamentalist' men and 'non-fundamentalist' women. This perceived threat has become an imminent reality with spiralling inflation and what Hamza Alavi calls the, "crisis of the middle and lower middle class household economy". While for the poor sections of society the division between the male-female space of operation is blurred, because of the exigencies of survival (in rural areas in any case the agricultural economy cannot be sustained without joint inputs of male and female members of the household) for the urban lower and middle classes, it presents a major problem. Both men and women are placed under stress. Men have to cope with the sense of failure emanating from the inability to fulfil their primary responsibility and the concomitant psychological loss of masculinity, in other words, their identity. Women have to assume roles they are neither conditioned nor prepared for, coming from highly segregated cloistered households. They have to deal with an unfamiliar and often mixed environment as the 'outsider' in both alien and insecure world. They need a reassuring anchorage and religion provides this. Thus, if women join obscurantist fundamentalist movement, it is because the latter do respond to some of the women's needs and allay some insecurities.

This, however, is only partial explanation of 'fundamentalist' women visible in Pakistan today, a point, which has been briefly mentioned earlier. An important factor was the resistance to Zia's Islamization by women and women's organizations from the platform of Women's Action Forum (WAF). It appears that WAF's questioning of the distorted interpretation of Islam to justify legal measures, rejection of Maulvis as self-styled guardians of Islam and challenging of the patriarchal structures underlying subordination has had a greater impact than warranted by their numbers. The obscurantist have felt compelled to promote a vocal women's lobby of their own to counter WAF's activities. The Jamaat-i-Islami had responded in a similar manner in 1974- 75, when a group of left wing women students formed the Women's Front (WF) in Lahore's Punjab University. The WF was perhaps the first instance of feminist expression of women's rights, that questioned patriarchal norms. Within a short period, the Jamaat had set up a women's section of its students' wing. That was the first time that women students in the burqa, associated with fundamentalist women made their appearance. The women students' section called Islami Jamiat Talebat is now a permanent subsidiary instrument of Jamiat-i-Islami. Its activists use aggressive strong arm tactics typical of the male students wing of the Jamaat-i-Islami (Jamiat-e-Tuleba) against liberal women students. The Islami Jamiat-e-Tuleba has the dubious distinction of introducing firearms in campus and using violence in student politics.

It was therefore, not a coincidence when Majlis-e-Khawateen, a women's organization unheard of before, came out with press statements against the progressive women's demonstrators in Lahore protesting against the law of Evidence in 1983. That the Majlis has the support of Jamaat-i-Islami and the President herself became obvious over the years. Nisar Fatima, the President of Majlis was elected member of the National Assembly of 1985, on the reserved women's seat with Jamaat-i-Islami support. She was also nominated with Jamaat-i-Islami's support and nominated by Zia to the council of Islamic ideology (an advisory body responsible for examining existing laws for their Islamic content and proposing new laws), as well as the 1984, Commission on the Status of Women. The Commission was composed of 13 women and three men besides ex-officio members. Of the women at least ten belonged to the professional elite class. Despite hand-picked by a military government, the Commission came out with an excellent report on women's oppression. It examined the prevalent social and cultural norms, critically reviewed the proposed and promulgated Islamic laws concluding that the latter has been a setback to women. Nisar Fatima, the only fundamentalist representative of the Commission wrote a dissenting note. Her basic disagreement was with the commission's perspective. For instance, she felt that the discussion on legal issues be undertaken by religious scholars only and that instead of demanding equal opportunities emphasis should have been on the importance of the family, responsibility of the male as earner, head of household and decision maker, women's place in the house as obedient wife and caring mother, strict segregation and women's exclusion from professions that do not need them. The unexpected candidness of the report and its obvious variance from the official policies resulted in it being shelved, the only part that received publicity was Nisar Fatima's dissenting note. In June 1990, Khawateen Nifaz-e-Shariah Mahaz (Women's Enforcement of Shariah Front) was formed with the blessings of the movers of the Shariah Bill following its adoption in the Senate in May 1990. A Nifaz-e-Shariat Conference was organized by the front in the same month, where 'fundamentalist' women rejected democracy as an imported ideology and made womens rights activists as well as the then Prime Minister Benazir Bhutto targets of its attack. Any action or statement of WAF or any non-fundamentalist women's organization had invited an immediate and vitriolic response from women of the religious right accusing the former of being westernized, alienated and non-religious.

The exploitation of Islam for political gains is not a new phenomenon in Pakistan. Successive rulers have repeatedly, used religion in an attempt to win political legitimacy and mobilize public support. But, such moves have never worked. Nawaz Sharif, like a true successor of Zia pursued the same retrogressive course, which served to fuel religious fanaticism. Religious minorities feel that with the enforcement, of the Shariat laws, they would become the targets of widespread discrimination and persecution. The worst dangerous aspect of the government's. Islamization policy is that it could fuel religious fanaticism and sectarian conflict, which will further fragment the social fabric. Women's right's organization and minorities particularly have vehemently opposed the Shariah Bill.

Now, it remains to be seen what is the dictator Perwez Musharraf's policy's impact on religious freedom in the country. However, there is little likelihood of soft peddling on religious matters by Musharraf, since he is closely associated with different religious fundamentalist groups.

WOMEN IN ISLAM

Financial Responsibilities

The Faith of Islam is a faith of mercy and compassion and it protects the Muslim woman from having to work for her sustenance and guarantees her subsistence so that she would not be subject to the evils that are frequently related to drudgery and toil. She is accordingly not required to earn her living and this is the responsibility with which men are charged.

If a Muslim girl or woman is not married, her expenditure is the religious and legal obligation of her male relations, according to the laws of jurisprudence. If there is no male relative financially capable of supporting her, her livelihood is the solemn obligation of the treasury of the state. This ruling is applied in all stages of a girl's or woman's marriage which include the period during which the girl or woman prepares for marriage, the duration of her marriage, and in the event of divorce the period during its procedures. Men are thus charged with the financial support of women in all the stages of women's lives.

During the period preceding marriage, the Faith of Islam imposes upon the prospective husband a number of financial obligations concerning his forthcoming marriage without incurring any expense upon the bride's family. The husband's responsibilities include the dowry and the preparation of the marital home.

The Laws of Inheritance

The Faith of Islam ordains that the males' share of inheritance be greater than the females' share, in most cases. The male inherits double the share of the female when the inheritance is shared between sons and daughters or between brothers and sisters. A widow's share of her husband's estate is half a widower's share of his wife's estate. Occasionally the father's share of his deceased son's estate is more than the mother's share. Nevertheless the mother's and father's share of the inheritance is sometimes equal if they have a son or more than two daughters.

The difference in the shares of the inheritance between males and females is based upon the financial responsibilities with which men alone are religiously charged. Men's financial obligations according to the laws of Islam are infinitely greater than women's financial responsibilities. A man is the head of his family and its custodian who is financially responsible for the maintenance of all its members if he is married and will be responsible for his family in the future if he is a bachelor. Islam also charges men with the financial support of their relatives whereas a Muslim woman, however wealthy she may be, is not even financially responsible for herself.

The laws of inheritance in Islam are accordingly fair in so far as they grant males a greater share of the inheritance, in order to enable them to fulfil their financial responsibilities with which Islam has charged them. On the other hand Islam does not burden Muslim women with any financial obligations.

The Islamic laws of inheritance for women are fair and generous for she is granted half the share of her male counterpart's inheritance although she is not obliged to spend any of it supporting herself or her family, since that is the religious duty with which her husband, father, brother, paternal uncle or her nearest male relative is charged.

There are certain cases when males and females are granted equal shares of the inheritance as is the case when the family consists of a father, a mother, a son and two or more daughters. If one of the children dies, the father and the mother each inherit one sixth of the inheritance as is stated in the following Quranic verse : "For parents, a sixth share of the inheritance to each, if the deceased left children ;..." [Surah IV verse]. Another case is when the deceased leaves no direct heir and maternal brothers and sisters all together inherit one third of the estate to be divided equally between them regardless of their sex. This is stated in the following Quranic verse "If a man or woman whose inheritance is in question, has left neither ascendants or descendants, but has left a (maternal) brother or a sister, each one of the two gets a sixth ; but if more than two, they share in a third ;..." [Surah IV, verse]. In this case the male does not take double the female's share. "In what your wives leave, your share is a half, if they leave no child but if they leave a child, ye get a fourth ; after payment of legacies and debts. In what ye leave, their share is a fourth, if ye leave no child but if ye leave a child, they get an eighth ; after payment of legacies and debts". [Surah IV, verse].

The Custodianship of the Family.

There are two reasons why the right to the custodianship of the family is granted to men by the Faith of Islam. The first reason is that men are charged with the financial support of their families and it is only fair that the person charged with the financial support and maintenance of any group of people should have the right of being that group's custodian who supervises their affairs.

The constitutions of the democracies of the modern world are likewise based upon this principle. The citizens of the state who pay taxes, which are spent on the public utilities of the state, have the right to have a say in their affairs and supervise the executive power of the land, in addition to participating in the legislation of the state. Referendums, general elections and representation in parliament are also based upon the same principle.

A referendum grants the citizens of a state direct supervision over the affairs of their country, whereas their indirect supervision is realised in the system of parliamentary representation by which they elect the members of parliament in a free election. Constitutional legislators sum up this principle in the following statement: "He who pays has the right of supervision". The second reason for granting a man authority and custodianship over his family is due to the indisputable fact that women are more emotional than men and that their disposition affects their judgement. God Almighty created women in this manner to enable them to pursue the principal role in their life namely that of motherhood and all that such a role entails, which includes nursing their babies and caring for them day and night. Such a vital role requires a sensitive compassionate nature more than its need for contemplation and meditation. On the other hand, men do not usually follow their emotions as is the case with women, and in most cases men are influenced by their reason and their perception. Accordingly a man's nature and disposition qualify him to be the head of the family and to supervise its affairs. These two reasons are stated in the following Quranic verse : "Men are the protectors and maintainers of women, because God has given the one more (strength) than the other, and because they support them from their means"

This custodianship which Islam grants man over his family is merciful, guiding and loving. It also includes principles that preserve a woman's dignity and protect her rights and welfare in every respect. The aim of this custodianship is one of protection and affection and not of absolute power or domination. Islam thus ensures the welfare of the family and of women themselves by taking into account all the circumstances and situations that exist in a woman's life.

If a Muslim girl or woman is unmarried, her father or her guardian is her custodian and he is therefore charged with supporting and providing for her financially so that she would not be forced to earn her living in a manner that might lead to her disgrace or the disgrace of her family. The custodianship in this case preserves the woman's dignity and protects her from any possible embarrassment.

A Muslim girl who is eligible for marriage, being of sound mind and body, has the right to choose the man she is going to marry, after the consent of her guardian be he her father or otherwise. Her guardian however cannot force her to marry any person against her will.

It has been related that a girl went to `A'isha, wife of the Prophet, blessings and peace be upon him, and complained to her that her father had married her to his brother's son in order to elevate her status. `A'isha told her to wait until the Prophet, blessings and peace be upon him, returned home so that he could advise her what to do. When he returned and heard the girl's complaint he said : "A girl has more right to her choice than her guardian". The girl said: "O Prophet of God, I will obey my father, but I came to you so that women will understand that men do not have the right to force women in this matter".

She meant that men did not have the right to force women into marriage against their will. If a girl or woman chooses a husband and her guardian refuses him, without having a legitimate reason for his refusal, she can take the matter to court and the Judge can marry her to the man of her choice. The following Quranic verse refers to not preventing divorced women from remarrying their former husbands if they desire to do so "When ye divorce women, and they fulfil the term of their (`Iddat), do not prevent them from marrying their (former) husbands, if they mutually agree on equitable terms".

Islam is greatly concerned with the issue of compatability between husband and wife. The wisdom of this ruling is that marriage is not only a relationship between two people but is a relationship between two families. An incompatible marriage usually brings more embarrassment upon the wife's family than the husband's family. Accordingly the Faith of Islam grants the girl's or the woman's guardian the right to prevent her from marrying a person who would bring disgrace upon her and upon her family. This is the guardian's right, yet he cannot force her to marry against her will but is permitted to advise her and convince her. The Faith of Islam also grants the judge of the State the right to intervene in matters of marriage in which guardians are unfair or exceed the limits of their authority.

Abu Hanifa, one of the four founders of the schools of Muslim Law, declared that a Muslim woman has the right to marry herself whenever she wishes provided that her husband is compatible by religious standards and that her guardian has no right to prevent her marriage except on the grounds of incompatibility.

The current laws in Egypt are based upon Abu Hanifa's ruling. Abu Hanifa's School of Muslim law and the other schools of Muslim law agree that the custodianship and supervision granted to men by Islam in this stage of a girl's or a woman's life, in common with the other stages of her life are for her welfare and protection.

After a woman is married, this custodianship and supervision is transferred from her father or guardian to her husband. This does not in any way belittle the woman nor does it affect any of her civil rights of purchasing, selling, entering into contracts or disposing of her wealth and property independently without requiring her husband's consent. In fact her husband does not have any right to intervene in her affairs without her consent or her granting him power of attorny, which she can cancel any time if she so wishes.

The man's custodianship and supervision over his wife as head of the family is manifested in his right to supervise the policy of the household with the cooperation of the wife, who must obey him within the recognized ordained limits. These rights granted to men impose upon them certain obligations such as financially supporting their wives and families in addition to protecting their rights. Husbands are also commanded to treat their wives fairly, kindly and generously. A husband must be tolerant and lenient when dealing with the problems that exist in every marriage. He is also religiously charged with correcting his wife's errors in a gentle and understanding manner. The Prophet, blessings and peace be upon him, stated that the best people are those who are kind to their families. The passage from the following Quranic verse summarizes the aforementioned relationship between husband and wife "And women shall have rights similar to the rights against them, according to what is equitable ; but men have a degree of advantage over them". In Islam women's rights are equal to their obligations and men's obligations are equal to their rights, and even the degree that God grants man is not without obligations since it charges him with the support, maintainance and protection of his wife and family.

The Testimony of Men and Women in Islam

Islam does not rely upon a woman's testimony in serious crimes such as adultery, and relies upon the testimony of women in matters concerning women that are understood only by women. In other matters the testimony of two women is equal to the testimony of a man and since Islam demands the testimony of two men in most matters, a man must corroborate the testimony of the two women. The reason for this discrimination is that God Almighty created women with extremely emotional and sensitive natures in order to enable them to fulfil their vital duties in life, the most important of which is the role of motherhood and all the love and affection it demands. Motherhood requires a sensitive, tender and compassionate nature and a woman's emotions are usually stronger than her reasoning and this in itself is not a shortcoming in a woman's character. Occasionally a woman's emotions overwhelm her to the extent that she may not be able to estimate an event clearly and may interpret it in a manner that may not be precise, without her realising it. Islam accordingly takes this into consideration and in order to ensure that justice is executed, ordains the above mentioned laws of testimony regarding women. The reason why the testimony of two women is equal to the testimony of one man is built upon the basis that there is hardly any possibility that two women would be emotionally affected in the same way by the same event. They can also correct each other's testimony if one of them forgets a fact or misunderstands a matter. This is mentioned in the following Quranic verse "And get two witnesses, out of your own men, and if there are not two men, then a man and two women, such as ye choose, for witnesses, so that if one of them errs, the other can remind her".

The Right of Divorce in Islam.

Many orientalists criticize the Faith of Islam because it grants the right of divorce to men only. It accordingly behooves us to explain the laws of divorce in Islam clearly and in detail. Many people have either misinterpreted or misunderstood the facts that govern the issue of divorce in Islam and have consequently presented a distorted picture of the matter.

The system of divorce in Islam is the most ideal system of divorce ordained by any religion. If we consider the system of divorce, in the countries of the Western world that adhere to Christianity we must understand the following facts. Christians follow one of three Churches, namely the Catholic, Orthodox or the Protestant Church.

The Catholic Church prohibits divorce and does not permit the annulment of marriage for any reason, however serious the reason may be. Adultery itself is not a justifiable cause for divorce and the only procedure permitted in the event of adultery is a separation between the husband and wife. The state of marriage nevertheless, exists legally between them and accordingly neither of them can marry again, since they would be committing the crime of bigamy. The Catholic Church ordained this law according to Mathew's Gospel which states: "What therefore God hath joined together, let no man put asunder." Certain groups that seceded from the Catholic Church permit divorce only in the event of adultery being committed by the husband or wife, but they also prohibit them from marrying again.

The Christian Churches that permit divorce in the event of adultery base their ruling on Mathew's Gospel as uttered by Christ : "Whosoever shall put away his wife, saving for the cause of fornication, causeth her to commit adultery".The prohibition of a divorced man and a divorced woman from entering into a second marriage is based upon the following ruling from Mathew's Gospel : "Whosoever shall marry her that is divorced committeth adultery" According to the original laws of Christianity, if discord between a husband and wife reaches a point when reconciliation is an impossibility and marital life becomes intolerable and the life of the whole family, adults and children alike, is threatened with disasterous consequences, they are commanded to remain in their miserable marriage whatever the consequences may be since : "What therefore God hath joined together let no man put assunder".

Even if a husband and wife hate each other and all human attempts fail to reconcile them to each other, since one has no control over one's emotions which are controlled by God alone, they are commanded by the Church to spend the rest of their lives together, however miserable their lives may be. If either a husband or a wife does not abide by the sacred contract of marriage and deviates from morality and all attempts fail to reform him or her, Christianity prohibits divorce and the injured husband or wife is commanded to remain married to the person who has sinned against the Law of God, for the rest of his or her life. Occasionally separation between a husband and wife is permitted, but neither of them is permitted to marry again, according to the aforementioned verses of Mathew's Gospel.

If either a husband or a wife becomes mentally deranged and is a threat and a danger to the family, Christianity does not permit a divorce. If a husband contracts a serious infectious disease for which there is no remedy, or if he is impotent or sterile and cannot father a child, the Christian faith prohibits divorce although the marital relationship between husband and wife and the birth of offspring are the foundation of marriage. A husband may abandon his wife and family for many years without his family knowing whether he was alive or had died or had been sentenced to life imprisonment, but the Christian faith will not grant the abandoned wife divorce. The same prohibition applies in the event of a husband who cannot or will not support his wife and family that has no other means of maintainance and may accordingly force the wife to lead a life of sin. An Egyptian Christian woman, Mrs Zahiya`Aziz Murqos, filed a suit of divorce against her husband who had abandoned her without any financial support and had been unable to pay her the money for her maintainance which the court had decreed, as a result of his straitened means. The court refused her suit on the grounds that the laws of Christianity ordain that the bond of marriage is a sacred bond as is stated in the Gospel and is one of the seven secrets of the Church, emphasizing that what God has joined, no human being should set asunder. The court stated that some church officials and members of the general religious board had responded to the demands of people of weak faith and had granted them divorce for reasons which had not been ordained in the Gospel, and that the only reason for divorce permitted by the Gospel was adultery. These were the reasons stated by the Court for refusing a divorce to Mrs. Zahiya `Aziz Murqos. The Christian faith also prohibits the divorce of a husband and wife whose treatment of each other may lead to their serious harm or injury, after all attempts to reconcile them fail. Even if a husband and wife both feel that their married life has become intolerable and they both desire and agree to terminate their marriage, so that each one of them may begin a new life, they are prohibited from doing so by the Church.

When the Christians in the countries of the Western world realized that they could not adhere to the rigid laws of divorce as ordained by the Gospel, they introduced civil laws which permitted them to annul the marriage contract in certain cases. The great English philosopher, Bentham, expressed his opinion on the matter of divorce in his book "The Principles of Legislation", in which he wrote that a permanent marriage is undoubtably the ideal state for people and the most suitable for their needs, in addition to being the most favourable for the welfare of the family. He then stated that if a woman should stipulate that her husband should never be separated from her even if hatred should replace love, that would be an intolerable situation.

He continued to state that this stipulation exists without women demanding it, since the laws of the Church declare to the bride and bridegroom that they marry in order to be happy, but that they must understand that they have entered a prison the door of which is locked and that they will never be allowed to leave the prison, even if they fight each other with the weapons of enmity and hatred. The English philosopher also declared that if death alone could terminate a marriage the number of murders would have increased greatly. Christians have introduced civil laws which permit divorce and thus deliver them from having to resort to murder or suicide in order to liberate themselves from this prison. Abiding by civil law in matters of marriage and divorce and abandoning the laws of their faith is a unique manifestation of the Christians of the Western world. People of other religions including the Brahmas, Budhists and even the Magians and Pagans adhere or adhered to the laws of their faith in matters of marriage and divorce even if they introduced laws in other matters. They were accordingly able to live their lives without the problems that arise from the prohibition of divorce.

Some Christians however disregarded the laws of theifaith marriage and divorce after realizing that these laws do not take human nature, with all its inherent weakness, into consideration. The Christian priests and clergymen could not stem the opposition to the laws of the Christian faith concerning divorce, nor could they deny the logic of man's natural needs, so they let matters drift and passed judgement on divorce only in the most serious and critical circumstances concerning royal families or other symbols of authority. They also chose the most opportune time from the political perspective in order to demonstrate their power and status. When King Edward the Eighth of England declared his intention to marry a divorced woman and the policy of the government was opposed to this marriage, the Church refused to grant him permission to marry Mrs Simpson and remain on the throne of Great Britain. He was consequently obliged to choose between his throne and the woman he loved, and he chose the woman he loved and relinquished the throne.

It beloves us to mention that neither the Church nor the nation objected to their king having an illicit relationship with Mrs Simpson but that they only objected to his intention of marrying her. When Princess Margaret Rose, sister of Queen Elizabeth the

Second of Great Britain, declared that she intended to marry Captain Townsend whom she loved, the Church refused to permit her to marry him as he had divorced his wife. The fact that Captain Townsend's divorce had been granted him by civil and religious law, since his wife had been found guilty of adultery for which sin, the Protestant Church of England permits divorce, had no influence upon the Church's refusal.

In Europe and in North America, the courts grant divorce to husbands and wives according to man-made civil laws, thereby violating the laws of their faith. The people who advocate that we abandon our Islamic laws of divorce and abide by these civil laws do not realize that such a procedure would result in chaos and corruption.

Although thousands of cases of divorce were filed and granted in Europe and in the United States of America, the Church did not object and did nothing to prevent such a phenomenum. An example of the Church's policy, which takes into consideration the political circumstances of the land, is that when the British Prime Minister, Sir Anthony Eden, divorced his wife, who had eloped with her lover to the United States of America, and married another wife, the Church did not object to his second marriage since it was not an opportune time to oppose the marriage.

The laws of Christianity concerning divorce and man-made civil laws concerning divorce are deficient with the result that the welfare of the family has invariably been sacrificed. There are two trends in the civil laws concerning divorce, the first of which is extremely lax in its attitude towards the sacred bond of marriage, and permits divorce on the slightest pretext. This is the case in certain states in the United States of America. It was therefore quite an ordinary occurrence in these states for a woman to be married in the morning and to be granted a divorce in the evening. Such laws of divorce are undoubtably responsible for the breaking up of family life.

The second trend in the laws of divorce bases its rulings upon the spirit of the Chritian faith although it is not as rigid in its rulings. It only permits divorce in certain cases with extremely complicated procedures. Accordingly such divorces are only valid after a lengthy period as is the case in France and most Catholic countries. The French civil law only permits divorce in three cases, the first of which is in the event of the adultery of either the husband or wife. The second case is in the event of either the husband or the wife being subjected to brutal treatment. The third instance is if either the husband or wife is sentenced to imprisonment for a criminal offence. A person's chronic malady, physical disability and insanity itself even if it results in harmful and cruel treatment to the spouse, are not, according to French law, legitimate reasons for divorce. Absence from one's husband or wife for a lengthy period of time and extreme discord between a husband and wife are also not considered legitimate reasons for divorce according to the French law, even if both the husband and wife desire the divorce. In order that divorce be granted if one's husband or wife is sentenced to prison, the crime committed must be a major crime. Proof of brutal and cruel treatment of wives and husbands is also a very difficult matter to prove to the court. Accordingly, most people who file for divorce do so on the grounds of adultery.

The concerned party presents the evidence of the adultery of his or her spouse to convince the court that adultery has been committed. On the other hand a husband and wife often present false evidence of adultery and perjure themselves in court in order to be granted a divorce. Divorce which is granted on the grounds of adultery brings disgrace upon the husband, wife and their children. In addition to this, divorce invariably incurs exorbitant expenses which can only be afforded by the wealthy. The final decree of divorce also takes years before it becomes valid during which time the husband and wife are separated from one another. As a result of these complications and the lengthy period that the divorce takes to become legalized, many men take mistresses and women lovers thereby completely destroying any family life that had previously existed. Such relationships have become so common in the United States of America and in Europe, that they are regarded as ordinary occurrences. In addition to the fact that the family has lost its value in society, the fatherhood of many children is unascertained and a source of doubt.

Thus the civil laws of divorce either destroy the sacredness of the bond of marriage by permitting divorce on the slightest pretext, or are so rigid that divorce is only granted after disgracing the family concerned and subjecting its members to a most complicated and expensive procedure. In both cases the family is sacrificed. After presenting the laws of Christianity concerning divorce and the civil laws introduced in the matter of divorce and the complications of both the religious and the civil laws, it behoves us to present the laws of divorce as ordained by the Faith of Islam. These laws have been severely criticized by non-Muslims who claim that these laws are not based upon equality between men and women. The Faith of Islam permits divorce because it ordains laws that take human nature into consideration and divorce is sometimes the only solution to serious problems of marital discord. However, Islam does not permit divorce without enforcing definite terms which ensure safeguarding the rights of both the husband and wife and guarantee the execution of their obligations and duties in a just and fair manner. The bond of marriage in Islam is a sacred bond which is venerated and solemnly respected. The following Quranic verse refers to the marriage bond "And how could ye take it when ye have gone in unto each other, and they have taken from you a solemn covenant ?"Such a bond is thus regarded with the utmost veneration. Islam does its utmost to make people detest divorce and urges Muslims not to resort to it as far as is humanly possible. The Prophet Muhammad, blessings and peace be upon him, said "Divorce is the most detested permissible legitimate act in the eyes of God". He also said "Marry and do not resort to divorce, for the Throne of God Almighty shakes with every divorce In addition to discouraging divorce on principle, Islam ordained certain rulings that guaranteed avoiding divorce except when it was the only solution to marital discord.

Islam states that one should not resort to divorce as a result of any matter that can be remedied or that might improve in the future. Even if a husband dislikes some qualities in his wife's nature, Islam does not consider this a justification for divorce. He should not contemplate divorce if his feelings for his wife have undergone a change or if he has begun to dislike her. Any minor matters that aggravate a husband in his wife's conduct-providing that this does not include immorality or disobedience of the Faith - are not justifiable reasons for divorce, since one's emotions are fickle and inconstant.

One should consequently never allow oneself to be controlled by one's whims when making decisions concerning important matters upon which the future of one's family depends, for a person whom one dislikes today may be beloved on the morrow. A husband who dislikes a certain trait in his wife might discover that she possesses other qualities that appeal to him. This is mentioned in the following Quranic verse : "...live with them on a footing of kindness and equity. If ye take a dislike to them, it may be that ye dislike a thing, and God brings about through it, a great deal of good".

The Prophet Muhammad, blessings and peace be upon him, said that a believer should not hate his believing wife for if he dislikes a certain quality in her, she may possess another quality that pleases him.

A man went to `Omar ben Al Khattab, the Second Rightly Guided Caliph, to ask for his advice about divorcing his wife. `Omar told him not to divorce her and when the man replied that he did not love her, `Omar said "Woe betide you ! Are homes built only upon love? Where then is the role of care, affection and avoiding censure ?" He meant that if a marriage were not built upon love, it could be built upon two other important factors, one of which includes the care, affection and consideration which binds the members of the family to one another and teaches them their rights and their obligations. The other important factor is avoiding being the object of censure or blame for one's actions such as breaking up a home and family and being the cause of their misery.

The system ordained by Islam aims at avoiding divorce and the husband and wife who are at discord with each other are commanded to do their utmost to overcome their differences by dealing with each other compassionately and considerately as is mentioned in the following Quranic verse "If a wife fears cruelty or desertion on her husband's part, there is no blame on them if they arrange an amicable settlement between themselves ; and such settlement is best".

When a husband and wife fail to reconcile their differences with each other, Islam ordains that the matter of their discord be discussed at a family meeting in which the husband and the wife are each represented by a member of their families. These representatives act as mediators, and it is their duty to discuss and consider the problems that had caused the discord and to do their utmost to reconcile the points of view of the husband and wife until a reconciliation between them is effected. The Faith of Islam, in its concern for the happiness of the family, does not wait until discord actually takes place, in order to resort to this method of reconciliation, but it commands the husband and wife to do so if they fear that discord may occur and they feel that they are unable to deal with the matter.

This is stated in the following Quranic verse : "If ye fear a breach between them twain, appoint (two) arbiters, one from his family, and the other from hers ; if they wish for peace, God will cause their reconciliation : for God hath full knowledge, and is acquainted with all things". The Faith of Islam has also ordained certain financial and social obligations in the event of divorce, so as to discourage people from resorting to it. Islam ordains that when a man divorces his wife, he must pay her the delayed dowry agreed upon in the marriage contract, in addition to the expense of her maintainance of food, drink and living quarters for a certain period of time, known as the " iddat ". The custody of the children is granted to the mother until they grow up. In the event of her death or inability to look after her children, the custody of her children is granted to her relations. The husband is legally and religiously charged with his children's financial maintainance, and for wet nurses to breast feed them even if their mother breast feeds them herself, as is stated in the following Quranic verse "And if they suckle your (offspring) give them their recompense"

If all attempts at reconciliation made by the mediators of both families fail, and the husband insists upon divorce, that in itself signifies that the stability of the family is in danger and that the chief elements upon which a marriage is founded no longer exist.

In such circumstances Islam permits divorce and at the same time guarantees the welfare and the future of the family. Even if a divorce takes place, Islam grants the husband an opportunity to reconsider the divorce if there is the slightest possibility that married life be resumed.

The Faith of Islam ordains that after a husband divorces his wife once, he is given two options, one of which is to restore his wife during her " iddat " or period of waiting which is approximately three months for a wife who is not pregnant. The wife's return to her husband in this case needs no legal procedure and is valid as soon as the husband utters the words "I have restored my wife", or words to that effect. In order to encourage a husband to restore his divorced wife, Islam ordains that she live in her marital home during her period of waiting. This is stated in the following Quranic verse "O Prophet When ye do divorce women,divorce them at their prescribed periods,.nd count (accurately) their prescribed periods and fear God your Lord and turn them not out of their houses, nor shall they (themselves) leave, except in case they are guilty of some open lewdness".

Islam also favours restoring one's divorced wife as is stated in the following Quranic verse : "And their husbands have the better right to take them back in that period, if they wish for reconciliation "The Quranic verse describes the restoration of the divorced wife to her marital life as redressing the divorce. If a husband does not restore his wife during her period of waiting, she will have been divorced for the second time. Islam, which always guards the welfare of the family, permits the husband after the second divorce to restore his wife, but charges him with paying her a new dowry and contracting a new marriage contract. In the event of the husband restoring his wife during her period of waiting or marrying her for the secondtime with a new marriage contract and a new dowry, and then deciding to divorce her, he is permitted the same opportunities of restoring his wife that he had previously been granted. After a husband divorces his wife twice he is left with the right to divorce her only one more time. A third divorce signifies that married life has become intolerable and that the husband and wife have failed to make a success of their marriage. It is at this stage that the Faith of Islam ordains permanent divorce between them. The only chance of their remarrying is if the wife marries another man after her final divorce from her first husband and is divorced by her second husband. If she and her first ex-husband believe that after their long separation from one another, and after the change in their circumstances, they can succeed in living a happily married life, Islam permits them to do as, as is expressed in the following Quranic verses "So if a husband divorces his wife (irrevocably), he cannot after that, re-marry her until she has another husband and he has divorced her. In that case there is no blame on either of them if they re-unite, provided they feel that they can keep the limits ordained by God. Such are the limits ordained by God, which He makes plain to those who understand".

The Imam Malik related that during the lifetime of the Prophet Muhammad, blessings and peace be upon him, Abdullah, the son of `Omar ben Al Khattab divorced his wife during her menstrual period, and Omar asked the Prophet, blessings and peace be upon him, his opinion on the matter. He told `Omar that his son must restore his wife until her menstrual course be terminated and she purifies herself from it then to wait till she purifies herself from the following menstrual course, after which he can divorce her or restore her.

Such is the system of divorce in Islam and these are the laws ordained according to the Quran and the Traditions of the Prophet, Divorce that does not adhere to the laws of Islam is not valid. This is clear from the ruling given by the Prophet - blessings and peace be upon him - concerning `Omar ben Al Khattab's son who had divorced his wife during her menstrual course, which is not considered a period during which divorce can be pronounced. Ibn Jurayh related through Abu Al Zubayr that he had heard `Abdel Rahman ben Ayman ask Abdullah ben `Omar about this matter and that `Abdullah had replied that the Prophet, blessings and peace be upon him, had told him that his utterance of divorce had not been legitimate.

`Omar ben Al Khattab, the Second Rightly Guided Caliph legalized a certain system of divorce which was not founded upon the aforementioned laws of divorce. This included considering a divorce irrevocable if a man uttered the vow of divorce three consecutive times in one sitting. The reason for enforcing this ruling was that `Omar ben Al Khattab noticed that many men had made light of the sanctity of marriage and had underestimated the gravity of divorce.

These men had often uttered the oath of divorce in order to intimidate their wives or to force them to obey them, so `Omar ben Al Khattab punished them by introducing this new system of divorce to make them realize the sanctity of marriage so that they would not utter false threats of divorce.

He told them that God had granted them an opportunity for tolerance and deliberation in the Islamic laws of divorce, but that they had not heeded them, so they deserved a penalty in keeping with their sin. `Omar's ruling was only temporary as a remedy for the ill use of divorce that had spread and was thus a disciplinary measure. The Egyptian law of the year decreed that any oath of divorce that specifies more than one divorce is considered only one divorce. In fact there is no valid law of divorce that is not mentioned in the Qur'an or the Traditions of the Prophet. The laws of divorce in Islam guarantee every person his or her rights and it is sinful for any man to believe that he can divorce his wife whenever he pleases, since the laws of divorce in Islam are based upon a precise and just system which God ordained for mankind, men and women alike, in order to remedy the discord and misery to which some families are subjected.

The laws ordained by Islam concerning divorce are divine laws and the following Quranic verses dealing with divorce invariably state that the laws are ordained by God who prohibits breaking these laws and warns against the harm that ensues "These are the limits ordained by God ; so do not transgress them. If any do transgress the limits ordained by God, such persons wrong (themselves as well as others)." Also "Such are the limits ordained by God, which He makes plain to those who understand". "Those are limits set by God and any who transgresses the limits of God, does verily wrong his own soul.. " "But do not take them back to injure them, (or) to take undue advantage ; if any one does that, he wrongs his own soul. Do not treat God's Signs as a jest,..." "And know that God knoweth what is in your hearts, and take heed of Him..."

The Faith of Islam ordains certain provisions and stipulations concerning divorce so that it would not be the result of a whim. Islam grants the husband the opportunity of reconsidering his decision and grants the relations of the husband and wife an opportunity to intercede and reconcile them. Even after the failure of all the aforementioned attempts at reconciliation, the Qur'an states that two witnesses must witness the divorce : "Thus when they fulfil their term appointed, either take them back on equitable terms or part with them on equitable terms ; and take for witness two persons from among you, endued with justice, and establish the evidence (as) before God. Such is the admonition given to him who believes in God and the Last Day. And for those who fear God, He (ever) prepares a way out....". "A way out" can be interpreted to mean a way out of divorce. The Shiites decree that there must be witnesses to a divorce, and that this is an essential factor without which the divorce is not valid and has no consequences. This opinion adheres to the Quranic verses and grants the husband a final opportunity to reconsider his intention and not finalize the divorce. It is also an opportunity for the two witnesses who are summoned to witness the divorce, and are usually close friends or relatives of the husband and wife, to make a final attempt to deter the husband from concluding the divorce.

If divorce occurs, the Faith of Islam does its utmost to ensure generous and compassionate treatment of the divorced woman in addition to guaranteeing her her rights and safeguarding her from any harm to which she might be subjected. The laws of financial support for the divorced wife and her children, the custody of the children, financial support during the period of waiting, financial maintenance for nursing the children are all in the divorced woman's favour and this is verified by the following Quranic verses : "When ye divorce women, and they fulfil the term of their (Iddat), either take them back on equitable terms or set them free on equitable terms; but do not take them back to injure them, (or) to take undue advantage ; if any one does that, he wrongs his own soul. Do not treat God's Signs as a jest, but solemnly rehearse God's favours on you, and the fact that He sent down to you The Book and Wisdom for your instruction. And fear God, and know that God is well acquainted with all things. When ye divorce women, and they fulfil the term of their (Iddat), do not prevent them from marrying their (former) husbands, if they mutually agree on equitable terms. This instruction is for all amongst you, who believe in God, and the Last Day. That is (the course making for) most virtue and purity amongst you. And God knows and ye know not."

Also : "O Prophet ! When ye do divorce women, divorce them at their prescribed periods, and count (accurately) their prescribed periods and fear God your Lord : and turn them not out of their houses, nor shall they (themselves) leave, except in case they are guilty of some open lewdness ; those are limits set by God :nd any who transgresses the limits of God, does verily wrong his (own) soul : thou knowest not if perchance God will bring about thereafter some new situation. Thus when they fulfil their term appointed, either take them back on equitable terms or part with them on equitable terms ;..." Also : "Let the women live (In Iddat) in the same style as ye live, according to your means annoy them not, so as to restrict them. And if they carry (life in their wombs), then spend (your) on them until they deliver their burden and if they suckle your (offspring), give them their recompense :nd take mutual counsel together, according to what is just and reasonable. And if ye find yourselves in difficulties, let another woman suckle (the child) on the (father's) behalf ". Also : "But if ye decide to take one wife in place of another, even if you had given the latter a whole treasure for dower, take not the least bit of it back would ye take it by slander and a manifest wrong ? And how could ye take it when ye have gone in unto each other, and they have taken from you a solemn covenant ?"

In addition to divorce between a man and his wife who consumated their marriage and lived together as man and wife, Islam permits the divorce of a man and his bride who have signed the marriage contract, but have not consumated their marriage, if there is a good reason to do so, so that each one of them can begin a new life with the Grace of God. In such a situation, Islam ordains that the man must pay the girl or woman half the dowry agreed upon, in addition to compensation for divorcing her. This procedure is ordained as compensation for the divorced bride and the compensation is estimated by the ruler of the state according to the means of the husband and the extent of the injury caused to the bride by the divorce.

The following Quranic verses mention this matter : "There is no blame on ye if ye divorce women before consumation or the fixation of their dower ; but bestow on them (a suitable gift), the wealthy according to his means, and the poor according to his means ; - a gift of a reasonable amount is due from those who wish to do the right thing.

And if ye divorce them before consumation, but after the fixation of a dower for them, then the half of the dower (is due to them), unless they remit it or (the man's half) is remitted by him in whose hands is the marriage tie ; and the remission (of the man's half) is the nearest to righteousness. And do not forget liberality between yourselves. For God sees well all that ye do." In addition to the aforementioned cases of divorce there are four other kinds of divorce, the first of which is if a wife stipulates in her marriage contract that the right of divorce be in her hand and her husband agrees to the condition, she has the right to divorce her husband according to some schools of jurisprudence with certain provisions.

10

Muslim Festivals in India-Pakistan Subcontinent

Muhammad (Pbuh), who is regarded as by his followers as the last Prophet, the Messenger of God, introduced Islam in the seventh century AD. All muslims agree on the following five basic obligations for believers, which Sunnis term "Arkan" or the "Five Pillars of Islam" and Shia Muslims would consider being elements of the Roots of Religion and the Branches of Religion.

The Pilgrimage to Mecca during the month of Dhu al-Hijjah, is compulsory once in a lifetime for every follower of Islam. The Islamic calendar followed by the Muslims started on the Hijrah. The migration of the Prophet Muhammad from Mecca to Madina in 622 AD is called Hijrah. The beginning of Hijrah 1407 corresponds to the Gregorian year 1987(January). The months of Hijrah year are: Muharram, Safar, Rabbi-ul-Awwal, Rabi-us-Sani, Jamad-ul-Awwal, Jamad-us-Sani, Rajab, Shaban, Ramzan, Shawwal, Zil Qaid and Zil-Hajj (Dhu al-Hijjah. Islamic festivals mostly are religious. There are mass gatherings for Namaz (prayers) during these festivals. Thus, the festivals, which the Muslims celebrate according to their customs, include Barah Wafat, Haj, Id-Ul-Azha, Id-Ul-Fitr and Muharram. It also includes regional festival like the Sair-E-Gul Faroshan held in Delhi.

MUHARRAM

Muharram is the tenth day of the first Muslim month. It commemorates the martyrdom of the Prophet`s grandson Hussein and the battle at Karbala in 680 CE. The long Muharram processions with their Taziahs (gorgeous replicas of the martyr`s tomb), masked dancers and colourful crowds; give the appearance of a happy festival.

However in reality the apparent pageant is an expression of grief and distress. After the death of the Prophet, the question of succession arose. Islam believes in the finality of Muhammad in the prophetic tradition. One faction maintained that succession could remain only in the Prophet`s family while another faction rejected this. Muhammad himself named no successor.

In the end, Abu Bakr, who had been a staunch ally of the Prophet during the early days of his mission, was elected Caliph. He was an able man. During his reign Umar and Uthman were assassinated. When Ali was elected the fourth Caliph, there was open rebellion. Ali too was assassinated. His son Hasan, who succeeded him, was poisoned. Now the war of succession assumed serious proportions. Hussein, Ali`s other son, was killed in action in very tragic circumstances at the battle of Karbala.

The Shias consider the killing of Hussein at Karbala a particularly heinous crime and give themselves up to public lamentations during Muharram. Since, Hussein was martyred on the tenth day of Muharram, the first ten days are spent in fasting, prayer and mourning. A procession is taken out on the 10th day, and the mourners give themselves up to frenzied expressions of grief. A horse is led in the procession, along with the Taziahs, in memory of Husseins`s horse Dul Dul.

Some parts of India masked dancers lead the procession. After the procession, the Taziahs are buried or sunk in tanks, rivers or the sea. A person does not have to fast for the whole month. On the contrary, each fast during this month has merit. Muslim observes fast on this day; give as much charity as he can afford; performs Nafl Salat prayers and recites Surah Ikhlas 1000 times. Some sects of Muslims hold meetings where speeches are made on the happenings of Karbala and on the lives of martyrs.

The Shias observe this festival in a different fashion. They put on black clothes, as black is regarded as a colour of mourning.

Majalis (assemblies) are held every day during the first nine days where Shia orators relate the incident of the martyrdom of Hazrat Imam Hussein and his party in a great detail. On the 10th day of Muharram, large processions are formed and the devoted followers parade the streets holding banners and carrying models of the mausoleum of Hazrat Imam Hussein and his people, who fell at Karbala. They show their grief and sorrow by inflicting wounds on their own bodies with sharp metal tied to chains with which they scourge themselves. This is done in order to depict the sufferings of the martyrs.

It is a sad occasion and everyone in the procession chants "Ya Hussein", with loud wails of lamentation. Generally, a white horse beautifully decorated for the occasion is also included in the procession, to mark the empty mount of Hazrat Imam Hussein after his martyrdom.

Some of the elegies sung by the Shias especially in Uttar Pradesh in their Muharram procession include uncomp-limentary references to certain Caliphs, held in honour by the Sunnis who register the protest by pelting the singers with stones. The Muslims also believe that Allah created Adam and Eve on the tenth day of Muharram. Mosques provide free meals (nazar) on certain nights of the month to all people.

The Tenth of Muharram and Ashurah

The Islamic year begins with Muharram ul Haram, the first month of the Hijri Calendar. While followers of other religions spend their opening month in worthless merriment, the first month of Islam teaches us lessons of admonition, good counselling, knowledge of Allah Ta'ala, sacrifice, selflessness, patience and seeking the pleasure of Allah Ta'ala.

The tenth day of Muharram (Ashurah) has many distinctive qualities and features. Allah Ta'ala created the heavens and the earth on this blessed day. On this day He gave His infinite blessings and bounties to many of His Prophets and delivered them from the clutches of their enemies.

Allah Ta'ala created Hazrat Adam (Alaihis-Salam) in this month, pardoned him of his mistake, and Hazrat Noah's (Alaihis-

Salam) Ark landed successfully on Mount Judi, and he saved Hazrat Ibrahim (Alaihis-Salam) from fire and rescued Hazrat Musa (Alaihis-Salam) from Pharaoh. On the first of Muharram offer 2 rakats Nafl prayer. In each rakat after Surah Fateha recite Surah Ikhlas 3 times. After the Salam pray to Allah Ta'ala for all your needs and desires. From the blessing of this prayer, Allah Ta'ala will appoint an angel for such a person. The angel will guide him or her to do only good deeds and prevent them in engaging in sinful acts.

On the eve of "Ashurah" offer 100 rakats Nafl. In each rakat recite Surah Ikhlas 3 times after Surah Fateha. After Salam recite first 'Kalimah' 100 times. Allah Ta'ala will forgive all the sins of such a person.

Dua-e-Ashurah-An Insurance for a Year's Life: Hazrat Imam Zainul Abidain (Radi Allah Anhu) reports that who ever recites this dua on the tenth of Muharram, any time after sunrise and before sunset, or listens to its recitation from someone else, Allah Ta'ala will certainly make it an insurance for a years' life for him, by keeping death away from him. However, if one is to become the victim of death in that year, they will by some strange coincidence not remember to recite it.

Nafl Salat for the Eve of Ashurah: On the eve of Ashurah offer 4 rakats Nafl Salat as follows: In every rakat after Surah Fateha recite "Ayetul Kursi" once and Surah Ikhlas 3 times. After completing this Namaz recite Surah Ikhlas 100 times. Allah Ta'ala will purify such a person of all their sins and grant them endless bounties and blessings in paradise.

The Fast of Ashurah: On the 9th and 10th of Muharram, one should fast. If it is not possible to fast on both days, then every effort should be made to fast on the 10th day of Muharram, as there is great reward for this fast. (Muslim Shareef).

The following are some of the desirable acts one should do on the day of Ashurah:

1. To observe fast on this day.
2. To give as much charity as you can afford.
3. To perform Nafl Salat prayers.

4. To recite Surah Ikhlas 1000 times.
5. To visit and be in the company of pious Ulema.
6. To place a hand of affection on an orphan's head.
7. To give generously to one's relatives.
8. To put surma in one's eyes.
9. To take a bath.
10. To cut one's nails.
11. To visit the sick.
12. To establish friendly ties with one's enemies.
13. To recite Dua-e-Ashurah
14. To visit the shrines of Awliyas and the graves of Muslims.

Hazrat Abdullah bin Masood (Radi Allah Anhu), a Companion of the Holy Prophet Muhammad (Sall Allahu Alaihi wa Sallam) reports the following saying of the Messenger of Allah Ta'ala, "Whosoever prepares ample food and drink for his family on this sacred day and delights in feeding them generously, Allah Ta'ala will increase His provisions for that year and place much blessings and good therein."

Imam Hussain (Radi Allah Anhu) and his companions were martyred on the tenth of this month. Like any month in the Islamic Calendar there are in this first Islamic month, many anniversaries which are celebrated every where in the world.

Muharram festival commemorates the martyrdom of Hazrat Imam Hussain, the grandson of the Holy Prophet (peace be upon him). This festival starts at the 1st day of Muharram and lasts for 10 days until 10th of Muharram. Muharram is the first month of Islamic calendar.

During this month, while on a journey, Hazrat Imam Hussain, his family members and a number of his followers were surrounded by the forces of Yazid, the Muslim ruler of the time. During the siege, they were deprived of food and water and many of them were put to death. The incident happened at a place called Karbala in Iraq in 61st year after Hijra. This dispute was result of a disagreement among Muslims on the question of succession after the demise of Hazrat Ali, the fourth caliph.

Some sects of Muslims hold meetings where speeches are made on the happenings of Karbala and on the lives of martyrs. The Shias, however, observe this festival in a different fasion. As Muharram, the first month of the Muslim year, approaches, they put on black clothes, as black is regarded as a color of mourning. Majalis (assemblies) are held every day during the first nine days where shia orators relate the incident of the martyrdom of Hazrat Imam Hussain and his party in a great detail. On the 10th day of Muharram, large processions are formed and the devoted followers parade the streets holding banners and carrying models of the mausoleum of Hazrat Imam Hussain and his people, who fell at Karbala. They show their grief and sorrow by inflicting wounds on their own bodies with sharp metal tied to chain with which they scourge themselves. This is done in order to depict the sufferings of the martyrs. It is a sad occasion and everyone in the procession chants "Ya Hussain", with loud wails of lamentation. Generally a white horse beautifully decorated for the occasion, is also included in the procession, to mark the empty mount of Hazrat Imam Husain after his martyrdom.

During these first ten days of Muharram, drinking posts are also set up temporarily by the Shia community where water and juices are served to all, free of charge.

The 1st of Muharram is New Year's Day, and with it marks the beginning of the Islamic (Hijri) Calendar. Its real significance lies in the major turning point in the course of Islam. As told in the Noble Qur'ân: "Verily the number of months with Allah is twelve months (in a year), so was it ordained by Allah on the Day when He created the heavens and the earth; of them four are Sacred. That is the right religion, so wrong not yourselves therein ...". Today itself, as we usher in the new year, many of us take the time to at least briefly reflect on the major lessons in the past year and anticipate new experiences in the fresh year of 1422 Hijrah. This is also the day that we should be reminded of the Prophet's last pilgrimage and the message that he wants us to carry in our hearts.

The prophet offered the noon and afternoon prayers in Arafah along with 100,000 worshippers, and the victory of Islaam over blasphemy became decisive and final. Thereafter, the Prophet mounted his camel, and delivered the historical sermon. In it, he had said: "... All mankind is from Adam and Eve, an Arab has no superiority over a non-Arab nor a non-Arab has any superiority over an Arab, also a white has no superiority over black nor a black has any superiority over white except by piety and good action. Learn that every Muslim is a brother to every Muslim and that the Muslims constitute one brotherhood. Nothing shall be legitimate to a Muslim which belongs to a fellow Muslim unless it was given freely and willingly. Do not, therefore, do injustice to yourselves...".

The Period of mourning is observed in the first month of the Islamic calendar, and it commemorates the death of Hazrat Imam Hussain in the battle of Karbala. Muharram means 'respected'. It is the first month of the Islamic calendar.The first ten days of this month are observed as a period of mourning by Muslims, particularly by those belonging to the Shiah sect, in memory of the tragedy of 680 AD. Hazrat Imam Hussain, the grandson of Muhammad the Prophet was killed in the battle of Karbala. This event, called Muharram, is named after the month in which it took place. The tenth day, called Ashura, is observed as the day for a public expression of their grief and is the most important day of the month.

During the pre-Islamic period in the Arabian penninsula, fighting was prohibited in four months of the year.These months, of which Muharram was one, were considered sacred. This period of inactivity was a necessity in heavily decorated replicas of the tomb of the Imam and his family are made for Muharram the era of warring tribes. The tradition was maintained even after the advent of Islam, though provisions to accommodate and accept war in special situations, like a threat to the sovereignty of an empire, were introduced. The gory battle of Karbala was fought against this law and tradition of Islam. The inhabitants on the banks of rivers Euphrates and Tigris were traditional rivals. Their animosity was contained to some extent by Muhammad. But when his son-in-law Hazrat Ali was the Caliph, the old enmity re-surfaced. Hazrat Ali had two descendants, Hazrat Imam Hussain and Hazrat Imam Hassan. Hussain was the ruler of the part of the empire known today as Iran. The other part in modern Iraq was ruled by the Umayyads. Hussain was called upon by the Shiahs of Kufa, a small town in the Umayyad kingdom, to accept their allegiance and claim his place as the leader of the Islamic community. This was against the wishes of the ruler of Kufa, Yazid, who instructed his governor, Ibn-e-Ziad to take appropriate action. Meanwhile, in response to the call of the Shiahs, Hussain accompanied by his family members, headed for Kufa. When they reached Karbala, enroute to Kufa, the forces of the governor surrounded them and their 70 men. Hussain, his family and his troops were tortured and killed, and Hussain's head was severed and presented to the king. They received no help from the Shiahs of Kufa. This happened on the tenth day of Muharram and it was called Ashura.

To commemorate this tragedy, the 40 days starting from the first day of Muharram to Chehalum, are observedas a period of mourning by the Shiahs. During this period, women foresake alladornments, even their bangles. All kinds of celebration like marriage are disallowed during this period. Shiah Muslims are celibate for these 40 days. The first 10 days however, are the most important and are passionately observed asa period of mourning. During the first nine days of the month, majlish (enacted grief-stricken scenes from the battle of Karbala) are organised in Shiah mosques. Huge Shiah crowds wearing black assemble at imambaras, where plaintive verses in memory of Imam Hussain are recited. These nine days are also spent in making Taziahs. On Ashura, the most important day, processions with Taziahs are taken out in commemoration of the sad event. The procession also includes a well-decorated horse, representing the horse of Imam Hussain. Emotional plays, enacting scenes from the battle of Karbala, are performed by bare-chested Shiah men. They strike their body with chains while some walk with bare feeton burning coals. Crying "hai Hussain hum na rahe", meaning 'Oh Hussain, we were not there', they express their anguish at their in ability to have prevented him from being tortured. By beating themselves, the Shiahs relive the pain Hussain suffered and thus express their sorrow. They also distribute water, soft drinks and fruit juices to passers-by in an effort to quench the thirst of the six-month old son of Hazrat Imam Hussain and many others who are believed to have died asking for water. The Taziah processions from allover the town terminate at the Karbala of the city. Most old habitations with a Muslim tradition have a specially marked place to represent the original Karbala.

The Taziahs are buried there. Sometimes they are dismantled so that they can be used again. Often they are immersed in a river. Accordirig to a popular belief among the Shiahs, the mud on the grave of Hazrat Imam Hussain turns blood red on Ashura. Muharram is also a time for making vows. People pledge their promises to the Taziah of Hussain. They can do this in two ways. The first is by sending milk,a soft drink, dates or refined sugar to the craftsman who is making the Taziahs. The craftsman recites the Al-Fatiha breaks a coconut and distributesits water with the soft drink or milk in small cups to those present.

The second method of making a vow is by performing an act of penance or self-torture before the Taziah. This is generally practiced by woman who volunteer to stand and watch over the Taziahs for a night or more.

They go to the place where it is built, and accompany it through its route to the Karbala. This commitment is performed on the ninth night of the month of Muharram. Some people offer to roll on the ground for a certain distance in front of the Taziah as thanksgiving for favours that have been granted or for wish fulfillment. Though the 10 days of Muharram are a period of mourning for the Sunni sect too, they do not indulge in passion plays and nor do they cry out Hussain Hussain because their tradition stipulates grieving in silence. They keep a two-day roja on the ninth and tenth of the month, wear only black clothes and read the Namaz and AlFatiha five times a day.

Contrary to popular belief, Muharram is not a particular day, but the name of a month that marks the beginning of the year according to the Islamic calendar. Muharram is one of four months that have been designated as holy according to the Islamic calendar, the other three being – Dhul-Qa'adah, Dhul-Hijjah and Rajab.

Fasting in the Month of Muharram: Fasting is advocated in the month of Muharram. The Prophet is believed to have said: "The best fasts after the fasts of Ramadan are those of the month of Muharram." Although the fasts of the month of Muharram are not obligatory, yet one who fasts in these days out of his own will is entitled to a great reward by Allah Almighty. Fasting on the tenth day of Muharram, called Ashura, is particularly important, as it supposed to lead to great rewards. A person does not have to fast for the whole month. On the contrary, each fast during this month has merit.

Muharram – an Auspicious Time: The month of Muharram is also associated with many auspicious events in Islamic history. Allah is supposed to have created the heavens and the earth on this blessed day. On this day He give His infinite blessings and bounties to many of His Prophets and delivered them from the clutches of their enemies.

Allah created Hazrat Adam in this month and pardoned him of his mistake. Hazrat Noah's Ark landed successfully on Mount Judi during this time centuries ago. God is also said to have saved Hazrat Ibrahim from fire and rescued Hazrat Musa from the Pharaoh during the month of Muharram.

You must be wondering what there is to mourn about then? The tenth day of Muharram or Ashura is of supreme importance for Shia Muslims as they celebrate the death anniversary of Hussain, the grandson of the Prophet Muhammad.

The Tragedy at Kerbala: In the month of Muharram many centuries ago, (approximately October 20th 680 A.D.), an event took place in Iraq at a place known as Kerbala on the bank of the river Euphrates.

A large army, which had been mobilised by the Umayyad regime, besieged a group of persons numbering less than a hundred and put them under pressure to pay allegiance to the Caliph of the time and submit to his authority. The Caliph was a man much taken with earthly pleasures that deviated from the Islamic way of life. The small group resisted and a severe battle took place in which they were all killed. The leader of the small band of men who were martyred in Kerbala was none other than Imam Husain, the grandson of the Holy Prophet. Imam Husain's martyrdom at Kerbala represents a conscious confrontation with anti-Islamic forces and a courageous resistance for a sacred cause. The tragedy was that the one who stood up to defend Islam was cut down in so cruel a manner. It is for this reason that the death of Imam Husain is mourned annually in the Muslim world.

The Observances: "Among the Shias in India the following ceremonies are common, although considerable differences in detail may be observed according to regions. As soon as the new moon appears, people assemble in the imam bara (lit, enclosure of imam), a permanent meeting place built in stone or, as mostly in southern India, they assemble in the 'ashur khanah (lit, ten-day house), a temporary structure. There they recite thefatihah over some sherbat (sweetened, cool drink), rice or sugar in Husain's name. The cool drink is meant to remind the faithful of the terrible thirst Husain and his family and retinue had to suffer. Food and drink are later distributed to the public, especially to the poor. In some places a pit is dug in which a fire is lighted every evening of the festival, and young and old people fence across it with sticks or swords. Or they run around it calling out: Ya'Ali! Ya'Ali! Shah Hasan! Shah Husain! Dulha! Hae Dost! Rahiyo! Oh 'Ali! (Noble Hasan! Noble Husain! Bride-groom! Friend! Stay! Stay!)

"The'ashur khanah is usually draped with black cloth on which texts of the Quran are written. The imam bara, too, will be decorated. Inside are placed the tazian-s or tabuts, wooden structures covered with silver paper, coloured paper and tinsel fringes. They are made with imagination and artistic sense and are meant to represent Husain's mausoleum, erected on the plains of Karbala, or else the Prophet's tomb at Medina or even the Taj Mahal of Agra. Nearby are placed imitations of articles which Husain is supposed to have used at Karbala, e.g., a turban of gold, a sword, a shield, a bow and arrow. There are also'alam-s or standards of different shapes, each one having its own special name and history. Often the 'a lam has the form of a human hand (panjab) fixed on top of the pole. This is the popular emblem representing the five members of the prophet's family: Muhammad, Fatima, 'Au, Hasan and Husain."

Processions and Other Ceremonies: "From the seventh to the tenth of Muharram processions are held to commemorate the martyrdom of Hasan's son, Qasim, who was slain shortly after his wedding, as well as the martyrdom of Husain. Along with the procession goes a white horse (duldul or dhu'l-janah) which represents the horse on which Husain rode, or it refers to the bridal horse of Qasim, who was married to Husain's favourite daughter Fatimat-us-sughra (as distinguished from Fatimah, the daughter of Muhammad), just before the battle of Karbala. With this in mind the people shout at intervals: Bride-groom! Bridegroom! On the eighth day a lance or spear is carried to represent Husain's head, which was carried on the point of a javelin by order of Yazid. In addition to these representations ta 'ziya h-s or tabut-s and standards of Hasan, Husain and Qasim are carried. All the time people beat their breasts, saying: Hasan, Husain! Sometimes the pro-cession halts, and then a group of men and boys, naked from the waist, beat themselves with a bundle of sharp blades so that the blood streams down their backs or, forming a large group, they beat their breasts in a uniform rhythm crying all together: Ya Hasan! Ya Husain! The tenth day is 'ashara 'ashurah. On this day the tabut-s or ta 'ziah-s are either stripped and thrown into the water, or they are taken to a ground set apart for this purpose (called Karbala) and literally buried in specially dug graves.

On the evening of the twelfth day people sit up all night, reading the Quran and reciting marsiyah-s and verses in honour of Husain. On the thirtieth day a quantity of food is cooked and, after saying the fatihah over it, it is given to the poor. With this act of charity the Muharram celebrations end."

The Memory of Karbala: Husain was the second son of Ali ibn Abu Talib and Fatimah bint Muhammad, the last Prophet. He was born in the 4th year after the hijra. His older brother, Hasan was named as the successor to his father, after Ali was murdered in the mosque in Kufah, Iraq. After Ali's death, people pledged their allegiance to Hasan as the khalifa (successor). Soon after he took office, however, Mu'awiyah, who had fought with Ali over the caliphate, formed an army to attack Hasan. In the interests of peace and unity, Hasan handed over the position of khalifa to Mu'awiyah who ruled until his death and passing of the caliphate to his son, Yazid.

Mu'awiyah, who was the son of Abu Sufyan (the arch enemy of Islam until he accepted Islam after the Muslims returned to Makkah), was not well liked among the "religious" Muslims. They disliked his son, Yazid, even more. Yazid's open disregard for Islamic law (shariah) and practices made many Muslims cringe at the thought of him taking the caliphate. Mu'awiyah, however, who insisted on turning the caliphate into a monarchy, pushed people to pledge allegiance to his son. On his deathbed, Mu'awiyah told Yazid not to try to force Imam Husayn to give allegiance to him because this would cause too much trouble. Soon after, in 60 A.H., Mu'awiyah died.

Little time passed before Yazid made it clear to his governors in Madinah that they were to force Imam Husayn to pledge allegiance to him or send Imam Husayn's head to him in Damascus. Representatives of Yazid came to Husayn in Madinah and asked for his allegiance. Imam Husayn asked for some time before he made his decision. In the meantime, he was able to move his family to Makkah where they were protected by the Sacred Precincts, Masjid-al-Haraam. It is forbidden in Islam to harm anything within these precincts.

Many people in the Ummah at that time who were already dissatisfied with the caliphate began to send letters to Imam Husayn urging him to join them in the city of Kufah in Iraq. They swore to defend him to the death and gave their allegiance to him.

To investigate the situation, Imam Husayn sent his cousin, Muslim ibn Aqil to Kufah. After discussing the situation with the people of Kufah, he was killed and beheaded by supporters of Yazid on Wednesday, 9th of Dhul-Hijja, the Day of Arafat, in the year 60 A.H. (680).

It was the time of pilgrimage in Makkah, and Imam Husayn had begun to perform the pilgrimage rites. When he learned that some of Yazid's men had come dressed as pilgrims to kill him in Makkah, he gathered his people together to leave for Iraq. He did not want his blood to be spilled within the sacred precincts and to have the sacred rite of Hajj dishonored by that violence. Thus, he, some members of his family, and a group of followers set out towards Kufah on 8th of Dhul-Hijjah.

As the Imam approached Iraq, he was informed that many of the people who had voiced their support for him had turned and now supported the reign of Yazid, possibly to save their own lives. It was then that many of his representatives, including Muslim Ibn Aqil were abused and killed.

As he and his followers marched closer to Iraq, a person that he met along the way who learned where he was going urged and pleaded with him not to continue his journey towards Kufah, but the Imam replied:

"Servant of God," he answered, "wise decisions are not hidden from me. yet the commands of God, the Exalted, cannot be resisted. By God, (my enemies) will not leave me till they have torn the very heart from the depths of my guts. If they do that, God will cause them to be dominated and humiliated until they become the most humiliated of the factions among nations."

Before the Imam and his followers were able to reach Kufah, Yazid's army surrounded them about 44 miles outside of Kufah in a desert called Karbala. At this point, Yazid's army cut off Imam Husayn's water supply, and his followers began to suffer from extreme thirst. Among these people were members of the Prophet's family, companions, and some women and children.

As the days passed in the month of Muharram, the first month of the new year on the Islamic calendar, Yazid's army, numbering 30,000, closed the circle around Imam Husayn's followers who were suffering from dehydration.

On the tenth day of Muharram, called Ashura, Imam Husayn and his followers went out with less than 100 people to meet the army of 30,000.

Ali Zayn al Abidin, son of Imam Husayn, peace be upon them, reported: When the cavalry began to approach al-Husayn, he raised his hands and said:

"O God, it is You in Whom I trust amid all grief. You are my hope amid all violence. You are my trust and provision in everything that happens to me, (no matter) how much the heart may seem to weaken in it, trickery may seem to diminish (my hope) in it, the friend may seem to desert (me) in it, and the enemy may seem to rejoice in it. It comes upon me through You and when I complain to You of it, it is because of my desire for You, You alone. You have comforted me in (everything) and have revealed its (significance to me). You are the Master of all grace, the Possessor of all goodness and the Ultimate Resort of all desire."

The Imam and his followers fought all day and fell to their deaths fighting in the cause of Allah. That day, all who fought were martyred. Among them were two children of Imam Hasan, and Imam Husayn's five year old child.

"When the Imam himself was ready to fight, he saw his six-month-old baby was dying from thirst. The Imam brought his infant near to the enemy and demanded some water for baby, saying: You want me but not this baby so take him and give him some water. The words of the Imam had not been finished that the thirst of the baby was quenched by a deadly poisoned arrow from the enemy which pinned the baby's neck to the arm of his father. The Imam threw some of his blood toward the sky saying: "O' Lord! Your Husayn has offered whatever You have given him. Bless me by acceptance of this sacrifice." Finally Imam came to the field and fought for a long time and was finally martyred. The army of Yazid having killed Imam Husayn, cut his head and raised it on a lance.

"The army of the enemy, after ending the war, burned the tents of the women and children accompanying the Imam and his companions, and plundered those helpless women. They decapitated the bodies of the martyrs, denuded them and threw them to the ground without burial. Then they moved women and children along with the heads of the martyrs to Kufah. They took with them the daughters and sisters of al-Husayn, peace be on him, together with 'Ali b. al-Husayn, peace be on him. The latter was still sick with a dysentery and was almost on the point of death. The bodies of the martyrs were under the sunshine for three days till a tribe passing that place found them and performed the burial.

"The event of Karbala, the capture of women and children of the Household of Prophet, their being taken as prisoners from town to town, and the speeches made by Zaynab, the daughter of Ali, who was one of the prisoners, became a scandal for the Umayyad Kingdom. Such abuse of the Household of Prophet nullified the propaganda which Muawiyah had built up for years. The scandal reached to the extent that Yazid denounced the actions of his agents in public. That was exactly what Imam Husain wanted to do, otherwise he would not bring women and children with him and sacrifice some, and let the rest to become captives. That was the only way to make a wave in order to awaken the Muslim nation.

"The event of Karbala was a major factor in the overthrow of Umayyad kingdom though its effect was delayed. Among its immediate results were the revolts and rebellions combined with bloody wars which continued for twelve years. During those riots none of the important elements in Karbala could escape revenge and punishment, including Yazid.

The Fast of Aashoorah The tenth day of this sacred month, Muharram is known as Aashoorah. It is one of the most important and blessed days of Allah in the Islaamic calendar. Some ulamaa (scholars) are of the opinion that before the fasts of Ramadhaan were made compulsory, the fast of the day of Aashoorah was compulsory upon the ummah. This is stated in a hadeeth reported by Aaishah radhiyallahu anha that the Holy Prophet sallallahu alayhi wasallam ordered the observance of the fast of Aashoorah. However, when the fast of Ramadhaan became compulsory, then whosoever wished, kept this fast and whosoever desired did not observe this fast. Bukhari Vol.1 Page 268 But, nevertheless the Prophet sallallahu alayhi wasallam continued to fast this day and encouraged his Companions to do the same.

Ibne Abbas radhiyallahu anhu says: I did not see Rasulullah sallallahu alayhi wasallam anxiously await the fast of any day, which he gave preference to over other days, but this day, the day of Aashoorah. Bukhari Vol.1 Page 268 Humayd Ibne Abdur

Rahamaan narrates that he heard Muaawiyah Ibne Abi Sufyaan radhiyallahu anhu on the day of 'Aashoorah, during the year he performed hajj, saying on the pulpit: "O the people of Madinah! Where are your ulamaa (scholars)? I heard Rasullullah sallallahu alayhi wasallam saying: This is the day of 'Aashoorah. Allah has not enjoined its fasting on you but I am fasting it. Whosoever wish, keep (this) fast and whosoever desires do not observe (this fast)." Bukhari Vol.1 Page 268. In another hadeeth, Ibne Abbas raahiyallahu anhu narrates that the Holy Prophet sallallaha alayhi wasallam came to Madinah and found the Jews fasting on the day of 'Aashoorah. Hence the Holy Prophet sallallahu alayhi wasallam inquired of them, "What is (the significance of) this day on which you fast?"

They replied, "This is a great day. On this day Allah saved Moosa and his people and drowned Fir'awn and his nation. Thus Moosa alayhis salaam fasted on this day as a token of thanksgiving, therefore we too fast on this day." The Messenger of Allah sallallahu alayhi wasallam said, "We are more worthy of Moosa and nearer to him than you." Thereafter, the Holy Prophet sallallahu alayhi wasallam fasted on this day and ordered (his Companions) that a fast be kept on this day. Muharram is observed by the Shia community of Muslims in commemoration of the martyrdom of Prophet Mohammed's grandson, Imam Hussain, who was killed in the Battle of Karbala in AD 680. The prophet's son-in-law Ali, and Ali's elder son Hassan, are also remembered during this period as having suffered and died for righteous causes.

The word muharram also means respect. The first ten days of the month are observed as a period of mourning. After the death of the Prophet Mohammed, the Quran was considered the final word. The Prophet had named no successor. One faction of his followers believed that succession should remain within Mohammed's family, while another disagreed. After a long dispute, Abu Bakr, a loyal follower of Mohammed, was elected his successor. His reign was peaceful, as was that of his successors.

However, during the reign of Ali, the Prophet's son-in-law, there was opposition from the masses. Ali was assassinated and his elder son Hassan was poisoned. His younger son Hussain, his family and his troops, were tortured and killed, and Hussain's head was severed and presented to the king. The killing of Hussain happened on the tenth day of month of Muharram, and the event was called Ashura. It is now observed as a day for public expression of grief. These circumstances divided the Muslim community into the Shias and the Sunnis. The Shias consider Ali, Hassan and Hussain the rightful successors of Prophet Mohammed and mourn their death during Muharram.

The Shias observe the entire month as a period of mass mourning. There is no celebration or expression of joy of any kind. Women are expected to forsake all adornments. Public enactments of grief, depicting scenes from the Battle of Karbala, are carried out in Shia mosques on the first ten days.

The Shias in India observe certain ceremonies in common, though the details differ considerably. As soon as the new moon appears, people clad in black assemble and recite plaintive verses over sweetened cold drink, in memory of Imam Hussain.

The cool drink is meant to remind people of the terrible thirst Hussain and his family had to suffer. Food and drink are later distributed to the public, especially to the poor. The first nine days are also spent in making bamboo and paper replicas of the martyr's tomb. On Ashura, the tenth day, decorated taziyas, or tombs embellished with precious metals, are carried through the city streets. A horse is led in procession in memory of Hussain's horse, Dul Dul.

Wrestlers and dancers enact scenes depicting the Battle of Karbala. Bare-chested Shia men strike their body with chains or walk barefoot over burning coal while uttering cries of anguish for the torture that Hussain suffered. Apart from reliving his suffering, it is also an expression of the people's inability to save Hussain from the brutalities.

Muharram or the 'sacred month' is the first month of the Islamic or Hegira calendar. The Hadith instructs to observe fasting on the 9th and 10th of this month. Fasting on *Ashura* (the 10th of Muharram) was a *faraz* (obligatory) until fasting in ramadan was made faraz. Both in pre-Islamic times as well as at the time of the

Prophet *Muhammad* (Sm), it was *haram* (forbidden) to be in war in this month. Muslims of the Shiah group observe the first ten days of the month as a period of mourning for the death of Imam Husain (R), the grandson of Hazrat Muhammad (Sm). The tenth day of Muharram is called Ashura. Imam Husain (R) was killed on this day at the hands of the troops of Yazid, the son of Muawiyah, the Umaiyya caliph. Shiahs take out processions with tazia, the replica of the tomb of Imam Husain (R) and they show their grief by clapping on their chests or flagellating themselves with knives or chains. The mourning continues for forty days till the first ten days of the next month Safar. Muharram had been observed since the 10th century. In Bengal also it has been observed for the last few centuries.

The centre of observances of Muharram in Dhaka is the *Husaini* dalan Imambara. As mark of mourning, Shiahs dress in black for at least ten days of Muharram. During this time, they refrain from merrymaking, listening to music, or seeing plays or movies. They also do not arrange weddings during this month. Keeping in mind that Imam Husain (R) and his followers suffered from unavailability of water, some Shiahs refrain from eating fish. During these first ten days of the month, *majlis* (mourning assemblies), are held at the imambaras, separately for men and women.

The story of the martyrdom of Hazrat Husain (R) is told and *marsiyas* (elegies) are sung or recited in the assemblies. At the end of the service, food is distributed to the people. On the seventh of Muharram, *shirni* (special offerings) are made and the people pray for Allah's blessings. Food and fruits in large quantities and varieties are distributed on the occasion. Those who pray for Allah's blessings, pick out a food item, and make a *manat*, or promise, not to eat that food for a year. In case the prayer is deemed accepted, they promise to offer shirni the next year. Along with the shirni, some also offer silver *panja*, the model of an open palm with five fingers that represent the five holy figures, the Prophet Muhammad (Sm), his daughter Fatima (R), his son-in-law Ali (R), and his two grandsons Hassan (R) and Husain (R).Muharram processions were common in Bengal in the 18th century. Horses and elephants were also used in the processions.

Processions nowadays are much smaller. In Dhaka, the procession begins at Husaini Dalan and, after winding its way through the streets, terminates at a place designated Karbala on the banks of the Dhanmandi Lake. The replica of *Duldul*, the horse of Imam Husain (R) and the flags in the procession show a symbolic presence of Imam Husain (R). Also latikhela (stick fights) are organised to remind of the battle between the troops of Imam Husain (R) and Yazid. As with other festivals in Bangladesh, Muharram has become an occasion for fairs at various places.

BARAH WAFAT

Barah Wafat is observed as the birth anniversary of Prophet Muhammad. It is also known as Id Milad-un-Nabi. It is the twelfth day of Rabi-ul-Awwal (September- October), third month of the Muslims calendar. This sacred day is both the birth and death anniversary of the Prophet. Prophet Mohammed was born in 571 A.D. on April 12th, in Mecca in Arabia. In Circa 610 AD, the Prophet is said to have gained revelations from Allah through the angel Gabriel that he was His Messenger. In 622 A.D. Mohammed along with his followers went to Medina. This flight from Mecca to Medina is known as Hijrah and marks the beginning of the Islamic era. By 630 AD, Islam came to be accepted as a religion and Muhammad as ruler by a large number of people. However, in 632 A.D. Muhammad led the pilgrimage to Mecca, preached his farewell sermon and died soon after.

The name, Barah Wafat, is taken to indicate the twelve days of sickness of the Prophet, which ended in his death. On this day, there are no grand celebrations, as the birth and death anniversary of Prophet Mohammed coincidently falls on the same day. Hence, Muslims spend this period in spiritual activities. The Quran is recited for the twelve days. The stories of his birth and death and of miracles performed by him are narrated. In the evenings, people assemble and have sacramental meals along with porridge of rice cooked in milk and even the Sayidut-Tam; favourite dish of prophet is prepared. Namaz, prayer, is offered throughout the night. Fatihah, prayer, is read over food in the name of the Prophet. Sweetmeats are distributed and friends and relatives are invited to feasts.

In some mosques, a ceremony known as `Sandal Rite` ceremony is performed. The symbolic footprints of the Prophet engraved in a stone are worshipped. A representation of Buraq the horse on which Prophet Mohammed is said to have ascended to his heavenly abode is placed near the footprints and anointed with sandal paste or scented powder. Besides, the house and casket containing this are elaborately decorated. Hymns are sung and Marsiya or elegies are recited. Food is distributed to the poor. The twelfth day is the Urs proper, is observed quietly and is spent in prayer and alms-giving.

RAMADAN

Ramadan is the month in which Muslims refrain from eating, drinking and sexual intimacy with their partners during daylight hours. This aims to teach Muslims about patience, spirituality, humility and submissiveness to God. Muslims offer more prayer than usual. The dates of Ramadan month vary, moving backwards by about eleven days. Each year depends on the moon. Muslims believe that Ramadan is an auspicious month for the revelations of God to humankind. It is also the month in which the first verses of the Holy Quran were revealed to Prophet Muhammad.

The word Ramadan is derived from Arabic root R-M-D which means intense heat, scorched ground and shortness of rations. Hilal is a day after the astronomical new moon. The new moon indicates the beginning of the new month; Muslims can safely estimate the beginning of this holy month.

Ramadan is a time of pious reflection and worship. Muslims avoid obscene, irreligious sights and sounds. Sexual intercourse among couples is allowed after one has ended the fast. During fasting eating and drinking and resistance of all temptations is persuaded. There should be purity on both thoughts and action. It is believed that the act of fasting redirects the heart away from worldly activities. Fasting helps to cleanse the inner soul. It also teaches to practice self-discipline, self-control, sacrifice, and empathy for those who are less fortunate. When one reaches puberty fasting begins. The elderly, constantly and mentally ill are exempted from fasting. Pregnant woman are also exempted from fasting. Muslims are also encouraged to read entire Quran. The entire Quran is completed at the end of the month. Ramadan is a time when Muslims should slow down from worldly affairs and focus on self-reformation, spiritual cleansing and enlightenment. As it is a festival of giving and sharing they prepare special foods and buy gifts for their family and friends. These are also offered to the poor and the needy.

Iftar is a social gathering that involves preparation of special foods to invited guests. At sunset, the family gather and break the fast and this meal is known as Iftar. The meal starts with the eating of three dates. Thereafter takes place the Maghrib prayer, which is the fourth of the five daily prayers.

Charity is important during Ramadan. The Muslims spend more in charity and many pay their zakat during Ramadan, to receive the blessings. It is believed that if a person helps a fasting person to break their fast, then they receive a reward for that fast.

Laylat al-Qadr is referred to as "the night of decree or measures". It is considered as the most holy night of the year. Muslims believe that Laylat al-Qadr is the night in which the Quran was first revealed to the Prophet Muhammad. Id ul-Fitr marks the end of the fasting period of Ramadan and the first day of the following month after another new moon has been seen. Id ul Fitr means the back to the fitrah.

ID UL FITR

Id-Ul-Fitr occurs at the end of Ramzan, the ninth month of the Muslim year, on the first day of the new moon in Shawwal. Id-Ul-Fitr means the `festival of breaking the fast`. `Fitr` is derived from the word `fatar` meaning `breaking`. Another allegation suggests that it is derived from fitrah or `alms`. Certain Sunni Muslims believe that fitr comes from fitrat meaning `nature` and Id-Ul-Fitr is the celebration of god`s magnanimity in providing nature to man. A 30-day fast of the month of Ramzan, is broken on Id-Ul-Fitr. It is broken with special prayers and festivities with sumptuous feasts. People embrace each other three times, as is laid down in the Quran (The Holy Book of Muslims). The festival originated after proclaiming Ramadan as the period of fasting and austerity. Prophet Muhammad announced this day for celebrations to reiterate the feeling of Id-Ul-Fitr, brotherhood.

It was during this month that Allah gave Prophet Muhammad the Holy Quran for the first time on one of the odd nights of the last ten days of the month of Ramzan. The exact date is not known. Muslims keep a fast every day during this month and the completion of the period, is decided by the appearance of the new moon. Prayers are offered in mosques and Idgahs and elaborate festivities are held.

`Do Rakat Namaz`, the Id-special prayer is performed in the morning in the mosque. These prayers can be read anytime between sunrise and just afternoon. Charitable gift, called Sadaqah Fitr, is to be given to a needy person as thanksgiving. Even one who has not kept the rojas is expected to give alms. The amount to be gifted must be in excess of one`s essential needs and free from all the burden of debt. Food grains or their cost can be donated. The Quran also specifies, the grain and their quantities. A person should give 3.5 lb of wheat or its flour per head, or 7 lb of barley per head or their cost. Do Rakat Namaz is performed. Even women in veil attend the prayers in special chambers. On the festival of Id, many people decorate their houses and people also buy new clothes to wear. In the morning, everyone gets up very early to attend the prayers. These are special prayers, held only at Id. They are held only in very big mosques, or in large open areas, such as football stadiums. They are held about 80 minutes after sunrise, so in the summer months it is very early. Every Muslim is required to pray with his brethren in faith. Before joining the prayer, every Muslim gives alms to the poor. After the alms have been distributed, the gathering goes to the house of the Muslim religious official for Id prayers.

At the end of the prayer, the Kazi delivers a sermon and then offers special prayers to Allah for the welfare of the faith, remission of sins of all Muslims, for the safety of pilgrims and travellers, for the recovery of the sick, for timely rain, for protection from misfortune and for freedom from debts. Thereafter, people visit friends and relatives to say Id Mubarak and to attend Id fairs to buy toys and trinkets. Id-ul-Fitr is an occasion for general goodwill.

Each day of the holiday is spent with one of the relatives, so that everyone is visited. In the evening, the visits start up again. This goes on for three days, but money is normally given to the children on the first two days. Women prepare sweets at home. Vermicelli cooked in sweetened milk, is popular. People then get together for celebrations. Some people visit cemeteries and stay there for many hours. This is perhaps to honour their ancestors and to be with their spirits. To a devout Muslim, Id is a time to forget all past grievances.

HAJ

Haj is pilgrimage to Mecca. Haj is mentioned in the Hadith (traditions) and it is the fifth of the Arkan or Pillars of Islam. Haj is also an imperative duty (Fardh) for all Muslims who have the resources to carry it out and a compulsory pilgrimage to be performed once in a lifetime. However, one may perform it more than once. Haj is an ibadah in which money is spent in Allah`s way and strength is sacrificed for the pleasure of Allah. At the same time, it is a test of patience. Haj also provides Muslims from all parts of the world an opportunity to meet at a central venue to strengthen the bonds of Muslim Brotherhood. Haj starts on the eighth day of the Zul Hijjah or Dhu al-hijah, the twelfth month of Muslim year.One can send a proxy, if he is unable to perform the Haj. The one who completes the Haj is called Haji. About three million pilgrims leave for Mecca during this month. Pilgrims travel to Mecca in groups with their friends or family, or people from their local mosque in order to save money. A woman is permitted to go to Mecca only in the company of a male relative (father, husband, or brother). The Saudi government permits an unaccompanied woman to go, provided, she travels in a group with other women and has written permission to do so from a male relative (even if the relative is not a Muslim or is younger than she is). The `ihram` or pilgrim`s dress in Islam symbolises leaving behind the material world and entering into a state of godliness or spirituality. It is made of two plain unstitched lengths of cloth. Most Muslims wear these clothes during Haj. Many female pilgrims wear a simple white or black dress with a head covering. Ihram is symbolic of the equality between the believers of Allah. An invocation called Talbiyah is chanted when a pilgrim dresses himself in Ihram in the Miqat (a place provided to change into ihram). After changing into Ihram, pilgrims leave for the nearby town of Mina.

On the second day of Haj, pilgrims assemble in the plains of Arafat. Here, a pilgrim thinks of the Doomsday or the Judgement day by Almighty, when he shall have to account for the deeds he committed in this world. The stay at Arafat is called "Wuquf." At night, they collect stones at Mujdalif, a place between Arafat and Mina.

On the third day, pilgrims return to Mina. This day is called Eid-ul-Adha. Pilgrims throw seven of the collected stones at the pillars of Jamarat. This act confirms symbolically, that they will chase away Satan. On this day, they sacrifice an animal and pledge to detach themselves from the worldy attractions. On this day, pilgrims are not bound by the restrictions of ihram. They can shave their heads and can change out of the ihram garment. The head shaving is a symbol of rebirth, signifying that the pilgrim`s sins have been cleansed by completion of the Haj.

On this day or the following day, the pilgrims visit the Masjid-al-Haram in Mecca for a tawaf called the Tawaf-az-Ziyarah (Tawaf al-Ifadah), which is an obligatory part of the Haj. Tawaf is walking around the Kaaba (holy house of Mecca) four times, at a hurried pace. Three more rounds in a counter-clockwise direction follow this, more closely and at a leisurely pace.

On the afternoon of the fourth day (the 11th of the month), pilgrims must stone all three pillars at Jamarat in Mina. The same ritual is performed on the following day. Here, the pilgrims must perform the stoning ritual again on the sixth day, if they are unable to leave Mina before sunset on the fifth day of Haj. Haj teaches complete devotion to the Almighty. It teaches one to use his thoughts, words and deeds in service of Allah. Haj is a complete and compact form of worship in the performance of which one learns about the spiritually vital aspects of life. However, only only those who perform Haj in its true spirit can experience these benefits.

ID UL ZUHA

Id-ul-Zuha commemorates Hazrat Abraham`s sacrifice of his own son in obedience to a command of god. Id-ul-Zuha is celebrated from the tenth to the twelfth day of Zil hijja (Twelfth month of Islam). It is, also called Bakr-id or Id-ul-Zuha and is a festival of great rejoices. It also marks the completion of Haj (pilgrimage to Mecca). The day also coincides with the day when the holy Quran was declared complete. God had put Hazrat Abraham to a dreadful test. He was asked to sacrifice whatever was dearest to him and he decided to sacrifice the life of his son, Ismail. Thus, he blindfolded himself, so that his paternal affection should not interfere with his duty. He sacrificed his own son at Mina near Mecca. But, after opening his folds, he found his son alive and a slain ram at the altar. It was revealed to him that this was meant only to test his faith, and it was enough, if instead he sacrifices only a ram in the name of Allah.

On Id-ul-Zuha, the Muslims go to the mosques in the morning to offer prayers to Allah. On Id-ul-Zuha, special `Dua` (prayer) is recited by thousands of Muslims for peace and prosperity. The wealthy are expected to sacrifice one animal per family and distribute two-thirds of the meat among poor. Those who cannot afford it, one animal per family can be offered. Very poor, seven or seventy families together offer one animal. A full-grown camel, cow, goat or sheep, free from disease, is considered the best offering. The sacrifice can be offered at any time before the afternoon of the third day. In India, too, goats and sheep are sacrificed all over the country and prayers are offered.

It is day for feasting. Special delicacies are prepared and served among family and friends on the occasion. People wish Id Mubarak to each other on this day. Women apply mehndi (henna) and deck themselves out in their finest ornaments. Special prayers and exchange of greetings and gifts mark the Id-ul-Zuha (Bakrid). Id-ul-Zuha is a festival of sacrifice, celebrated with traditional fervour and gaiety in India. The animal sacrifices made during Bakr-Id are mainly to provide food to the poor and to commemorate the noble act of Ibrahim. This spirit of sacrifice is what truly underlines the spirit of Id-ul-Zuha.

Bakr-Id: The feast of Bakr-Id is an occasion to give and to sacrifice. It is a day to thank the Almighty for one's good fortune and to share it with the less fortunate brethren.

Legend has it that Allah commanded Hazrat Ibrahim (Abraham) to sacrifice his son Ismail on Mount Mina near Mecca. Ibrahim, unable to see himself kill his son, blindfolded himself and carried out the pronouncement of God. When he took off the blindfold, a lamb lay slaughtered on the altar and his son stood there unharmed. Ibrahim understood then that this willingness on Ibrahim's part to give up his only son was what God sought, and not the sacrifice of human flesh and blood. The legend ascertains that all God requires of man is a surrender of his will and self. Like Ibrahim, who willingly surrenders his beloved son to God, a true follower of Islam is expected to sacrifice something that is dear to him.

The animal sacrifices made during Bakr-Id are mainly to provide food to the poor and to commemorate the noble act of Ibrahim. This spirit of sacrifice is what truly underlines the spirit of Bakr-Id. Incidentally, the day also coincides with the day when the holy Quran was declared complete. Bakr-Id is celebrated from the tenth to the twelfth day in the Islamic month of Dhul Hijjah. Every year, while pilgrims to the Mount of Mina make animal sacrifices as part of the pilgrimage rituals, Muslims the world over celebrate Bakr-Id in a similar fashion.

Every true Muslim who possesses wealth equal to or more than 400 grams of gold or is capable of affording two square meals a day, is expected to sacrifice an animal. A goat (also called bakri, hence Bakr-Id), sheep, camel or any other four-legged animal is slaughtered during one of the three days of the festival, and the meat is distributed. The sacrificial offering is divided in three parts-one for the self, another for friends, and the third, most importantly, for the needy. The sacrifice can be offered at any time before the afternoon of the third day.

Festivities mark the first day, when people wear new clothes, offer prayers at the mosque, and greet friends and relatives. Special prayers are offered on all three days. It is said that the celebrations are carried on over three days to ensure that the entire Muslim community partakes in the noble of act of giving and sharing. Bakr-Id is celebrated all over India with much fervour, as it is in the rest of Islamic world. The name Bakr-Id, however, is most popular in India. In Arabic, the feast is usually referred to as Id-ul-Azha or Id-ul-Zuha.

Besides Hinduism, India is also the home of innumerable other faiths and the religious and cultural diversity of this nation is manifested in the large number of non-Hindu festivals. The sizeable Muslim communities have their Ids in common with Muslims across the world. *Id-ul-Fitr, Id-ul-Zuha* and *Id-i-Milad* are the three festive occasions widely celebrated by Muslims in India.

Id is celebrated with great enthusiasm all over the country, and one can see Muslims of all age groups and from all stratas of society attired in new clothes, visiting mosques to offer *namaaz.*

The tombs of many Sufi saints attract devotees of all religious persuasions, especially during the urs or death anniversaries. The best known urs are centred at tombs in towns like Ajmer, Delhi, Manakpur, Nagore and Dongri.

The Id-ul-Azha commemorates the ordeal of Hazrat Ibrahim, who had been put to a terrible test by God when he was asked to sacrifice whatever was dearest to him and he decided to sacrifice the life of his son. As he was on the point of applying the sword to his son's throat, it was revealed to him that this was meant only to test his faith, and it was enough, if instead he sacrifices only a ram in the name of *Allah*. This is celebrated on the tenth day of *Zilhijja,* when the *Haj* celebrations at Mecca are rounded off by the sacrifice of goats or camels. In India, too, goats and sheep are sacrificed all over the country and prayers are offered.

Bibliography

Abbas, Nadwi Abdullah : *Learn the Language of the Holy Quran,* Kitab Bhavan, New Delhi, 2002.

Abdali, M.R. : *Scientific Thought in Islam*, Pious Publications, Hyderabad, 2001.

Acquinas, St. Thomas : *The Political Ideas of Islam,* Hafner Publishing Company, New York, 1953.

Ahmad, Aziz : *Islamic Modernism in India and Pakistan,* Oxford University Press, 1970.

Ahmad, K. N. : *Muslim Law of Divorce,* Kitab Bhavan, New Delhi, 1988.

Ahmad, Moinuddin : *Religions of Mankind,* Kitab Bhavan, New Delhi, 1994.

Ahmad, Naseem : *Liberation of Muslim Women,* Gyan Books Pvt., Ltd., New Delhi, 2001.

Ahmed, Hasanuddin : *A Handbook of Muslim Belief,* Goodword Books Pvt. Ltd., New Delhi, 1995.

Ali, Kattani : *Muslim Minorities in the World Today,* Ashish Publishing House, New Delhi, 2001.

Allchin, Bridget : *The Rise of Civilization in India and Pakistan,* Cambridge University Press, New Delhi, 1989.

Anwarullah : *The Islamic Law of Evidence,* Kitab Bhavan, New Delhi, 2000.

Arvind, Sharma : *Women in World Religion,* New York Press, New York, 1990.

Asad, Majda : *Indian Muslims : Festivals and Customs,* Publication Division, New Delhi, 1989.

Azmi, Majaz : *Muslim Wife,* Idara Ishaat-e-Diniyat Pvt. Ltd, New Delhi, 1991.

Binder, L. : *Religion and Politics in Pakistan,* University Press, Berkeley, 1961.

Briffault, Robert : *The Making of Humanity,* Islamic Book Foundation, Lahore, 1980.

Bukhsh, S. K. : *Contribution to the History of Islamic Civilization,* Kitab Bhavan, New Delhi, 2000.

Carl, Bockleman : *History of Islamic Peoples,* Oxford, New York, 2003.

Divine, Epiphany : *Man and Transformation,* MacMillan, London, 1964.

Gibbon, Edward : *History of the Decline and Fall of Roman Empire,* Oxford, New York, 2000.

Haykel, Bewnard : *Revival and Reform in Islam : the Legacy of Muhammad al-Shawkani,* Cambridge University Press, New Delhi, 1963.

Ikram, S.M. : *Muslim Civilization in India*, Oxford, New York, 1981.

Irfan, Habib : *The Agrarian System of Mughal India,* Popular Prakashan, Bombay, 1963.

Kalim, M. Siddiq : *Studies in Pakistan Culture : an International Perspective,* Manohar Publications, New Delhi, 1993.

Landau, R. : *The Philosophy of the Ibn Arabi,* Century Pub., London, 1959.

Malik, Jamal : *Colonization of Islam : Dissolution of Traditional Institutions in Pakistan,* Manohar Publication, New Delhi, 2000.

Mclver, R.M. : *The Community,* Macmillan & Co., London, 1928.

Misra, Neeru : *Sufis and Sufism : Some Reflections,* Manohar Publisher , New Delhi, 2004.

Nabith A. : *The Foundations of the Articles of Faith,* Feroz Pub., Lahore, 1963.

Nasr, Syed Husain : *Three Muslim Sages,* Cambridge, New York, 1959.

Qazi A. Qadir : *The Changing World of Islam,* Royal Pub., Lahore, 1992.

Richards, J.F. : *Mughal Administration in Golkonda,* Oxford, New York, 1975.

Sardar, Ziauddin : *The Future of Muslim Civilization,* Croom Helm, London, 1979.

Shaikh, N. M. : *Women in Muslim Society,* Kitab Bhavan, New Delhi, 1991.

Sharif, M.M. : *A History of Muslim Philosophy,* Feroz Pub., Lahore, 1993.

Subhan, J.A. : *Sufism : its Saints and Shrines,* Kitabiyat Pub., Lucknow, 1960.

Ullah, M. : *Administration of Justice in Islam,* Kitab Bhavan, New Delhi, 1990.

Wahed, Husain : *Administration of Justice during the Muslim Rule in India,* Ashish Publishing House, New Delhi, 1977.

Winer, L. : *Contributions towards a History of Arabico-Gothic Culture,* Oxford, New York, 1917.

Zaehner, R.C. : *Hindu and Muslim Mysticism,* Oxford, London, 1960.

Index

❑❑❑